Liberty, Market and State

Liberty, Market and State

Political Economy in the 1980s

James M. Buchanan
Harris University Professor and General Director,
Center for Study of Public Choice
George Mason University

 NEW YORK UNIVERSITY PRESS
Washington Square, New York
1985

First published in the USA in 1986 by
NEW YORK UNIVERSITY PRESS,
Washington Square, New York, N.Y. 10003

© James M. Buchanan, 1986

Library of Congress Cataloging-in-Publication Data

Buchanan, James M.
  Liberty, market and state

  1. Economic policy—Addresses, essays, lectures.
2. Liberty—Addresses, essays, lectures. 3. State, The—
Addresses, essays, lectures. 4. Distributive justice—
Addresses, essays, lectures. I. Title.
HD82.B76 1985   338.9   85-15367
ISBN 0-8147-1085-9

Typeset in 10/12 point Times by Witwell Ltd
Printed in Great Britain by Oxford University Press

Contents

Introduction

All of the papers collected in this volume were written in the early years of the 1980s; the subtitle is temporally accurate, even if the political economy is personal rather than public. As the titles of the separate chapters suggest, my concerns turn increasingly to the fundamental questions that seem as important in the 1980s as they were in the 1780s and as they will remain in the 2080s. These questions are those of political, legal, and social philosophy—order, liberty, justice, efficiency, progress. The political economist brings to these questions a disciplinary perspective that makes his contribution complementary to the inquiries of others. Any arrogance of scientific authority seems wholly out of place. The papers here are my own inputs in an ongoing dialogue and discussion in which many scholars participate. They are presented in the hope that my sometimes confused groping for understanding will be transferable to others who are similarly concerned.

The separate papers were written initially with no explicit long-range plan for inclusion in a volume such as this book. For the most part they were prepared for seminar, lecture, or conference presentation. As I have found in other collected volumes, both my own and those of others, there is more 'spontaneous order' or integration among the separately written items than any mere observation of the production process might suggest. Because the papers were done separately, however, there is necessarily more redundancy and repetition in argument among the different chapters than should ever have been permissible in a well-organized book. I have tried to minimize the damage here, both by carefully restricted selection and by editorial revision.

The book is organized under five main headings, which seem reasonably descriptive of content, although there are a few items that simply do not fit well. In Part One my concern is with alternative perspectives of social order. In these chapters I make some effort to define and describe my own vision and, also, to appreciate and to understand that of others who have seemed to have difficulty with my own. In parts of Chapters 1 and 2 the discussion is unabashedly autobiographical, a feature that was occasioned both by the purpose of the initial presentations and by the possible value to be gained by placing important philosophical questions in a personal context. The fifth chapter, entitled 'The Potential for Tyranny in Politics as Science', is I think the most important as well as the most controversial in the entire book.

Part Two contains five items under the heading 'The Emergence of Order.' These chapters reflect both my continuing methodological critique of orthodox or mainstream economics and my critique of those who would extend evolutionary explanations too far. These are themes that will be familiar to those who know my work elsewhere, but the particular applications here may clarify remaining ambiguities. I have included Chapter 10 in this Part for lack of a better location in the volume, even if the material does not quite fit. It is related to other items in Part Two only in that I rely on the Hayekian distinction between genetic and cultural evolution.

Problems of justice are discussed in the chapters of Part Three. The material is not offered as any comprehensive treatment of justice, even from my own perspective. The chapters include, instead, portions of what I have written about a limited subset of the issues that the word 'justice' conjures up. Jointly with Geoffrey Brennan and Loren Lomasky, I have, in other papers written during the period and published elsewhere, extended the set somewhat, but my own contributions remain, at best, severely constrained.

Part Four contains four closely related chapters that will be interpreted to fall more clearly within 'political economy' as normally understood than other chapters in the volume. This work was motivated, for me and for those who invited me to write the papers initially, by the topicality of the issues of debt and deficits. My efforts here reflect a return to or continuation of earlier work done when the problems of debt and deficits seemed much less urgent than they did in the 1980s. The central argument in these chapters is controversial primarily because of the differing philosophical foundations for analysis that are implicitly accepted by those who reject my position. With the philosophical foundations, discussed in other chapters in the book, the analysis of debt and deficits becomes straightforward, indeed elementary.

Part Five contains four chapters. In Chapter 21 the influence of the choice setting on individual behaviour is examined. In Chapters 22 and 23, which are related, I discuss the relationship between the general contractarian position and constitutional democracy. In Chapter 24, I try to place political economy in a broader context of social philosophy. This chapter is an appropriate conclusion to the whole volume.

The papers included were all individually written, but during the period of their gestation and production I worked with several colleagues whose help was instrumental in the work presented here. Geoffrey Brennan, how of Australian National University, was my colleague during the whole period and he made valuable comments on the papers as they were written. Dwight Lee, my colleague at the Center for Study of Public Choice, George Mason University, and earlier at Virginia Polytechnic Institute, worked with me on the material discussed in Chapter 20, extensions of which we have published elsewhere as joint papers. Gordon Tullock, my colleague for more than a quarter-century, has always strengthened my resolve in the analysis of debt and deficits through his ability to cut through to the elementary logic of my position.

Permissions to reprint the papers previously published are specifically acknowledged at the beginning of each chapter. I should express my appreciation for the research atmosphere provided by the Center for Study of Public Choice during the whole period when these papers were first prepared. Without the external support provided for the Center's overall programme, these papers could never have materialized. Much the same comment applies to my several colleagues and members of the Center's staff and students.

Finally, and as has come to be expected in the acknowledgements in all my books, Betty Tillman remains a necessary part of the whole production process.

Fairfax,   James M. Buchanan
Virginia   December 1984

Part One
Alternative Perspectives

1 Liberty, Market, and State[1]

I recall hearing 'my professor', Frank Knight, say on numerous occasions that he could never tell whether those who opposed the market did so because they thought the market worked well or because they thought it failed. Like so many other statements made by Frank Knight, this one is worth a bit of pondering. I want to suggest here that opponents of the market or market order fall into two quite distinct groups along the lines Knight indicated, and, further, that the two groups are quite different in terms of the potential receptiveness to the ideas of economic theory on the one hand and to public choice theory on the other.

The theme for these remarks emerged from my resolution of a puzzle that I had thought about for more than three decades. I was invited to deliver the G. Warren Nutter Memorial Lecture in April 1983 (included here as Ch. 2). In that lecture, I referred to the experience that Warren Nutter and I shared at the University of Chicago in the late 1940s. I noted that both of us had initially come into economics as dedicated socialists, an experience shared by so many members of our age cohort. But I also noted that both Warren Nutter and I had been converted into strong advocacy of the market organization of the economy, in my own case through a mere six-week exposure to Frank Knight. My puzzle was why the other dedicated socialists in our group, who shared precisely the same academic experience, including the exposure to Frank Knight, did not undergo comparable conversion. Why did they remain as firmly dedicated to the socialist alternative after they 'learned economics' as they did before. And they obviously did 'learn economics', since there was no distinction in levels of observed academic achievement.

Only after I had written the draft for the Nutter lecture, and as I was going over the draft for presentation, did I come on my answer to the puzzle. I had always assumed implicitly that most of those persons whose attitudes might best be described as 'socialist', broadly defined, were in most essential respects similar to me before I was converted, before I became a born-again free-market advocate. I now realized that this essential similarity applies only to a subset, only to members of one of the groups who oppose market organization, and that the distinction has important consequences.

3

Members of one of these groups, those who may be described as having basically my own preconversion mentality, are vulnerable to the analytical arguments of economic theory. Members of the other group, by contrast, remain almost totally immune to such arguments. By comparison, the analytical arguments of public choice theory may be considered unnecessary, irrelevant, redundant or worse (after conversion) by members of the first group, but for members of the second group the public choice arguments may possibly engender a paradigm shift, even if not accompanied by a conversion to any positive alternative.

I want to discuss these two quite distinct anti-market mentalities in some detail. It is useful, even if sometimes misleading, to assign labels. I shall refer to a member of the first group as a *libertarian socialist*, and to a member of the second group as an *anti-libertarian socialist*.

Objection may be raised to the juxtaposition of the two words 'libertarian' and 'socialist'; my joining them may seem internally contradictory. Nonetheless, I think that the term 'libertarian socialist' does best describe the position I held before I 'saw the light'. (There did exist a Libertarian Socialist party in Weimar Germany.) The person who shares this perspective places a primary value on *liberty*, as such. He personally disputes, rejects, resents, opposes attempts by others to exercise control or power over his own choice behaviour. He does not like harness. There is an exhilaration in simply being free.

Consider, now, the thought processes of such a person who does not really have the foggiest notion of the way the market works. He remains blissfully ignorant of economic theory and, notably, of its central principle of spontaneous coordination, and he is not blessed with any intuitive sense of the interaction process. At the same time, however, the person observes what goes on about him. He lives in and participates in an economy. He works for his wages; he pays money for his consumables. Economic decisions are made by someone, somewhere.

How can such a person fail to view the economy as a system through which some persons control and exploit others? The direction and control of the economic process seems totally arbitrary, and a single participant seems to be at the mercy of those who manipulate the lives and fortunes of others to further their own private greed, to promote their own whims and fancies. If such ideas did not emerge more or less naturally, they would be encountered almost universally in the popular media and in the academic-intellectual establishment. And these ideas would find alleged intellectual legitimacy in the many variants of the Marxian dialectic, the 'science of historical development'. The abiding genius of Karl Marx lies precisely here, in his acute understanding of the possible reaction of the ignorant intellectual to the workings of the capitalist or market order.

In the attitude of the person whose mentality I am trying to describe here, there is little or no positive value placed on collective action, as such. There need be no sense of community, no thought about the organic unity of the social group, the state, or any such things. The person that I am describing here is socialist only because he is strongly anti-capitalist. In a very real sense, his socialism stems from his very libertarianism. Rejecting the control over his own destiny by the whims of the arbitrary 'money managers', 'robber barons', 'Wall Street tycoons', 'gnomes of Zurich', and 'members of the Eastern establishment', what is left as the organizational alternative? 'Throw the rascals out', but who is to replace the rascals? The libertarian socialist falls back, almost desperately, on some form of populist democracy. At the least, he reckons, come the revolution, he will exercise potentially equal powers in shaping his own fate, powers equal to those exercised by others. The person I am trying to describe here probably never goes much beyond his negativism. He really does not think much about the pragmatic problems of organizing a genuinely democratic socialism. (Again, witness the genius of Marx in remaining silent on the post-revolution organizational problems.)

Consider now how such a person will respond when he encounters the solid arguments of economic theory. Think about his reaction when he finally comes to understand the principle of spontaneous order of the market economy. Consider how his whole vision of the world might be affected by exposure to someone like Frank Knight, whose intellectual honesty and integrity were beyond question. Such a person now *understands* that the choices in the market are not arbitrary, that there are narrow limits on the potential for exploitation of man by man, that markets tend to maximize freedom of persons from political control, that liberty, which has always been his basic value, is best preserved in a regime that allows markets a major role. Such a person is both morally consistent and intellectually honest when he undergoes the apparent conversion into market advocacy. He has, quite literally, seen the light.

Let me now try to contrast the position of the libertarian socialist, just discussed, with that of the anti-libertarian socialist. Description of the mentality of a member of the latter group is much more difficult for me since, after all, in describing the first position I am describing my own former self. But let me try to get into other persons' minds. The anti-libertarian socialist is not an individualist, and he does not place primary value on individual liberty. He could never have written, or sympathized with, the slogan of the American revolutionaries, 'don't tread on me'. His initial anti-market or anti-capitalist mentality stems not from any anger, rage, or loathing at the arbitrary powers that others seem to exercise over him, and not from any apparent limits placed on his own liberty by others. Instead, this person opposes the market order for a much more basic reason. He does not think that individuals *should* choose their own destinies. He objects to the market just as much if he knows how it works as he does if he remains ignorant. And he objects just as much to a market that works well as to a market that fails. The level of economic understanding and sophistication possessed by the anti-libertarian has little or no influence on his ideological stance in opposition to market order.

The socialism of the anti-libertarian is essentially positive rather than negative. He actively supports collective control over the lives and liberties of men because he does not consider that persons should be allowed to control their own lives, that they should retain their liberties. There is a 'better' way. The community, the society, the organic unity of the group, the state—these entities command his loyalties. The anti-libertarian may be, but need not be, paternalist. He may, but need not, think that his own values should be imposed on others. The central element in this position is the rejection of the notion that individuals should be allowed to determine their own values, independently of the collective, which is presumably guided in its search for 'truth' and 'goodness' (see Ch. 5).

Consider how such a person might react to the teachings of the economic theorist. He may take these teachings as the duck takes water off its back. He may fully understand the logical structure of the market, while at the same time he remains an ardent advocate of socialist or collective initiatives. Such a person is basically immune to economic argument. The dispersion and limitation of power that the market insures is precisely the reason for his opposition to this organizational form, rather than the converse. The anti-libertarian remains anti-libertarian.

Interestingly enough, however, it is precisely this sort of person who may, if he remains intellectually honest, be reached by the teachings of public choice theory. If such a person comes to recognize that the idealized collectivity does not, and indeed cannot, exist, that persons in politics are like persons elsewhere, including the market, that they remain pursuers of their own private and individualized interests, despicable as these might be, he may waiver considerably in support for collectivistic schemes. How much waivering will take place is unclear, however, since such a person cannot really be expected to become a market zealot. There is no way that the true anti-individualist can be brought to a position of advocacy for the market order, regardless of some removal of romance from his image of the state. The socialist god may die for the anti-libertarian, but no other god appears. The temptation toward drift into nihilism is strong, and this stance does seem to me to be descriptive of many jack-socialists in our world of the 1980s.

In this preliminary chapter I have done nothing more than to share with you how I resolved the puzzle I mentioned. I have found the excursion useful in clarifying my own confusions about the anti-market mentalities. I do not want to argue that my two ideal types are located in their pure forms anywhere, in any person, past or present, living or dead. We are all mixtures of many persons, so that those who oppose the market order may well reflect some blending of the two abstract positions I have tried to outline here, as well as others that may be constructed. Further, even among those of us who remain basically proponents of market order, there remain remnants of the two mentalities I have sketched. For myself, I can empathize much more closely with those who advance the pseudo-Marxist criticisms of monopoly capitalism than I can with those who advance the arguments about the potential benevolence of the state.

My ultimate justification for these remarks is the hope that understanding the mind-set of those who differ with us is a first step toward commencing dialogue and discussion at the most fundamental level of political philosophy.

NOTE

1. The material in this chapter was first written for presentation as an Occasional Lecture at the Liberty Fund Series Conference, Fairfax, Virginia, in July 1983.

2 Political Economy: 1957–82[1]

1. INTRODUCTION

I have chosen this chapter's title, 'Political Economy: 1957–82', with deliberation. The symmetry of a quarter-century has an appeal all its own, but my
choice was also prompted by events at the beginning and the end years of the
period selected. It was in 1957 that Warren Nutter and I founded the
Thomas Jefferson Center for Studies in Political Economy at the University
of Virginia. It was in 1982 that I engaged in a modern struggle to sustain an
institutional setting for a political economy that Warren Nutter would have
endorsed enthusiastically. I want to trace the lineage between these terminal
points of my narrative. In so doing, I shall be largely concerned with what
members of the academies were and are doing and how they interpret their
own social, scientific, and philosophical roles. I do not apologize for this
emphasis to those among my readers who are not of the academy. I remain
convinced that what goes on in the groves has profound effects on the
development and transmission of ideas and, ultimately, on the translation of
these ideas into practice.

II. POLITICAL ECONOMY: 1957

In 1957 the anti-libertarian socialists (see Ch. 1) were in the ascendancy in
the academies. I refer to those who were driven by an ideological commitment to the benevolent leadership of the national state on all matters
economic. (The French have a more suitably descriptive word, *dirigistes*.) In
1957 the Keynesian 'digression', to employ Leland Yeager's apt
phraseology, was still accelerating if measured by its acceptance in the
universities. Those were the days before the Stalinist terror had fully seeped
into modern intellectual consciousness. The debacle of post-war socialist
experiments elsewhere had not then been fully recognized. The dirigistes in
the academic establishment, those who would have run our lives for us, were
in positions of dominance. They controlled major departmental
programmes; they made basic decisions on who should be appointed,
tenured, and promoted; they approved what was to be published; they

controlled the flow of funds from the major foundations, which had by that time floated free of any desires of the initial donors.

When Warren Nutter and I joined the faculty at the University of Virginia in late 1956 and early 1957, we found, I think to our own surprise, an academic setting that was genuinely different, in a commonwealth that had a different history that mattered for its academies. Under the leadership of T. R. Snavely, and bolstered by the imaginative ideas of David McCord Wright and Rutledge Vining, the economics programme at Virginia had already become 'different' from its counterparts. The University of Virginia administration was more than passively receptive to our announced intention to make some effort to counter more explicitly the dominating thrust in economics, and in political economy, circa 1957. (Almost surely, any statement of such an intention would have met immediate resistance at most of the leading universities in the United States at that time.) I recall vividly a meeting with William Duren, then Dean of the College of Arts and Sciences, and Colgate Darden, then President of the University. When I somewhat hesitantly put forward the notion that Warren and I had discussed about establishing a Political Economy Center, the simple response was 'go ahead'. Given this lead, we waxed enthusiastic, and establish such a Center we did.

In the initial brochure for the Thomas Jefferson Center for Studies in Political Economy and Social Philosophy that Warren and I jointly prepared, we stated that our purpose was to set up a 'community of scholars who wish to preserve a social order based on individual liberty'. Little did we reckon on the difficulties that the phrase 'individual liberty' would cause us in the intellectual-academic atmosphere of that time. We were told, quite openly, by an officer of a major foundation, that the explicit encouragement of scholars who believed in individual liberty, as implied in the brochure, was 'particularly objectionable', and that the Thomas Jefferson Center's stated purpose reflected a clearly defined ideological bias. We were placed under suspicion precisely because we had indicated our intention to study the problems of a free society.

In retrospect I can recognize our naïveté in thinking that rational argument could have been effective in countering the dominant mind-set of the time. But we did make such argument, and I remain pleased with one of my own statements included in a letter to Kermit Gordon, our primary adversary:

> I categorically refuse to acknowledge or to believe that a program such as ours, one that is unique only in its examination of the search of free men for consensus on social issues and which assumes that individuals are free to discuss all issues openly and fully, violates in even the slightest way the Jeffersonian spirit.

But all of this belongs in a much longer story than is appropriate in this chapter.

Let me then shift my level of discourse and try to outline for you what our thinking was in establishing the Thomas Jefferson Center. What differences in programme did we have in mind? How did Warren Nutter and I aim to make the Virginia programme in political economy distinct?

We were concerned, first of all, by what seemed to us to be a developing neglect of the basics of economics. Both Warren Nutter and I were Chicago economists, and Chicago economists of the Frank Knight, Henry Simons, Lloyd Mints, Aaron Director vintage. The basics of economics were those of *price theory*, not formal mathematics, and *price theory applied to real world issues*. The economic organization, the market process, was the focus of attention and the working of this organization operating through the pricing structure was the subject matter of the discipline. Political economy was nothing more than this subject matter embedded within the framework of society, described by the 'laws and institutions' about which Adam Smith wrote. To us, quite simply, political economy meant nothing more than a return to the stance of the classical political economists. Aside from Chicago, we saw programmes elsewhere in economics neglecting these very foundations of our discipline.

Let me also admit, openly and without apology then or now, that we were motivated by our conviction that if these foundations are neglected, a society in which individuals retain their liberties is not sustainable. We had faith that an *understanding of the price system* offered the best possible avenue for the generation of support for free institutions. We did not feel any need for explicitly ideological polemic. Our faith in *understanding* was intensely personal. Both Warren and I became economists when we were dedicated socialists (see Ch. 1). We experienced 'conversion' as a result of our own enlightenment through an understanding of market process, and we translated our own shared experience into the positions of our peers and students. We were convinced that the apparent persuasiveness of the socialist arguments seemed so only to those who were ignorant in economics. Our ultimate purpose was to enlighten prospective graduate students, to help them reach an understanding comparable to our own, to produce economics who knew what their proper subject matter was all about, economists who might be able, by presenting their own hard-nosed analysis, to then lead generations of others to their own enlightenment. It was as simple as that, even if we could not state our purpose so straightforwardly then as I can do now. And let me also now acknowledge that, in the dominant anti-libertarian mind-set of the later 1950s, our purpose was indeed *subversive*.

III. THE CHARLOTTESVILLE DECADE: 1957–67

By both our own and by external standards, the 'Virginia School', over the decade 1957–67, was highly successful. The Thomas Jefferson Center for Studies in Political Economy was generously supported by several special, non-mainstream foundations as well as by the university and the commonwealth. The graduate programme was expanded. Leland Yeager, Ronald Coase, Alexandre Kafka, Andrew Whinston, Gordon Tullock, and William Breit were added to the faculty. Visiting scholars, political economists all, and all of worldwide eminence, came to the Center for extended half-year visits. These included Frank Knight, F. A. Hayek, Michael Polanyi, Bertil Ohlin, Bruno Leoni, Terence Hutchison, Maurice Allais, Duncan Black, and O. H. Taylor.

We commenced to attract outstanding graduate students. For a period our graduate students were among the best in the United States. Out of several cohorts, and with my advance apologies to an equally large number whose names could well be added, let me mention only a few by name here: Otto Davis, Charles Goetz, Matt Lindsay, Jim Miller, John Moore, Mark Pauly, Charles Plott, Paul Craig Roberts, Craig Stubblebine, Bob Tollison, Dick Wagner, Tom Willett. These were all products of the 'Virginia School of Political Economy'. A mere listing of these names is sufficient without elaboration on my part. The Virginia initiative was successful.'

During this 'Charlottesville decade', which seems so productive when viewed retrospectively, things were, of course, happening in economics and in political economy, both in and out of the academies. As I noted earlier, the socialist ideal, as a motive force for intellectual-moral-emotional energies, was perhaps at its zenith in the 1950s. This force was spent by the middle of the 1960s. The somewhat lagged Keynesian apogee was attained in the very early 1960s, and fine tuning went the way of all flesh in the latter part of the decade.

The dirigistes of our discipline shifted into neutral or else joined the flower children. The Virginia programme in political economy lost any putative ideological taint it might have had to external observers as its scholars and students produced ideas that came to command respect and attention. There came to be an increasing awareness of the importance of the institutional setting and of institutional constraints for the operation of an economy. Property-rights economics, law and economics, public choice—these three closely related but distinct subdisciplines emerged, each of which is derivative from political economy, broadly defined, and each of which also finds some of its origins in the work of scholars then associated with the Virginia School.

The active and identifiable programme at the University of Virginia was not, however, destined to persevere much beyond the decade. Despite its dramatic success story, the programme was too different from mainstream academic attitudes within the university itself and, notably, from attitudes held by those outside economics. At the very same time that the graduate programme was being so widely praised for its success by those beyond the Lawn, there were active internal efforts aimed at its destruction. I personally recall that one of my proudest moments was recorded when Jack Gurley, then editor of the *American Economic Review*, sometime around 1963 or 1964, stated in a general meeting of the American Economic Association that Virginia's graduate students were submitting more interesting manuscripts than those of any other institution in the country. Almost simultaneously with this, however, and unknown both to Warren Nutter and to me, the university had, in 1963, organized a secret study of our programme, by a committee explicitly motivated by a desire to offset the 'political motivation' of the Center, and whose report concluded with a description of the Department of Economics as 'rigidly committed to a single point of view' which it labelled as 'nineteenth-century ultra-conservatism'. All of this was produced with no consultation from the Department or the Center. The committee went on to recommend, of course, that economists of a 'modern outlook' be appointed.

By the mid-1960s, the University of Virginia, which had indeed been so different in the 1950s, had joined the ranks of academic orthodoxy, albeit belatedly and almost out of date. Over a period of some four years, from 1964 through 1968, the university made no effort to hold onto members of the dramatically successful research-educational unit that we had so fortunately managed to organize at Virginia. Through a policy of deliberate neglect and even active encouragement, scholars were allowed to shift to other institutions. By 1968, Coase, Whinston, Tullock and myself had moved to other universities, and in 1969 Warren Nutter became a participating rather than an academic political economist.

At this point my necessarily autobiographical narrative loses direct contact with Warren Nutter. I saw him only rarely after I left Charlottesville in 1968, and after he joined the United States Department of Defense in 1969. I cannot, therefore, bear personal witness to the continuing struggle within the university that was waged by Warren Nutter after his return to academia, a struggle in which Warren was joined by Leland Yeager, William Breit, and others and which continued over the decade of the 1970s. On the few occasions that Warren and I did meet, however, I felt that there had been no change in our long-standing consensus on the purpose and objective of any programme in political economy. There was really no need for us to discuss this commonly held commitment to what we considered to be the moral obligation of those in our discipline. For this reason I feel that it remains appropriate for me to continue my personal approach to developments in political economy after 1968.

IV PUBLIC CHOICE—THE NEW VIRGINIA SCHOOL: 1969–82

As I noted above, 'public choice' emerged as an independent, or quasi-independent, subdiscipline within political economy and had its inception at the Thomas Jefferson Center in the early 1960s. What was to become the Public Choice Society was initially organized by Gordon Tullock and me at the Old Ivy Inn in Charlottesville in October 1963. When, six years later, Tullock and I found ourselves relocated in Virginia once again, this time at Virginia Polytechnic Institute, we established the Center for Study of Public Choice.

This new centre had a somewhat narrower purpose than the Thomas Jefferson Center. Experience had shown us that an understanding of the market process was a necessary but not a sufficient condition to secure the intellectual-analytical foundations of a free society. This understanding is greatly strengthened in practice by a complementary understanding of the political process. And we found that the study of public choice, which in summary terms is nothing more than the application and extension of economic tools to politics (see Ch. 3), opened up exciting new vistas for social scientists, some of whom could never have been affected by exposure to old-fashioned, hard-headed price theory alone. Public choice quickly gained prominence in intellectual circles more generally, both in and out of the academies. Our programme in Blacksburg, supported initially by the exciting administrative leadership of T. Marshall Hahn, was a success in a way quite different from the earlier programme in Charlottesville. Graduate students came to Virginia Polytechnic Institute, and many of these now carry forward the public choice perspective in their research and teaching at many instituions. But perhaps the most dramatic impact of the programme was reflected in the internationalization of public choice over the decade of the 1970s. Public choice emerged as the 'new political economy' in Europe, Japan, and elsewhere. Blacksburg, Virginia, of all places, became a mecca for economists, political scientists, philosophers, sociologists, and other scholars from all corners of the globe.

As was the case with the Charlottesville center a decade earlier, however, public choice research, like Virginia political economy, its parent, was too unorthodox, too different, indeed too successful, for the orthodoxy, whose members command positions of influence in modern academies. The year 1982 marked a turning point. The Center for Study of Public Choice at Virginia Polytechnic Institute, like the Thomas Jefferson Center before it, was a victim of its own successes. In 1982 a new story commenced. A decision was made to start anew, to shift the centre's operations as a unit (faculty, staff, facilities) to George Mason University.

V   THE ORTHODOXIES OF 1982

I repeat my apologies for too many lapses into autobiographical detail that will interest only selected readers. But I have a larger purpose in detailing these experiences. I want to compare and to contrast the challenges that Warren Nutter and I thought we faced in 1957 with those challenges that seem to face anyone who seeks to promote a research-educational programme in political economy in the decade of the 1980s.

Recall that I said earlier that the 1957 mind-set of the academy's members was dirigiste or anti-libertarian socialist. Among economists, market failure was all the rage, and a demonstration that markets could fail by comparison with a totally imaginary idealized construction was widely held to be evidence that political-governmental intervention was justified. The macro economic fluctuations in employment, output, and the price level were held to exist only because old-fogey politicians had not yet learned the Keynesian policy lessons. Recall how economists of that time laughed with scorn when President Eisenhower said that public debt imposed burdens on the generation's grandchildren.

It is easy to criticize the attitudes of the economists of the 1950s. But let us also give them credit due. They were wrong on so much; we are allowed to say this in hindsight. But they were interested in ideas, and they thought that ideas mattered. They were not frauds and they were not conscious parasites on the community.

A quarter-century is a long time. But the shift in the mind-set of the economists who dominate the academies seems a whole century away from that of the 1950s. Surely for the better, anti-libertarian socialism has almost disappeared. Even under the most inclusive definition that might be possible, the economists of 1982 who could be enrolled under socialist banners would make up a tiny minority of the profession, and they control almost no programmes or funds. The dominant dirigisme of the 1950s has vanished, but it has not been replaced by any comparable offsetting ideological commitment.

Economics, as a discipline, became 'scientific' over the quarter-century, but I put the word in inverted commas and I deliberately pronounce it pejoratively here. As it is practiced in the 1980s, economics is a 'science' without ultimate purpose or meaning. It has allowed itself to become captive of the technical tools that it employs without keeping track of just what it is that the tools are to be used for. In a very real sense, the economists of the 1980s are illiterate in basic principles of their own discipline, even if in a quite different manner from those of the 1950s. Their motivation is not normative; they seem to be ideological eunuchs. Their interest lies in the purely intellectual properties of the models with which they work, and they seem to get their kicks from the discovery of proofs of propositions relevant only for their own fantasy lands.

Command of the tools of modern economics is a challenging intellectual achievement, and I do not question for a minute the brilliance of the modern 'scientists' who call their discipline by the same name that I call my own. I do deplore the waste that such investment of human capital reflects. The intellectual achievement comes at major resource cost, and, as with any such commitment, the opportunity cost is measured in benefits that might be expected from the alternative that is sacrified. In modern economics, that which is sacrificed is an understanding of the principles of market process and of the relationship of this process to the institutional setting within which persons choose. In other words, learning to master the tools of modern economics, as exemplified in the educational programmes of our major graduate schools today, does not leave time for the achievement of an understanding of political economy in the classical meaning of the term.

Our graduate schools are producing highly trained, highly intelligent technicians who are blissfully ignorant of the whole purpose of their alleged discipline. They feel no moral obligation to convey and to transmit to their students any understanding of the social process through which a society of free persons can be organized without overt conflict while at the same time using resources with tolerable efficiency.

The task faced by those of us who would attempt to restore political economy to its proper place of attention as the central research programme of our discipline is then quite different from that which we faced in the 1950s, and it is in many respects much more difficult. The socialist commitment was dislodged in part by the simple observation of the cumulative historical experience, which finally does affect human consciousness, even of those who are long immunized within the ivoried towers. The success of some of our earlier efforts in instilling an understanding of the elementary principles of market and political order was made possible only by the sweep of events over the three decades. To say that events overwhelmed the intellectual arguments is not, of course, to deny the relevance of the latter. Public choice theory did offer an intellectually sophisticated government failure analogue to the earlier market failure thrust of welfare economics. But general attitudes about governmental failures were much more directly affected by straightforward observation of those failures in action.

Our job in the 1980s is therefore less one of ideological displacement and more one of methodological revolution in our parent discipline of economics itself. We find ourselves in the bizarre position where those of us who seek to define our central research programme as it was defined for the first century and one-half of our discipline's history are now the methodological revolutionaries.

Our task is made difficult because of the genuine awe that partially trained mathematicians feel for mathematics itself. It is useful to try to understand just why this awe arises and why it tends to create such serious inferiority complexes in those economists who do not fully understand economic process. Why do the acknowledged masters in mathematics itself not feel some comparable awe at the understanding possessed by the genuine political economists? What is the ultimate source of the one-way awe?

I suggest that the asymmetry emerges because of the methodological revolution in economics that did take place, almost unnoticed, in the twentieth century and, notably, since Alfred Marshall wrote his *Principles*. Once the 'economic problem' is the research programme of the discipline, and the search is on for maximizing or optimizing solutions within the constraints of specified wants, resources, and technology, we are unwittingly trapped in a *mathematical perspective*. In this perspective, we *must* defer to those among us who have superior command of the tools and techniques that only sophisticated modern mathematics can provide. In this perspective, those among us who cannot 'border the Hessians' *are* ignoramuses, and we should be made to feel pedestrian and second rate, left behind by the mainstream scholars of the 1980s.

The basic commitment to the mathematical perspective in economics may be challenged, however, and outside this perspective we need feel no more awe for the mathematicians than we do for the logician, the linguist, or the fiddle player. In comparison with these specialists, we simply acknowledge that we are trained to do, and do, different things. So it should be with the mathematicians. The methodological revolution that is required in political economy must remove the awe by shedding the mathematical perspective; unless this perspective is modified, we shall remain the slaves of the economist-cum-mathematician.

Let me be quite specific at this point, and let me try to illustrate my argument. It is necessary to be clear, especially since many of our colleagues who are outstanding political economists, in the way that I should define the term, remain trapped in the mathematical perspective, even if they remain unconscious of its affect on so many lesser lights. It is their own ability to have become solid political economists while not having been awed by the mathematicians that distinguishes members of this group, but this very ability does tend to blind them to the genuine methodological trap that the mathematical perspective places upon the whole discipline.

I suggest that the mathematical perspective takes hold once we so much as define persons as utility or preference functions and implicitly presume that these functions exist independently of the processes within which persons make actual choices. The utility function apparatus can be properly employed as an *ex post* reconstruction of the choices that may have been made, but it becomes totally misleading to postulate the independent existence of such functions. By postulating such functions independently, and by imposing the resource constraints, it then becomes possible to define, at least conceptually, the 'efficient' allocation of resources, quite apart from any voluntary processes of agreement among trading parties. This formalization of the efficiency norm then allows the market to be conceptualized as merely a means, a mechanism, one among others, to be tested or evaluated in terms of its efficacy in attaining desired results in the utilization of resources.

It is indeed hard for almost anyone trained in economics almost anywhere in this part of our century to exorcise the false constructions and presuppositions that characterize the mathematical perspective. It is not easy to give up the notion that there does indeed exist an 'efficient' resource allocation, 'out there' to be conceptually defined by the economist and against which all institutional arrangements may be tested. Despite the emerging emphasis on process as opposed to end-state philosophizing, economists will only reluctantly give up major instruments of their kit of tools.

VI PROSPECTS

In any short-term context, I am not at all optimistic that the required methodological revolution will take place. Academic programmes almost everywhere are controlled by rent-recipients who simply try to ape the mainstream work of their peers in the discipline. These academic bureaucrats will not be easily displaced, and it is only in fortuitous circumstances that favourable academic settings will present themselves to those who would take the foundations of their discipline seriously.

I remain thoroughly convinced, however, in 1984 as in 1957, that those of us who do place a value on the transmission of the intellectual heritage of political economy face a moral imperative. We must exert every effort to ensure the survival of the ideas that were formative in generating what Hayek has properly called 'the great society'.

Warren Nutter was fond of saying, in the sometimes bleak days of the 1950s and early 1960s, that one of our most important functions was to 'save the books'. Interpreted in the way that I know Warren meant that statement, our function remains basically unchanged. Classical liberalism—the ideas and the analysis that nurtured these ideals for a society that became a near reality—need not perish from the earth. As the saying on Fred Glahe's Colorado T-shirt goes, 'Adam Smith was right—pass it on'.

NOTE

1. Material in this chapter was first presented as the G. Warren Nutter Memorial Lecture at American Enterprise Institute, Washington, D.C., On 20 April 1983

and was published under the chapter's title by American Enterprise Institute (Washington: © American Enterprise Institute, 1983). I acknowledge permission to reprint relevant portions. I have made some revisions from the initial lecture, both the delivered and the published versions.

3   The Public Choice Perspective[1]

I INTRODUCTION

On several different occasions in recent years, I have offered my interpretation of the history, development, and content of public choice.[2] What I want to do here is something different from the earlier efforts. The very word 'perspective' is helpful in allowing me to get some focus on the very general comments I want to make.

Let me start by indicating what the public choice perspective is *not*. It is not a method in the usual meaning of the term; it is not a set of tools; it is not a particular application of standard tools with standard methods, although we are getting somewhat closer with this last statement. Public choice is a *perspective* on politics that emerges from an extension-application of the tools and methods of the economist to collective or non-market decision-making. But this statement, in itself, is inadequately descriptive, because, in order to attain such a perspective on politics, a particular approach to economics is required.

In these notes I shall refer to two separate and distinct aspects or elements in the public choice perspective. The first aspect is the generalized *catallactics* approach to economics. The second is the more familiar *homo economicus* postulate concerning individual behaviour. These two elements, as I shall try to demonstrate, enter with differing weights in the several strands of public choice theory, inclusively defined.

II   CATALLAXY, OR ECONOMICS AS THE SCIENCE OF EXCHANGES

My 1962 presidential address to the Southern Economic Association in the United States was published in 1963,[3] and, incidentally, about the same time that Gordon Tullock and I founded what was to become the Public Choice Society (it was initially organized under the rubric 'Committee on Non-Market Decision-Making'). In 1979, by way of a special celebration, several of my papers on methodology were published in a volume under the title

19

What Should Economists Do?[4] which was directly taken from the title of my 1962 essay, which was included in the volume. In June 1982 I had occasion to rethink my general position in response to this old question I had posed, for an address in Giessen, Germany.

What should economists do? My 1962, as well as my 1982, response to this question was to urge that we exorcise the maximizing paradigm from its dominant place in our tool kit, that we quit defining our discipline, our 'science', in terms of the scarcity constraint, that we change the very definition, indeed the very name of our 'science', that we stop worrying so much about the allocation of resources and the efficiency thereof, and, in place of this whole set of ideas, that we commence concentrating on the origins, properties, and institutions of *exchange*, broadly considered. Adam Smith's propensity to truck and barter one thing for another—this becomes the proper object for our research and inquiry.

The approach to economics that I have long urged and am urging here was called 'catallactics', the science of exchanges, by some nineteenth-century proponents. More recently, Professor Hayek has suggested the term 'catallaxy', which he claims is more in keeping with proper Greek origins of the word. This approach to economics, as the subject matter for inquiry, draws our attention directly to the *process* of exchange, trade, agreement, or contract. And it necessarily introduces, quite early, the principle of spontaneous order, or spontaneous coordination, which is, as I have often suggested, perhaps the only real 'principle' in economic theory as such.

I could, of course, go on with an elaboration and defence of this approach to economic theory, but such is not my purpose here. You may well be asking what this methodological argument has to do with the public choice perspective, which *is* my assignment. My response is straightforward. If we take the catallactics approach seriously, we then quite naturally bring into the analysis complex as well as simple exchange, with complex exchange being defined as that contractual agreement process that goes beyond the economists' magic number 'two', beyond the simple two-person, two-commodity barter setting. The emphasis shifts, directly and immediately, to all *processes of voluntary agreement* among persons.

From this shift in perspective on what economics should be all about, there follows immediately a natural distinction between 'economics' as a discipline and 'political science' or 'politics'. There are no lines to be drawn at the edges of 'the economy' and 'the polity', or between 'markets' and 'governments', between 'the private sector' and 'the public sector'. Economists need not restrict their inquiry to the behaviour of persons within markets (to buying and selling activities as such). By a more or less natural extension of the catallactic approach, economists can look on politics and on political process in terms of the exchange paradigm. So long as collective action is modelled with individual decision-makers as the basic units, and so long as such collective action is fundamentally conceived to be reflective of complex exchange or agreement among all members of a relevant community of persons, such action or behaviour or choice may readily be brought under the catallaxy umbrella. There is no 'economists' imperialism', as such, in this inclusion. There remains a categorical distinction between 'economics as catallaxy' and 'political science' or 'politics'. The latter, that is politics as an academic-research discipline, is then assigned the whole realm of *non-voluntary* relationships among persons, those relationships involving power or coercion. Interestingly enough, this dividing line between the two areas of social science inquiry is the same as that proposed by some political scientists and sociologists (e.g. Talcott Parsons).

Almost any observed empirical relationship among persons will incorporate some catallactic and some power elements. The idealized setting of perfect competition is defined in part for the very purpose of allowing a description of a situation in which there is no power or one person over another at all. In the world where each and every buyer of each and every commodity and service confronts many sellers, among whom he may shift costlessly, and where each and every seller of each and every commodity or service confronts many buyers, among whom he may shift costlessly, there is no power of one person over another. In such a setting, 'economic power' becomes totally without meaning or content.

As we depart from this conceptualized ideal, however, as *rents*, actual or potential, emerge in the relationships between and among persons, elements of power and potential coercion arise, and behaviour becomes amenable to analysis by something other than pure catallaxy.

I do not propose to elaborate the myriad of institutional variants in which both exchange and power elements coexist. I make the categorical distinction largely to suggest that the perspective of economics-as-catallaxy, with its quite natural extension to institutional settings in which persons interact collectively, offers one way of looking at politics and governmental processes, a 'different window', to use Nietzsche's metaphor. And, in a very broad sense, this is what the public choice perspective on politics is about, a different way of looking at political process, different in kind from that way of looking which emerges from the politics-as-power perspective.

Note that in applying the catallaxy perspective to politics, or in applying public choice, to use the more familiar term, we need not, and indeed should not, make the mistake of implying, inferring, or suggesting that the power elements of political relationships are squeezed out as if by some methodological magic. The public choice perspective, which does model politics ultimately in the exchange paradigm, is not necessarily offering an empirically refutable set of hypotheses to the effect that politics and political process is exclusively or even mainly reducible to complex exchange, contract, and agreement. It should be evident that elements of pure rent, and hence of power, emerge more readily in settings of complex than those of simple exchange, and hence more readily in many-person than in two-person relationships, in political than in market-like arrangements. Hence, an appropriate division of scientific labour would call upon the discipline of 'political science' to concentrate more attention on political arrangements and for that of economics to concentrate more attention on market arrangements. There are, nonetheless, major contributions to be made by the extensions of both perspectives across the whole spectrum of institutions. In this sense, the public choice perspective on politics becomes analogous to the economic power perspective on markets.

There are important normative implications to be derived from the public choice perspective on politics, implications that, in their turn, carry with them an approach to institutional reform. To the extent that voluntary exchange among persons is valued positively while coercion is valued negatively, there emerges the implication that substitution of the former for the latter is desired, on the presumption, of course, that such substitution is technologically feasible and is not prohibitively costly in resources. This implication provides the normative thrust for the proclivity of the public choice economist to favour market-like arrangements where these seem feasible, and to favour decentralization of political authority in appropriate situations.

Even without the normative implications, however, the public choice perspective on politics directly draws attention to an approach to reform that does not emerge from the power perspective. To the extent that political interaction among persons is modelled as a complex exchange process, in which the inputs are individual evaluations or preferences, and the process itself is conceived as the means through which these possibly diverging preferences are somehow combined or amalgamated into a pattern of outcomes, attention is more or less necessarily drawn to the interaction process itself rather than to some transcendental evaluation of the outcomes themselves. How does one 'improve' a market? One does so by facilitating the exchange process, by reorganizing the rules of trade, contract, or agreement. One does not 'improve' or 'reform' a market-like exchange process by an arbitrary rearrangement of final outcomes.

The *constitutional* perspective (which I have personally been so closely associated with) emerges naturally from the politics-as-exchange paradigm or research programme. To improve politics it is necessary to improve or reform the *rules*, the framework within which the game of politics is played. There is no suggestion that improvement lies in the selection of morally superior agents, who will use their powers in some 'public interest'. A game is described by its rules, and a better game is produced only by changing the rules. It is this constitutional perspective, as it emerges from the more inclusive public choice perspective, that brings public choice closest into contact with current policy issues in the 1980s. I have, as an economist, always felt very uneasy about proffering advice on particular policies (e.g. on this or that proposed change in the tax law). On the other hand, and by contrast, I do feel it to be within our potential competence to analyze alternative constitutional regimes or sets of rules, to discuss the predicted workings of alternative constitutional arrangements. Hence, as you might suspect, I have been personally (both indirectly and directly) involved in the various proposals for constitutional change that have been made in the 1970s and early 1980s. I refer, of course, to such proposals as Propositions 1 and 13 in California in 1973 and 1978 respectively, the one unsuccessful the other successful; or to Proposition $2\frac{1}{2}$ in Massachusetts, or Proposition 6 in Michigan; and, at the federal government level, to the proposed balanced-budget amendment, and to the accompanying tax limit or spending limit proposals, as well as to proposed changes in the basic monetary regime.

Let me backtrack to the suggestion made above to the effect that the public choice perspective leads directly to attention and emphasis on rules, on constitutions, on constitutional choice, on choice among rules. The Buchanan-Tullock 'classic' book, *The Calculus of Consent*, was the first attempt to derive what we called an 'economic theory of political constitutions'.[5] It would, of course, have been impossible to make that effort without the methodological perspective provided in economics-as-exchange, or catallactics. The maximizer of social welfare functions could never have written such a book, and indeed, even today, the maximizer of such functions cannot understand what the book is all about.

I have identified the first element or aspect of the inclusive public choice perspective as the catallactics approach to economics, the economics-as-exchange paradigm. I referred to nineteenth-century economists who urged the catallactics framework for emphasis. I should be remiss here, however, if I should fail to mention that, for me personally, the acceptance of the catallaxy framework for economic theory emerged, *not* from inquiry into economic methodology directly, but rather from the constitutional public choice perspective that I got from Knut Wicksell.[6] I have often remarked that Wicksell is the primary precursor of modern public choice theory. Wicksell warned as early as 1896 against the presumption that we, as economists, give advice to the benevolent despot, to the entity that would indeed try to maximize a social welfare function. Wicksell stated that if reform in economic policy is desired, look to the rules through which economic policy decisions get made, look to the constitution itself. This 'politics as complex exchange' notion of Wicksell was the stimulus for me to look more closely into the methodological presuppositions of economics itself, presuppositions that I had really not questioned independently.

III. HOMO ECONOMICUS

The second element or aspect embodied in the inclusive public choice perspective that I identified in the introduction is the behavioural postulate familiarly known as that of *homo economicus*. Individuals are modelled as behaving so as to maximize utilities subject to the constraints they face, and if the analysis is to be made at all operational, specific arguments must be placed in the utility functions. Individuals must be modelled as seeking to further their own self-interest, narrowly defined in terms of measured net wealth positions, as predicted or expected.

This behavioural postulate is, of course, part and parcel of the intellectual heritage of economic theory, and it has indeed served economists well. It stems from the original contributions of the classical economists themselves, whose great discovery was that individuals acting in pursuit of their own interests may unintentionally generate results that serve the overall 'social' interest, given the appropriate framework of laws and institutions. Since these eighteenth-century roots, economists and economics have relied on the *homo economicus* postulate to analyze the behaviour of persons who participate variously in markets and, through this, to analyze the workings of market institutions themselves.

No comparable postulate was extended to the behaviour of persons in their political or public-choice roles or capacities, either as participants in voting processes or as agents acting for the body politic. There was no such postulate stemming from the classical economists or from their successors. There was no 'economic theory of politics' derived from individual choice behaviour.

We might, in retrospect, have expected such a theory to be developed by economists, as a more or less obvious extension of their *homo economicus* postulate from market to collective institutional settings. Once economists turned their attention to politics, they should, or so it now seems, have modelled public choosers as ultility maximizers. Why did they not do so? Perhaps the failure of the classical economists, as well as that of their nineteenth-century successors, to take this step might be 'excused' by their implicit presumption that collective activities were basically unproductive and that the role of the state was limited largely to what has been called minimal or protective functions. These economists simply could not conceive that much 'good' or 'goods' could be generated by collective or governmental action.

But why did their twentieth-century descendants fail similarly, despite some suggestive models as advanced by Wicksell and the Italian public-finance scholars (De Viti De Marco, Puviani, Pantaleoni, and others) in the waning years of the nineteenth century? My own interpretation of the modern failure is that twentieth-century economists had been converted to the maximization-scarcity-allocation-efficiency paradigm for their discipline, a paradigm that is essentially at variance with that which classical economics embodies and which draws attention away from individual behaviour in exchange contracts and toward some presumably objectifiable allocative norm that remains conceptually independent of individual choices. By the third decade of this century, economic theory had shifted to a discipline of applied mathamatics, not catallaxy. Even markets came to be viewed as 'computing devices' and 'mechanisms', that may or may not secure idealized allocative results. Markets were not, at base, viewed as exchange institutions, out of which results emerge from complex exchange interaction. Only in this modern paradigm of economic theory could the total absurdity of the idealized socialist structure of Lange-Lerner have been taken at all seriously, as indeed it was (and, sadly, still is) by practising economists. We may well ask why economists did not stop to ask the questions about why socialist managers would behave in terms of the idealized rules. Where are the economic eunuchs to be found to operate the system?

Or, to bring the discussion somewhat further forward in time, why did the economists of the 1930s, 1940s, 1950s, and into the 1960s take the Keynesian theory of policy seriously? Why did they fail to see the elementary point that elected politicians will seek any excuse to create budget deficits?[7]

It all seems so simple in retrospect, but we should never underestimate the difficulties, indeed the moral costs, that are involved by a genuine shift in paradigm, a change in the very way that we look at the world around us, whether this be economists looking at politics or any other group. It was not easy for economists before the 1960s to think of public choosers as utility maximizers in other than some tautological sense. In part, the intellectual blockage here may have stemmed from a failure of those who did advance self-interest models to incorporate the politics-as-exchange paradigm in their own thinking. If politics is viewed only as a potentially coercive relationship among persons, at all levels of conceptualization, then the economist must be either courageous or callous who would model public choosers (whether voters or agents) as net wealth maximizers. Few want to reap the scorn that Machiavelli has received through the ages. Such a world of politics is not at all a pretty place. And analysis based on such a model and advanced as 'truth' becomes highly noxious. The very unpleasantness of these models of politics may have been the root cause that explain the neglect of what now appear to be clear precursors of this element in the public choice perspective. Some of the early Italians, and notably Pareto, who were themselves perhaps influenced importantly by Machiavelli, and in the middle of this century, Schumpeter, seem to have had little or no impact on the thinking of modern social scientists about political process.

It is only when the *homo economicus* postulate about human behaviour is *combined* with the politics-as-exchange paradigm that an 'economic theory of politics' emerges from despair. Conceptually, such a combination makes it possible to generate analysis that is in some respects comparable to that of the classical economists. When persons are modelled as self-interested in politics, as in other aspects of their behaviour, the constitutional challenge becomes one of constructing and designing framework institutions or rules that will, to the maximum extent possible, limit the exercise of such interest in exploitative ways and direct such interest to furtherance of the general interest. It is not surprising, therefore, to discover that the roots of a public choice perspective which contains both elements here identified are to be found implicitly in the writings of the American Founders, and most notably in James Madison's contributions to *The Federalist Papers*.

I look on *The Calculus of Consent* as the first contribution in modern public choice theory that combined and balanced the two critical elements or aspects of the inclusive perspective. This combination might well not have occurred but for the somewhat differing weights that Gordon Tullock and I brought to our joint venture in that book. I think it is accurate to say that my own emphasis was on modelling politics-as-exchange, under the acknowledged major influence of Knut Wicksell's great work in public finance. By comparison (and interestingly because he was not initially trained as an economist), Gordon Tullock's emphasis (stemming from his own experience in, and his reflections about, the bureaucracy) was on modelling all public choosers (voters, politicians, bueaucrats) in strict self-interest terms. There was a tension present as we worked through the analysis of that book, but a tension that has indeed served us well over the two decades since initial publication.

In the 1960s, 1970s, and early 1980s varying contributions have represented differing weighted combinations of the two central elements in the inclusive public choice perspective. Works on the theory of bureaucracy and bureaucratic behaviour and on the theory of regulation have been weighted towards the *homo economicus* element, whereas works on constitutional analysis have been more derivative from the politics-as-exchange paradigm.

These two wings of modern public choice theory are not mutually inconsistent. Even if politics and political process is ultimately modelled in an exchange paradigm, simple and direct observation suggests that politicians and bureaucrats are inherent components. And these persons act no differently from other persons that the economist studies. Recognition of this simple point followed by a positive analysis of the working out of its implications in the institutional settings of modern politics are essential inputs into the more comprehensive comparative analytics that must precede any discussion of constitutional reform. It is precisely because of the insights of the modern theories of bureaucracy and regulation that there has emerged the increasing awareness of the need for new institutional constraints.

NOTES

1. This paper was initially published in *Economia delle scelte pubbliche* (Rome), 1 (Jan. 1983), 7–15. I acknowledge the permission of the editor, Professor Domenico da Empoli, to reprint the paper here, substantially unchanged.
2. *See* James M. Buchanan, 'Public Finance and Public Choice', *National Tax Journal*, 28 (Dec. 1975), 383–94; 'From Private Preferences to Public Philosophy: Notes on the Development of Public Choice', in *The Economics of Politics*, ed. Arthur Selden (London: Institute of Economic Affairs, 1978), pp. 1–20; 'Politics Without Romance: A Sketch of Positive Public Choice Theory and Its Normative Implications', Inaugural Lecture, Institute for Advanced Studies, Vienna, Austria, *IHS Journal, Zeitschrift des Instituts fur Hohere Studien*, 3 (Wien, 1979), B1–B11.
3. James M. Buchanan, 'What Should Economists Do?', *Southern Economic Journal*, 20 (Jan. 1964), 213–22.
4. James M. Buchanan, *What Should Economists Do?* (Indianapolis: Liberty Press, 1979).
5. James M. Buchanan and Gordon Tullock, *The Calculus of Consent* (Ann Arbor: University of Michigan Press, 1962).
6. Knut Wicksell, *Finanztheorietische Untersuchungen* (Jena: Fischer, 1896).
7. On this point, *see* James M. Buchanan and Richard E. Wagner, *Democracy in Deficit: The Political Legacy of Lord Keynes* (New York: Academic Press, 1977).

4 The Related but Distinct 'Sciences' of Economics and of Political Economy[1]

I INTRODUCTION

'Science', in a narrowly defined sense that is descriptive of the 'hard science' disciplines, is explicitly positive. Scientists are presumably concerned with the discovery of the apparent reality that exists, that is 'out there', or (if they are somewhat more sophisticated) with the construction of models that enable refutable predictions to be made about the consequences of particular experiments. Science is about the 'is', or the conjectural 'is', not the 'ought'. It rarely occurs to the 'scientist' to ask himself or herself about his or her *raison d'etre*. Why does science have ultimate 'social' value? Once this question is so much as raised, however, the limits of the strictly positive posture are very soon exhausted. By more or less natural presumption, science is valued because it is precursory to its usefulness in control. Physics, as positive science, is antecedent to the miracle of modern technology, the space flights and the hydrogen bomb alike.

'Know the truth and the truth shall make you productive.' This implicit motto has served science well, and especially so until the emergence of the awful moral questions raised in the middle and late years of our own century. Knowledge of how the physical universe operates has allowed man to assume increasing control over the 'natural processes' that he observes about him. And, again excepting the new moral issues of our times, this control, made possible by the application of science, has been largely unidirectional in effect. It has dramatically improved man's lot. But how is 'improvement' measured? By man's own evaluation—this offers the only satisfactory response. But the normative step taken in such a response should be acknowledged. 'Improvement' follows upon the control made possible by science; therefore, science 'ought' to be pursued; there is apparent normative support for the exercise of the scientist's talents.

Man is of the world and his activities are 'natural processes'. Does it not then follow that increasing knowledge about man and his activities has its appropriate place in science? And should we not expect that such advance will yield results comparable to those demonstrated to have emerged from other aspects of general scientific development? Why should there exist a categorical difference between the 'science of man' and the science of anything else?

These questions point to unidirectional answers if the normative purpose of science is forgotten. The necessary linkage between increasing scientific knowledge and 'improvement' is provided by the control that the knowledge potentially offers, control that may be exercised to further objectives that individuals themselves evaluate positively. Can the 'sciences of man' be made to correspond to the non-human sciences in this respect?

II ROBINSON CRUSOE AS POSITIVE SCIENTIST

Consider Robinson Crusoe alone on his island. In one sense, much of his behaviour can be interpreted as that of a positive scientist who is making and testing hypotheses. 'This red berry makes me ill; this blue berry makes me well. Fish abound in the eastern lagoon; sharks are in the western lagoon.' Crusoe is testing hypotheses about his own body and temperament as well as about the external elements of his new environment. He is engaged in pursuing a 'science of man', as well as all of the other sciences. His standard of living improves, by his own reckoning, as he applies the newly acquired knowledge, as he controls the environment, and himself, in the light of this knowledge.

Let us now shift to Crusoe's situation after Friday is on the island. Friday is now a part of Crusoe's natural environment, and Crusoe will have an incentive to acquire knowledge about this part much as any other. He will, therefore, continue to behave as a positive scientist. He will advance and test hypotheses. As he does so, knowledge is acquired, and, as applied, this knowledge will allow Crusoe to control Friday's behaviour. As he does this, Crusoe will be able to improve his own well-being, in his own terms. For purposes of illustration, even if a departure from Defoe's narrative, suppose that Crusoe discovers that Friday is extremely superstitious about serpents, even to the extent of fearing images of serpents. Having made this discovery, which is genuinely scientific in the full sense, Crusoe can, perhaps by drawing images in the sand, modify Friday's behaviour in ways that seem desirable to him.

The story to this point neglects Friday's ability to behave also as a positive scientist. Robinson Crusoe is a part of the new natural environment for Friday, and the latter, too, will engage in advancing and testing hypotheses about Crusoe's behaviour. The two positive scientists, Crusoe and Friday, are discovering aspects of their environment, and they are controlling this environment through application of their scientific discoveries, each to the improvement of his own standard of living, as he himself evaluates it. Crusoe is 'exploiting' Friday's superstitious fear of serpents; Friday is 'exploiting' that which he learns about Crusoe. Each person, individually, is better off than he would be without the bit of scientific knowledge that he has discovered.

III ADDING UP

The moral of our illustrative Crusoe-Friday story should be clear. Each person, acting as a positive scientist and applying his discoveries for his own purposes, finds the activity rewarding. But, because there are now *two* sentient beings interacting *each upon the other*, there is no *a priori* basis for claiming that 'science,' as practised in the illustrative study, improves well-being for the group of two persons. The normative support for 'science' as an activity that seems so self-evident in both our introduction and in Crusoe's one-man setting, now seems questionable when applied to interactive behaviour. Science, as applied, implies control, and control for individualized private purposes *need* not lead to mutual gains.[2]

The problem that Crusoe and Friday confront in living together is not scientific in the standard sense, and no matter how rapid the advances in scientific knowledge by one or both persons, the problem will remain one of mutual adjustment. There is no reality 'out there' to be discovered that will be of assistance in accomplishing this mutual adjustment. Each person may come to know the properties of all the elements in the natural environment, and each person may model the behaviour of the other with reasonable accuracy in a variety of interaction situations. To the extent that Crusoe (Friday) discovers that Friday (Crusoe) will act in certain ways in response to increments or decrements in his stock of goods, each person may use something we might call 'economic science' in making his predictions about the behaviour of the other. But so long as each person acts independently, the setting will remain one of a non-cooperative game. In such a game, 'science' can, at best, indicate to the players something about optimal strategy selection. We suggest that a society of many persons is simply the Crusoe-Friday setting with complications.

IV THE IMAGINATION-EVALUATION OF ALTERNATIVE INSTITUTIONS: THE 'SCIENCE' OF POLITICAL ECONOMY

Let us suppose, however, that Crusoe (or Friday) *imagines* (dreams) a different world, one in which he and Friday (or Crusoe) remain alone on the island, but one in which the interaction between the two persons becomes cooperative. But what imaginary scenarios are feasibly worth consideration? Crusoe could, of course, imagine himself and Friday to be wholly different creatures, but he may reckon that such thoughts would reflect idle dreams. Within the realm of feasible scenarios in which both persons remain recognizable specimens of what they are observed to be, Crusoe (or Friday) can still imagine alternative 'possibles', to introduce a useful term from G. L. S. Shackle here. A world in which each person refrains from the exploitation of the other person's known vulnerability might be a better world for both persons. In his imagination of this alternative interaction, Crusoe is required to engage in 'science' of a categorically different sort from that which describes his search for 'truths' about the edible qualities of berries or the superstitions of Friday.

What is required here is some imagination of the behaviour of the other persons that is categorically different from the straightforward *reaction* pattern that would consist simply of a set of predicted responses to changes in the environment. Crusoe, acting as a positive scientist in the simplistic sense, and subsequently acting on the knowledge gained, can develop a set of predictions about Friday's reactions to external stimuli (Friday can of course do the same with Crusoe). This set of predictions will *not*, however, be of direct assistance in the imagination of the interaction that follows from a 'leap out of anarchy', a 'shift from the independent adjustment equilibrium' a 'move out of the dilemma'. Crusoe (or Friday) must imagine a *person* who is, in a sense, *morally equivalent* to himself in order to examine the prospects for mutual gains. Furthermore, he must model the predicted working properties of the interactive setting within which each party behaves within the limits of agreed rules of conduct. The 'science of political economy' describes this process of institutional evaluation.

An interaction with an animal could never provide the basis for such an imaginative construction. The difference between human and animal interaction was acutely sensed by Adam Smith in a passage that economists have too much neglected. Smith lodged the sources of human progress squarely in man's propensity to 'truck, barter, and exchange one thing for another', and he specifically stated that no one had seen 'a dog make a fair and deliberate exchange of one bone for another with another dog'.[3]

V SELF-SEEKING WITHIN CONSTRAINTS

It is essential to understand the precise meaning of the term 'morally equivalent' in the discussion above. Crusoe need not imagine Friday to be 'moral' in the ordinary sense of this term; he need not project or model Friday as a benevolent person, one for whom Crusoe's interests matter as well as his own, even to the slightest degree. That is to say, Friday need not be required to 'love' Crusoe, and vice versa, in the potentially productive interaction that will guarantee mutuality of advantage. Friday may be modelled as a self-seeking autonomous person, but one whose predictable behaviour is constrained voluntarily within the limits of mutual gain.

The central contribution of eighteenth-century moral philosophy was the recognition that such limits could be drawn, both conceptually and in institutional reality. Without such recognition there is no escape from the attitude that man must be 'ruled' so long as he remains immune from the full acceptance of the moral precepts of the church. 'Free man', as a legitimate philosophical idea, emerged only when it was recognized that the indicated behavioural limits were *minimal*, in the sense that they fall far short of some standard of 'ethical perfection' or 'universal love'. To the medieval philosophers, man could not be free *because* he could not attain sainthood.

To modern economists the wheel has come full circle. Many of them model man as a net wealth maximizer in *all* aspects of his behaviour. They fail to see that man cannot be 'free', in any normatively meaningful sense, unless he is constrained within the limits of mutual advantage. Unchained man *is* a beast; this is a simple and elementary fact that must be acknowledged by us all. And, as we have argued above, whereas intelligent 'beasts' may be very skilled in the usage of what may be called 'economic science', until and unless they acknowledge the normative relevance of imposing limits on behaviour, they cannot evaluate alternative schemes of cooperative social order. They cannot act as 'political economists'. 'Economic science', defined and used analogously to the hard sciences, requires that some persons be putty, subject to the manipulation and control of others.

More specifically stated, the eighteenth-century contribution was to construct the bridge between *homo economicus* on the one hand and 'social welfare' or 'group interest' on the other. Mandeville, Hume, and Smith did not invent the notion of self-seeking, autonomous man. Such a person had been around for centuries, and he had been emphatically brought to philosophical consciousness by Thomas Hobbes in the seventeenth century. By building on the Hobbesian contractual insights, and by postulating the possible existence of the limited sovereign in the sense articulated by John Locke, the eighteenth-century philosophers demonstrated that, within such constrained behavioural limits, the self-interested motivation on the part of individuals might promote the welfare of the whole community of persons.

To return again to the Crusoe-Friday illustration, and to concentrate only on the calculus of one party, Crusoe, we can see that he must imagine how the two parties might interact in a *limited* or *constrained* setting, where each party is motivated by self-interest but where the exercise of this interest is itself constrained by some adherence to mutually accepted 'law', which may itself be morally derived, externally imposed, evolved as custom, or contractually established. The 'imagination' of such an 'economy' of self-seeking persons who make their own choices within a system of law becomes a 'scientific' construction, but it is one that is categorically distinct from that which straightforwardly models persons as beasts and which embodies no limits on maximizing behaviour.

VI THE SCIENCES OF ECONOMICS AND OF POLITICAL ECONOMY

There are two quite different uses or applications for the exercise of the scientific imagination in relation to the interaction behaviour of persons within an economy under law. By postulating self-seeking behaviour of *other* persons, within the legal limits, the individual, acting as 'scientist', can make and test predictions about their behaviour, and these predictions may prove useful either for their own sake, or for improving the well-being of the scientist or those for whom he acts as agent. The predictive 'science of economics' is positively valuable to governmental agents, business firms, and private individuals. Persons can 'play better games' if they can predict their opponents' strategy more accurately.

But there remains a categorically different exercise, which we may call the 'science of political economy'. Its purpose is to evaluate the structure of the constraints, 'the law', with some ultimate objective of redesign or reform aimed at securing enhanced efficiency in the exploitation of the potential mutuality of advantage. This science of political economy requires more than the making and testing of predictions about behaviour under an existing set of constraints, some given system of laws, although the latter 'science' will of course continue to be a necessary input in the exercise. The second 'science', however, also requires some comparison of the results observed within an existing system of constraints and those that might be predicted to emerge under alternative systems. For the simple reason that it does not now exist, the results of an alternative set of constraints can never be observed. Alternative structures exist only as potentialities, as constraints that persons might *create* by their own choices, from the void as it were and not from some reality 'out there' waiting to be explored and discovered. At this level the discovery metaphor which has proven useful in describing the search activity of ordinary science becomes positively misleading in application to the comparative analysis of alternative constraints structures.

It is in its failure to distinguish between the two distinct sciences that it inclusively embodies that modern economics often defaults on its very *raison d'etre*. By modelling their own activities in the exploration-discovery metaphor of the ordinary sciences, and by misunderstanding the positive-normative relationship between science and control, modern economists often inadvertently lend support to the efforts of the subset of persons who seek always to treat other persons as potential responders to control stimuli, support to those putative authoritarians who act on behalf of, and as agents for, the modern state apparatus. Often in wholesale ignorance of what they are about, modern economists may invent the shackles by which they, along with their fellows, are bound by the modern state.

VII PREDICTIVE SCIENCE, BEHAVIOUR, AND CHOICE

Man cannot be, at one and the same time, a behaving animal that is subject to scientific prediction *and* a choosing agent that remains immune from control by the manipulation of rewards and punishments. This fact is applicable both for the single person and for the collectivity of persons in the 'representative' or 'average' sense. To put the point differently, there is no way to 'explain' the existence of civil order among persons by resort to the predictive science of behaviour alone. The eighteenth-century philosophers knew this; their modern counterparts have forgotten it.

Crusoe must initially imagine Friday to be a person, like himself, who acknowledges the desirability of imposing limits on the behaviour of *both* parties but who would, necessarily, reject the imposition of constraints unilaterally. The leap from anarchy into order is at the same time a leap 'beyond predictive science'. Civil order requires mutual agreement on and acceptance of the trading ethic, or, more simply, respect for contractual agreement, for promise-keeping. Civil order is based on *exchange*, in the most inclusive meaning of this term. Civil society requires and implies reciprocity in dealings among its members.

But what is 'truth' in reciprocal dealings? Predictive science is by its nature unidirectional in its search for and discovery of 'truth', an attribute of the reality presumed to be 'out there', quite independently of the means through which it is ascertained or discovered. 'The red berries are poisonous'—this scientific statement exists for Crusoe quite separately from the means through which he has found out about its validity.

But contrast such a statement with Crusoe's speculative philosophizing to the effect that *both* he and Friday can improve their lot, and on their own terms, by simple trade based on comparative productive advantage. The latter becomes, for Crusoe, a speculative hypothesis that he may test only by suggesting it to Friday and by securing the Friday's agreement, agreement that must be expressed behaviourally in terms of adherence to the limits of mutual gain.[4]

Within the agreed limits, Crusoe may, indeed, model Friday as *homo economicus*, as one who seeks to gain private advantage and who is unconcerned about the well-being of his partner across the exchange relationship. Reciprocally, Friday models Crusoe's behaviour in a similar way. It is important to recognize, however, that, in adhering to the limits, both parties may violate the strict *homo economicus* postulate of net wealth maximization. Each trader may stop short of maximal exploitation of his privately defined advantage, not from any benevolent concern for the well-being of his trading cohort, but instead from some recognition that the mutuality of gain to all parties is the *sine qua non* of stable civil order. Indeed, it may be argued that behaviour based on a recognition of such limits as here discussed is appropriately defined as 'rational' under an inclusive definition of rationality.[5]

VIII FROM SIMPLE TO COMPLEX SOCIETY

As we shift attention from the simple two-person interaction to a many-person community, however, any model of behaviour that requires voluntary adherence to the limits of mutual advantage for *all* persons must be questioned. Crusoe might well imagine a two-person society that incorporates mutual agreement on behavioural constraints that will be honoured; he might reckon plausibly on enlightened or long-range self-interest motivation to lead each of the two parties to extend precepts of rationality to include predicted behavioural feedbacks. But to imagine such voluntaristic limits on behaviour in the many-person setting may become scientifically naive in the sense that any attempts to organize one's own behaviour on such a prediction of voluntaristic limitation may lead to disastrous personal consequences.

In a many-person, complex society, it becomes necessary to model the actors as if they do not voluntarily restrict their behaviour to the limits defined by the mutuality of gains. Such models of behaviour do indeed embody the *homo economicus* (or net wealth maximization) assumption in the strict sense. But these models are *not* used as inputs for prediction and control in the sense of ordinary science. They are, instead, to be used for the purpose of allowing the individual (each individual) to make informed and sophisticated choices among alternative institutional constraints, constraints that are to be mutually acknowledged and accepted by all parties and which are to be *externally enforced* by the sovereign.[6]

In the complex society the enforcement role of the sovereign, of government, cannot be romantically neglected; this role must be squarely acknowledged. The sovereign must 'enforce the law', 'keep the peace', or, in the terminology of this paper, must 'keep the self-seeking behaviour of persons within the limits of mutual advantage'. The scope and range of the authority granted to the sovereign will critically depend on the analytical results that emerge from the construction of models of interaction. It is in precisely the construction of such models that the *homo economicus* postulate about human behaviour assumes maximal value. Only by examining the workings of models in which all persons are postulated to behave exclusively as self-seeking maximizers of privatized or individualized net wealth can appropriate 'limits of law' be defined and entered into the lists for effective constitutional dialogue. It would be folly to model persons as saints for the purposes of generalizing the results to form a basis for 'the law' to be enforced by the sovereign agent. But, on the other hand, to model persons in *homo economicus* terms for this purpose of deriving constitutional structure is not the same thing at all as advancing predictions that persons will necessarily behave as *homo economicus*, even in some average or representative sense. The legitimate 'science of political economy'—of interaction among persons who behave in accordance with precepts of net wealth maximization—is not, and should not be conceived to be, analogous to that 'science of economics' which is conceived to be exclusively concerned with the generation of refutable hypotheses. The 'positive science of political economy', which does embody persons behaving as net wealth maximizers, does not have as its ultimate normative purpose the accumulation of predictive knowledge about behavioural relationships in the observable real world, knowledge that may be of ultimate assistance in enabling some sovereign master to control those whose behaviour is so analyzed. Political economy has, instead, the ultimate purpose of enabling persons to analyze their own behaviour, along with that of others, in some imagined state and, from such analysis, to define the appropriate or desired set of constraints that will be then embodied in the law assigned to the sovereign for enforcement.

IX MODELS OF THE SOVEREIGN

Modern economists, who do not spend much thought on methodological questions, might not object strenuously to the distinctions sketched out above. If pressed, they would presumably agree that the knowledge about economic reality that they seek is primarily useful in genuine political economy as an input in the dialogue about constitutional-legal reform. Having done so, they would return to their chores, leaving open the whole set of issues raised concerning models of the enforcing agent, of the sovereign, of government, of persons who act on behalf of the modern state.

A major deficiency in the political-legal-social philosophy of the nineteenth and twentieth centuries has been the failure to model the behaviour of the sovereign, or, more precisely, to model the behaviour of those persons who are empowered or authorized to act on behalf of the state or government. This failure has been far more pervasive than any like failure to model what we may call 'private man'. The latter has often modelled as *homo economicus* for the legitimate purposes of assisting in the dialogues on law reform. By contrast, 'public man' has rarely been modelled at all, save implicitly as 'saint'. This perversity in analysis has only come to be recognized, and partially corrected, through the influence of public choice theory in the years since 1960.[7]

The reason for the perversity lies partially in the confusion about 'economic science' and the 'science of political economy' previously noted. 'Public man', the agent who acts in the name of the sovereign, the elected legislator, the judge, the bureaucrat, the person who chooses among the options that restrict and confine the liberties of the citizen, cannot be conceptually modelled as behaving to further his own self-interest and *at the same time* be justified or legitimated in his functional role on some grounds of 'general good'. By contrast and comparison, the profit-seeking businessman (Adam Smith's butcher) can be modelled as wealth-maximizing while at the same time be justified as furthering the 'general interest'. As noted above, however, the self-seeking in the marketplace must be assumed to be limited or constrained by the bounds of mutual advantage, even if the necessity of assuming such limits is not often explicitly recognized.

How can models of 'private man' and 'public man' be made consistent one with another? 'Public man' must be modelled in self-seeking terms if his behaviour is to be compared with those persons who interact in the accepted models of markets. But how, then, can any 'public man' role be justified at all?

The recognition of limits can be helpful in resolving what seems to be a dilemma here. It becomes necessary to differentiate between the predictive science of behaviour, the 'science of economics', and the modelling of interaction patterns for the purposes of designing appropriate legal and constitutional constraints, the 'science of political economy'. In the latter, only by modelling 'private man' to be exclusively seeking to maximize net wealth can the legal framework, the 'laws and institutions', of the marketplace be designed so as to further the 'general interest' and to prevent the undue exploitation of man by man. Comparable principles should tell us that 'public man' must be similarly modelled and for the same reasons. The person who is placed in a position to act on behalf of the state must be modelled as a net wealth maximizer in his own right if the legal-constitutional constraints that define his authorized powers and his behaviour within those powers are to be appropriately designed. 'Public man', like his counterpart in the market, can be constrained to behave within the limits of mutual gains. 'Public man' need not be allowed powers of exploiting his fellows provided that his behaviour is appropriately restricted.

The purpose of the scientific construction that embodies *homo economicus* is the same as between the two patterns of interaction, as between the relations of persons within markets and the relations of persons within politics or government. 'Economic theory', as it has emerged and developed, has been almost entirely devoted to analysis of persons within markets, and even here with a neglect or oversight of the ultimate purpose of the whole exercise. Prior to the 'public choice revolution', there was essentially no comparable theory of the interaction of persons within politics. In the absence of such a theory, persons who act on behalf of the sovereign were implicitly modelled as saints, with the predicted consequences. There was a near-total loss of the eighteenth-century wisdom that recognized the necessity of constraints on the agents of governance. There was a developing failure to understand and to appreciate the *raison d'etre* of constitutional limits on government and governors. There emerged the awesome normative gap in elementary social philosophy, a gap that seems clearly to be attributable to the absence of a scientific theory used in its appropriately constructive sense. It is perhaps not an exaggeration to suggest that millions of citizens in many modern states might have been spared the agonies and terrors of collectivism in almost all of its embodiments had the 'science of political economy' been properly rather than improperly used.

X CONCLUSION

Economists will of course continue to engage in both the 'science of economics' and the 'science of political economy'. In the former role they will try to construct more satisfactory models of human behaviour within historically observed institutional structures, with empirical tests being used as an important criterion of scientific progress. These efforts must go forward, and there is nothing in my argument in this paper that suggests otherwise. Economists must, however, understand that the underlying normative purpose of the whole exercise is that of facilitating comparison of institutional alternatives. 'Economic science' is not to be conceived as offering assistance to selected agents who seek to use scientific knowledge to control others. Even if these warnings are heeded, however, the role of the economist, as scientist, is not limited to 'economic science', as defined here. In the comparison of institutional alternatives, the 'science of political economy' emerges to occupy a role that is perhaps more important than its predictive counterpart. In the ultimate sense, this science, too, finds its normative purpose in *control*—that which is exercised upon our behaviour by the selection of the institutional-constitutional constraints within which we interact one with another. But the vital distinction between the use of science to assist in the control of subjects-objects (animate or inanimate) and the use of science to assist in the self-imposed control of the behaviour of those who are simultaneously the controllers and the controlled, must be kept in mind.

NOTES

1. This chapter was initially published in a special issue, 'Social Psychology and Economics', ed. W. Stroebe and W. Meyer, *British Journal of Social Psychology*, 21 (June 1982), 94–106. I acknowledge permission to reprint the material here.
2. We should stress that in the interactive setting any scientific knowledge can be used to damage some persons for the benefit of others. Crusoe's possible discovery of a plant that would induce sycophantic behaviour by Friday would be equivalent to the discovery of Friday's serpent mania.
3. Adam Smith, *The Wealth of Nations*, I, Ch. 2, p. 13, in Modern Library Edition (New York: Random House, 1937).
4. *See* James M. Buchanan, 'Positive Economics, Welfare Economics, and Political Economy,' *Journal of Law and Economics*, 11 (Oct. 1959), 124–38. Reprinted in James M. Buchanan, *Fiscal Theory and Political Economy* (Chapel Hill: University of North Carolina Press, 1960).
5. For a modern discussion, *see* J. R. Lucas, *On Justice* (Oxford: Oxford University Press, 1980).
6. *See* Geoffrey Brennan and James Buchanan, 'Predictive Power and Choice Among Regimes,' *Economic Journal*, 93 (Mar. 1983), 89–*105*, for an extended treatment of the bases for employing the *homo economicus* model in institutional comparisons.
7. As in all shifts in ideas, there are antecedents or precursors. The Italian public-finance theorists and sociologists, who worked in the last part of the nineteenth century, did introduce models of the 'ruling classes' that have much in common with modern public-choice theory constructions. And, of course, Machiavelli himself is the father of all such models. For a summary of the Italian public-finance contributions, *see* James M. Buchanan, *Fiscal Theory and Political Economy, op. cit.*

5 The Potential for Tyranny in Politics as Science[1]

I INTRODUCTION

My title may be extended to the positive statement: There is a potential for tyranny if the enterprise of politics is interpreted as being analogous to that of science. I am not directly concerned with an empirical description of the scientific process itself, a description that may be widely at variance with the representation of this process by those who concern themselves with the workings of politics. I hope that this proviso will forestall potential misdirected criticism from those who might consider my effort to fall within the philosophy of science, even broadly conceived. My subject matter is *politics*, not science, and concerns the illegitimate juxtaposition of two categorically distinct types of social interaction, along with the implications of this juxtaposition for politics. Quite a different, and possibly equally interesting, paper might be written on the implications for science that would emerge from its being modelled as politics. In jargon that George Orwell would have despised, my concern is 'scientized politics' not with 'politicized science'.

In its common representation, science is a process in which conflicts about truth are resolved. Those who participate in the process acknowledge the existence of a reality that is itself independent of any belief about it. The scientific enterprise is necessarily teleological, even when the provisional nature of any established truth is recognized. By comparison and contrast, politics is a process in which conflicts among individual interests are settled.[2] In this enterprise there is no independently existing 'interest' analogue to truth, towards which an interaction process converges. The end-states emergent in the two processes remain categorically different.

When politics is wrongly interpreted as being analogous to science, as a truth-discovery process, coercion may find moral legitimization for those who claim enlightenment. By contrast, when politics is rightly interpreted as a process for settling conflicts among interests, which are acknowledged to be individually derived, those who seek to impose preferred solutions do so without claim to moral superiority.

So much for a summary statement of the argument, one that seems almost self-evident to me but which has proved to be highly objectionable to critics whose views I otherwise respect highly. Their reactions suggest that an attempt to restate the argument in some detail may be warranted.

II BELIEF, SCIENCE, AND TRUTH

Individuals confront the world of reality with a set of beliefs about that which their senses perceive. They conduct personal experiments and, in the process, continually revise their earlier beliefs. They engage with others, directly and/or indirectly, in the discovery enterprise. The boundaries of the 'understood' are continually pushed outwards; the discovery process is never-ending. The 'truths' that are filed away in the category of the 'accepted and understood' are not totally frozen; these remain, at best, 'relatively absolute absolutes', always subject to challenge, exhumation, autopsy, and reversal.

In the scientific quest so interpreted, agreement among informed persons offers a test for the validity of a proffered truth, but agreement, in itself, does not intrinsically validate that which it seeks to establish. Agreement is a stage in the process of moving from personal belief to truth, and agreement signals a resolution of conflict among separate personal beliefs that were earlier advanced. Upon agreement, that proposition which is 'true' can be put away, as if in a filing cabinet or computer memory, and scientific inquiry may be shifted to territory that remains unexplored (Polanyi's metaphor of science as the 'society of explorers' is apt here). It is precisely because agreement does not intrinsically validate a proposition, however, that the possibility for re-examination always stands open. Much of what we accept as truth today, and which does command requisite agreement, will surely become error at some later date. Science does indeed make progress; genuine discovery does take place.

I want to concentrate attention on the position of the individual, any individual, in the discovery enterprise, so interpreted. Regardless of the state of his information, the individual confronts reality with a set of beliefs that enable him to exist and to function. But the individual does not consider these beliefs to be applicable uniquely to him as an individual member of the human species, or even to the species itself. He believes, and accepts as fact, that he cannot walk through the wall. But he also believes, and accepts as fact, that no other person can walk through the wall. That is to say, the individual's beliefs about reality are general in their potential extension. They describe a reality that the individual presumes to exist for everyone. They are not descriptive of a reality that is private and personal and, hence, unique to the person who holds them.

Recognition of this generalization of belief about the reality that exists does not involve imputing to the individual any commitment to Platonic ontological precepts. The individual may acknowledge that the physical theory of atomic structure may not describe the world as it might 'really exist'. The theory, instead, may be acknowledged to do nothing more than allow predictions that have not, as yet, been falsified. My concern here is not with correspondence between the theory of reality that the individual accepts and the underlying reality itself, in some deeper ontological sense.[3] My point is that, quite apart from the presence or absence of such correspondence, the individual extends his working hypotheses about reality to others than himself. It simply makes no sense for a person to believe that he, personally, confronts a reality that is different from that confronted by others than himself.

Important implications seem to follow from this generalization of beliefs. Because the individual lives in the same world as other persons, he may be willing to learn from others. The individual may recognize that his own personal, subjectively experienced set of beliefs about reality remain always incomplete and that this set does not facilitate an understanding of that which he may observe as well as a competing set held by others. To refuse to learn, to hold onto privately generated beliefs in the face of evidence that better explanations are available would reflect abnormality and would be taken as such.

The correction of error in beliefs previously held is so commonplace an event in all our lives that it is often not discussed at all. The farmer counts the number of cows in his herd; someone alongside counts the same herd and comes up with a different number. The farmer corrects the initial error and attributes it to earlier misperception. In the adjustment he may feel a minor psychological disappointment, but he has not compromised either his virtue or his honour. He simply acknowledges the error and goes on his way.

Much the same thing occurs when a person is shown that he has erred in the logical analyses that are employed to support a particular set of beliefs that are held. If the analytical errors are pointed out, the individual will change the emergent beliefs, and without undue psycholgical embarrassment. In the broadest definitional sense, as here interpreted, science is the process through which individual beliefs about reality are continually corrected, and a process within which individuals are brought into agreement about that which is, at least in the provisional filing-cabinet, relatively absolute absolute sense previously noted. The activity of 'science', more narrowly defined, takes place along the margins of established truths and is of course carried on by specialists in inquiry. For the overwhelming majority of persons, and for almost all of those elements of reality they confront, there are truths that remain unchallenged. And it is these truths and their generalization that persons utilize in their daily lives.

The social function of 'science', the activity of the specialists, is that of shutting off dialogue and discourse, of resolving conflicts among competing explanations of physical reality, and of allowing provisional truths to be put to everyday usage, at least until more acceptable alternatives emerge. Agreement among the specialists in inquiry, along with the subsequent acceptance by nonspecialists, signals the end of scientific conflict and the establishment of peace among the contending parties. The nature of this resolution is my point of emphasis here. Conflict is not settled by compromise. Conflict comes to be resolved by a 'victory' of sorts; those who give up a previously contending view of, or belief about, reality do so because they have been led to 'see the light'. They are genuinely 'converted' to the alternative vision that the now agreed-upon explanation offers. Agreement comes about when one protagonist gives up a competing set of beliefs and takes on another. (The farmer does not count twenty cows and his wife twenty-one on the way to a compromise agreement on twenty and one-half as the settled number.)

In the enterprise of science it would be folly to think of agreement among competing specialists as being settled by compromise, with some mixture of competing elements counterposed, one to another in the final terms. Truth tends to be mutually exclusive; agreement settles on the 'either' or the 'or'. Two competing and mutually contradictory explanations of reality cannot be simultaneously held, nor can two explanations be held by different persons and both deemed to be 'correct' in any meaningful scientific sense.[4]

The scientist who challenges a proposition in the widely prevailing structure of agreement does so as a genuine revolutionary. He seeks to overthrow the existing scientific regime on the point in question and to set up his own competing hypothesis as a new truth, to which all must eventually come to pay homage through their ultimate acceptance and agreement. Note that in the process of accomplishing this result, the individual scientist is not trying to get his hypothesis accorded equal weight with those that might be advanced by competitors on the subject matter of concern.

There is something profoundly misleading in the familiar metaphor of 'the free market of ideas'. Organizationally, the scientific enterprise may operate in ways of similar to a competitive market. But there remains a categorical difference. In the market, each participant pursues *his own* ends, purposes, or values. In science, each participant advances *his own claim* to truth that must ultimately be accepted by all. Each scientist is dedicated to the advance of the frontiers of 'truth' against 'falsehood'; each is seeking to impose his own emergently correct vision of reality on the great unwashed. In this sense, science is more akin to a war of annihilation than it is to a market process. It is improper, even metaphorically, to conceptualize scientists as 'trading', either with other scientists or with persons outside the scientific community. As many have recognized, science, as an activity, is much more analogous to religion than to trade, and the liberty of individual scientists to present their own hypotheses is analogous to the liberty of persons to promulgate their own faiths and to seek the conversion of others.

The activity of trade, by contrast, in which one person attempts to demonstrate to another an advantage of interest rather than a path to the light, is at the opposite pole of human interaction from that of science or religion.

The analogy between science and religion is helpful when we consider the attitudes that persons adopt towards one another. Consider a person who has 'seen the light', for example, as a born-again or evangelical Christian. To such a person, others who have not experienced conversion continue to live in sin. They are to be pitied, persuaded, perhaps tolerated, and possibly persecuted. But their views can never be respected in the sense that embodies granting them equal weight with those of the person who possesses the inner light. A person cannot, by nature of his belief, treat someone who holds a contrary belief with mutual respect if this treatment requires that both beliefs be acknowledged as being equal claimants to 'the truth'. To accord such respect to others in matters of belief would amount to a sacrifice of one's own, or rather to an acknowledgment that one's own beliefs, as such, are not generalizable.

How different is the activity of the scientific enterprise, broadly defined? The scientist who has discovered, or who has been convinced by the discoveries of others, that the world is curved rather than flat must hold all flat-earthers to be 'living in error', persons who may be pitied in their ignorance, persuaded so that they too can become enlightened, and possibly even to be persecuted if they remain too stubborn. The flat-earthers' claim to truth cannot be respected in any mutual or reciprocal interpretation of this term. The scientist who now sees the earth as spherical cannot respect the belief of the flat-earther as deserving of equal weight with his own in some measuring of 'truth'.

III INTERESTS, POLITICS, AND ORDER

My purpose in this chapter is not to make any direct contribution to the interpretation of science (or religion). As previously noted, my description is intended to convey the representation of the scientific enterprise as it is broadly interpreted by those who would extend its workings, at least by analogy, to politics, an extension that is both inappropriate and potentially dangerous for the preservation of individual liberties.

In the preceding section I commenced with the statement that individuals confront the world of reality with a set of beliefs. They also confront this world of reality, which includes other persons, with a set of evaluations over and above, and categorically different from, the set of beliefs. For my purposes here, I do not need to identify with any precision the sources of individuals' interests or to assign weights to differing components in what might be called an evaluation vector. Further, I need not express direct concern about the possible malleability of individual interests. My argument depends only on acceptance of the restricted proposition to the effect that an individual can be modelled as possessing (at any given moment) an evaluation or utility function reflecting interests or preferences and a set of beliefs and that these two ultimate determinants of action are logically distinguishable.[5]

The set of beliefs that an individual holds is, in one sense, necessarily prior to the evaluations that reflect his interests and which become relevant only within those beliefs. Indeed, it would be difficult to imagine a person expressing a preference for, an interest in, or value of, something that he did not believe to exist, actually or potentially. Or, to put the point differently, those interests that are potentially relevant must be those that are constrained by beliefs about reality; the values that emerge only in daydreams or fantasies are irrelevant.

Beliefs and evaluations exist simultaneously in the mind of the individual, but they serve totally different functions. Beliefs enable a person to understand reality, to impose a mental order on that which he observes, quite independently of any participation in that order. By comparison and by contrast, evaluations become conceptually necessary for participation in the order that a person's beliefs define as existing. A person totally without values or preferences would have no ability to choose. But, of course, the existence of such preferences is not sufficient to insure a power of choice, since actions may be totally constrained.

As in the discussion of section II above, my primary concern is about the individual's attitude toward his own values or interests and about his attitude toward the values expressed by others, and especially as these attitudes are compared and contrasted with those accorded to beliefs. At some fundamental level the individual must acknowledge that interests (values, preferences) are individually derived and privately held, an acknowledgement that is not extended to beliefs, as previously noted. This distinction is important for my argument, and it deserves detailed discussion.

Consider an example. A person faces a wall with a door in it. His set of beliefs suggest that he cannot walk through the wall but that he can walk through the open door. These beliefs are generalizable to other persons; they, too, must walk through the door to get to the other room. The individual whose calculus we examine, however, also has a set of preferences, values, or interests, which include some comparative evaluation of the two locations. Suppose that the person places a higher value on being in the room beyond the door than on staying put. This will provide the motivation for walking through the door. But the individual who acts in this way need not, and indeed does not, generalize this evaluation to others in any manner at all analogous to the generalization of beliefs as previously discussed. The individual may acknowledge that his own comparative evaluation of the two locations is different from, or can be different from, the comparative evaluation of another person who stands alongside him in the initial location.

Once this elementary distinction is made, however, it becomes evident that there will exist a categorically different relationship between the individual and the other person who holds contrasting or dissimilar evaluations and the relationship between the individual and the person who holds contrasting or dissimilar beliefs. The individual need feel no intellectual or moral superiority over the person who simply values the alternatives differently. In the example, the person who initially stands alongside and who chooses not to go into the room beyond is judged to be neither 'in error' nor 'in sin'. Such a person is acknowledged to have a different utility function, which carries the further and important implication that *differing values can coexist* with no relegation of any one set to a status of inferiority. The implication that is important for my purposes is that the individual, who may be quite secure in his own values, can accord respect to the values of others, respect that can embody the recognition that one person's values count for as much as another's and that, ultimately, each person's values can be assigned equal weight in social order. In summary, a 'democratic' attitude is possible with reference to individual values; a 'democratic' attitude is impossible with reference to individual beliefs.

The elementary distinction I have drawn here is applied by each of us in everyday life. We treat the person who claims that two plus two makes five as a fool; we treat the person who prefers coffee to tea to be entitled to his own preferences.[6]

In the introduction to this chapter, I defined politics as the process through which conflicts among separate individuals' interests are resolved or settled. As the above discussion makes clear, however, conflicts among individuals' separate interests need not arise at all in many settings of human interaction. In the example, each of the two persons can choose his preferred location, each can exercise his own choices. Freedom is possible because the spaces do not necessarily intersect. By contrast, conflicts over beliefs must always arise because of the mutually exclusive nature of 'truth' itself. Persons act as if 'that which is out there' is independent and apart from their own interpretations of it. We do not behave as if each of us lives in his own personal world, with our privately imagined models of reality. Potential conflicts over beliefs cannot be confined only to the intersections among 'private spaces', as is the case with interests or values.

Politics, in my definition, should be limited to that set of interactions where 'private value or interest spaces' come into potential conflict. The range of politics is, then, determined by the technology of interaction itself, including behavioural and institutional elements as well as those more normally considered. Values or interests come into potential conflict only at the edges, so to speak, of the behavioural spheres of action pursued by persons seeking their own purposes. Conflict arises when an individual's action, motivated by his interests, affects the interests of another person. That which one person does may invade the claimed domain of someone else. When such a conflict arises, there is nothing akin to the scientific enterprise that may be called on to suggest means of resolving the issues. You do not become my slave because I succeed in converting you to a new vision of the world, at least not in normal settings.[7]

In its most general sense, one of the functions of politics is the establishment of 'rules of the road' which enable individuals and groups with differing sets of interests to pursue widely divergent objectives without the emergence of overt conflict.[8] Politics in its constitutional, or rule-making, function resolves potential conflicts among individual interests by setting boundaries for private spaces, which, if respected, allow persons to pursue their own ends without interpersonal conflict. One interpretation that may be placed on the working of politics at this level is that the rules themselves can become elements in the belief structure of persons, despite the artifactual origins. That is to say, individuals may accept, as a part of the reality they live in, the existence of quasi-permanent rules that define the private spaces within which individuals may operate without overt conflict. In terms of our simple example, the individual who walks through the door may also prefer that his counterpart in the initial location also walk into the adjoining room. But if the other person does not share this value, potential conflict may be forestalled because the reference person may also accept, as a part of his structure of reality, the legal rules that allow persons to choose their own locations. In this setting there is a shared acquiescence in the possession and retention of differing values.

In this function of rule-making, politics may sublimate conflicts among interests and values by making explicit the appropriate limits within which individuals can act so as to secure their objectives. A set of property rights may be defined and contracts among persons in exchanges of these rights may be enforced. Within this defined structure of rights, persons may promote their own privately generated values without running afoul of other persons. The interests of the individuals are different in market-exchange interactions, but these interests do not come into overt conflict because the structure of legal rights does not allow nonvoluntary boundary crossings without penalty.

There may be near-universal agreement on many elements in a structure of legal rights. Laws against murder, rape, assault, and theft may command almost unanimous consent. Such laws represent the translation into politics of widely held and commonly shared moral values. In many respects such values seem analogous to truths of science. In the critical sense emphasized here, however, values, even if commonly shared, remain categorically different from truths because they emerge only from individuals and do not exist independently. There may be universal agreement that murder is wrong, but there is a distinction between this commonly shared value and a truth that is universally acknowledged to be non-falsifiable.

There may be types of personal interaction, however, where no structure of rules, no assignment of rights, can succeed in eliminating conflicts among individual values and interests. In our simple example, suppose that the two persons in the room should be Siamese twins. In the language of modern economics, the relationships among persons may involve elements of 'publicness'; either technological features of jointness efficiency and/or non-exclusivity make conflicts among interests inevitable. No arrangement or redefinition of individual rights can resolve the conflicts that may arise in such instances.

Consider a familiar classroom example. There are three persons in a room, A, B, and C. Each desires a differing ideal value for the thermostat setting, say, 60, 65, and 70 degrees Fahrenheit, respectively. There will be a range of conflict over the setting, which, because of technological necessity, must be the same for all three persons. In its ordinary function, post-constitutionally, politics is a process of settling such conflicts through institutionalized procedures that take the form of agreed decision rules, at least in nominally democratic politics, rules that take individual evaluation as inputs and then generate results that are applied to all parties. The way such instruments work is the central subject matter, positive public choice—a subject matter that is not germane to my purposes here. My stress is on the nature of the results or outcomes that are generated by the instruments or institutions of ordinary politics and, importantly, on the interpretation of these results or outcomes by those who are affected by and who are specialists in inquiry.

Let us stay with the thermostat example. If the preferences or interests of the persons are plausibly single-peaked, simple majority decision will produce the median-value outcome, or the 65-degree setting. This outcome is, in genuine respects, a *compromise*, a plausibly acceptable reconciliation of the conflicting values (interests, preferences) and *nothing more*. This outcome does not represent the 'community's value' or the 'society's interest', merely because it emerges from the decision rule that has, by presumption, been agreed on at some constitutional stage of rule-making for politics. Nor does this outcome, which in the example comes close to the ideal for the middle or median person in the group, have any claim at all to 'truth'. The persons whose preferred settings are not chosen in the process, A and C, are not, thereby, proven to be 'wrong'. They are not expected to modify their own value or preference orderings over the alternatives because the median result emerges from the operation of the decision rule.

There cannot of course be two thermostat settings; the alternatives for choice are mutually exclusive. But this feature is technologically rather than ontologically determined. There is no unique 'true' value for the room temperature that politics somehow mysteriously discovers and which comes to be established in the working out of history. Agreement may emerge in politics, either among all persons at the rule-making stage (where all may agree on laws against murder) or among only a required subset of persons at the post-rule stage of ordinary politics (where a simple majority may agree on the size of the education budget). But this sort of agreement is not at all analogous to that which occurs in science and the scientific enterprise. Agreement in politics reflects concurrence in individual interests, values, or preferences. At the rule-making or constitutional stage of deliberation, agreement may emerge among all or nearly all prospective participants in collective interaction if they are placed behind a sufficiently thick veil of ignorance and/or uncertainty so that their own interests, post-constitutionally, cannot be accurately predicted.[9] Or, at the post-constitutional stage of ordinary politics, agreement may emerge from a concurrence of individual interests or from a set of trades among members of the requisite coalition. In neither case does observed agreement among all persons or among the required subset provide a proximate way-station toward 'truth', as is the case in science. There is simply nothing analogous to truth in politics at all. There is no unique value 'out there' that exists, or that should be thought to exist, apart from the individual valuations. The individual participant in politics is not engaged in a discovery enterprise. His position is much closer to the role of the trader in the market-place. He expresses his own interests through the instruments available to him, and he accepts the outcome that emerges from the process. Politics is a 'market in interests or values' much as the ordinary exchange process. Its difference from the market lies in its more inclusive range. Politics has the functional task of settling conflicts among individual interests and values at several levels simultaneously, and not only within well-defined legal structures, which themselves emerge from politics in its rule-making stage.

A somewhat different way of emphasizing the relationship between economics and politics, as social processes, is to say that, in the formulation here, 'economics' is fully incorporated within 'politics'. Economics is one particular process through which potential conflicts among separate individual interests are settled. As noted earlier, at the rule-making or constitutional stage, politics may assign to the market the task of facilitating social interaction without overt conflict over a wide range of activities.

The central institution of the economic process, that of exchange, points up the distinction between interests and beliefs. In an ordinary exchange setting, traders possess initially differing endowments and they have initially differing preferences. So long as prospects for mutual gain exist, there are motivations for engaging in exchange or trade. The initially divergent valuations are resolved; at the relevant margins the relative evaluations are brought into equality. But the equality in marginal valuations does not, in any sense, imply that there is something intrinsically determinant in the outcome that is akin to the truth of a proposition, even provisionally interpreted. The agreement between traders does not signal the bringing of separate values into line with something that exists over and beyond the traders themselves. Traders are not 'converted' by the trading process into some modified version of the world of economic reality. The valuations or preferences over alternatives remain internal to the individuals who engage in trade, and there is no convergence to anything that exists over and beyond internal evaluations. Individuals, through trade, are enabled to maximize that which they seek to maximize, given the instruments that they are presented with and in accordance with the constraints that they face. The exchange process allow traders to realize the most from values that are internally based; the process may, in one sense, involve internal discovery of one's own values, but it does not involve exploration of anything beyond the individuals themselves.[10]

Economists have themselves been responsible for confusion at this point, in their definition of 'efficiency' in resource allocation. They have often talked as if 'an efficient allocation' exists quite independently of the process through which the outcomes of market exchange are generated. In a very real sense, therefore, many economists have putatively tested market or exchange institutions against an idealized criterion of 'efficiency' in a manner that has elements similar to the truth test of the scientist. Fortunately, this ultimate absurdity in economic method seems on the way to intellectual oblivion.

VI PROVISIONAL TRUTH AND ABSOLUTE VALUE

I have deliberately counterposed the processes of science and politics in extreme terms. The scientific enterprise that embodies the search for, and discovery of, truth, including the process through which truth comes to be established, has been sharply distinguished from the enterprise of politics, which embodies institutional means of resolving conflicts among individual values or interests. It should be clear, however, that to the extent that the 'truth' established by science and in science is, itself, acknowledged to be provisional (as implied in the discussion in section II above) and subject always to falsification by yet unknown explanatory hypotheses, there may be considerably less danger from modelling politics as science than would be the case were science to be interpreted in pre-Popperian terms. The developments in the philosophy of science in this century which have had the effect of removing scientific truth from the realm of the sacred could only have had salutary effects on the interpretation of political reality. The moral force of provisional truth is necessarily less than that of truth established as dogma. I should argue, nonetheless, that the moral force even of provisional truth, acknowledged to remain at best a relatively absolute absolute, remains categorically distinct from that of value, so long as value is acknowledged to be derivable only from sources within the individual psyche.

Conversely, of course, to the extent that values are themselves held to be independently determinate, and hence outside of and beyond individual scalar orderings over alternatives, there may be relatively little difference between modelling 'politics as science' and as the process for resolving 'conflicts among values'. Indeed, in some circumstances the direction of argument may be reversed. If values are deemed to exist 'on their own' and quite apart from human minds, and, further, if these values are deemed to be universal in application, over persons, places and times, then the moral force claimed for such values may well exceed those which could ever be claimed for the provisional truth of modern science. In such extreme cases, value is treated as some higher form of truth, revealed only to those who hold the sacred keys and hence undiscoverable and unchallengeable, even to those who might qualify as scientists. In these circumstances, those who suggest the appropriateness of modelling politics as science rather than as theology may actually exert an influence towards a less coercive social order. To the leaders of the Inquisition or to the Khomeni's of today, any move towards treating politics as Popperian science might indeed serve to reduce human suffering.

V CONCLUSIONS

In modern Western countries, however, the balance seems surely to be tilted in the manner that my argument has presupposed. Values are widely acknowledged to be derived from individuals, and there are not absolutes. God has been dead for a century, and attempts to revive him are likely to founder. The moral relativism of modern times may be, and has been, assigned a share in the responsibility for the social ills of this century.[11] And we might all agree that politics, modelled as a resolution of conflicts among competing individual values and interests, might have been quite different in a world of absolutes in ethics should have continued to exist. But is such a world of moral absolutes that which the Enlightenment promised? Must we sacrifice our nature as individual sources of valuation to ensure our survival in viable social order?

The thrust of my own argument, in this chapter and elsewhere, runs counter to that which calls for a return to absolute values in ethics, if such were possible. There is a positive side to value relativism that is too easily overlooked. Because values are relative, and because the individual recognizes that his values are indeed his own, it becomes possible for man to model an existence in social interaction with other persons that does not involve acquiescence in a single-value norm. This essential vision of the great eighteenth century social philosophers was somehow lost to the mind of this century. Without this vision, and in the face of earlier moral absolutes, it was perhaps natural that scholars should have promoted 'salvation by science', even in extension to the political enterprise itself.[12]

The social engineer would never have dared base his argument for constructive (destructive) change on his own, personal, and private preferences 'for society', which he would be forced to acknowledge as relative. He turned instead to science for intellectual and moral support and justification. He advanced the claim, directly and/or indirectly, and often in a confused way, that politics, like science, involves a search for truth. And truth, once discovered, carries its own moral justification. Those who do not 'see' must be 'shown the light', perhaps preferably by persuasion but, if necessary, by coercion.

Value is relative, truth is not, at least within the realm of ordinary discourse. To introduce the fallibility of post-Popperian science as a helpmate in the philosophy of politics seems to me to be misguided and ultimately to be dangerous.[13] It is not the recognition of fallibility in scientific truths that facilitates man's understanding of his social order and that renders him tolerant of dissent. It is, indeed, the recognition of the necessary relativism and *individualism* of values, along with the modelling of politics as the enterprise of resolving conflicting among such values, that makes the libertarian social order meaningful.

NOTES

1.   In 1967, I published a paper, 'Politics and Science,' *Ethics*, 77 (July 1967), 303–10; reprinted in my book, *Freedom in Constitutional Contract* (College Station: Texas A & M University Press, 1978), pp. 64–80. In that paper I attempted to clarify issues in an unresolved conflict of views between Frank H. Knight and Michael Polanyi. This earlier paper differs substantially in content from this chapter, but the overlap in subject matter should be acknowledged.

      This chapter was initially presented at a Liberty Fund Conference on George Orwell in Cambridge, England in August 1984. I am grateful to Dr Shirley Letwin, who organized the conference, and to Liberty Fund for permission to reprint the paper here.

      I am indebted to Geoffrey Brennan, Paul Heyne, David Levy, Karen Vaughn, and Viktor Vanberg for comments on earlier drafts.

2.   In a 1983 draft paper 'Science and Politics' I stated that politics is the process through which 'conflicts about values are settled'. This statement aroused such

criticism, particularly on the part of Geoffrey Brennan and Paul Heyne, that I have now substituted 'interests' for 'values' in some parts of the text. For my central argument, this change in terminology is not important. It is 'politics as truth-seeking' that I am directly concerned with, and not the possibility of there being 'truth in values', moral or otherwise. To the extent that the moral absolutist extends the discovery process to politics, my strictures of course apply. But I should recognize the position of someone who simultaneously restricts politics to conflicts of interests and engages in a non-political, non-scientific enterprise described as a search for moral absolutes. Nonetheless, the temptation facing the moral absolutist must remain omnipresent. Why not impose that which is true?

3. For a discussion of some of the issues here, *see* Colin McGinn's review of Hilary Putnam, *Realism and Reasons* (Cambridge: Cambridge University Press, 1983) in *Times Literary Supplement*, 25 Nov. 1983, p. 1307.

4. I am not of course rejecting the proposition that each of several alternative models or theories of reality may add explantory value in the search for a general or inclusive explanation. For example, the *homo economicus* model of man's behaviour, defined in operationally meaningful terms, explains some aspects of observed behaviour in almost all interaction settings. At the same time, an altruistic model of behaviour, again defined operationally, might be acknowledged to yield further explanatory insights. It is possible that these competing models be simultaneously used, each considered as partially explanatory. The statement to the effect that two competing explanations cannot simultaneously exist would arise in this example only if someone claimed that the *homo economicus* model fully explains human behaviour while, at the same time, holding to the view that the altruistic model explains any or all of the same behaviour.

5. In economic theory there is a distinction between preferences and constraints. Preferences are the same as interests in my terminology here, but note that the very definition of constraints presupposes agreement on a set of beliefs. (To use the earlier example, my interests or preferences may be to walk through the wall, but I am physically constrained from being able to do so, and act within this constraint because I hold the belief that I could not carry out my preferences, even if I tried to do so.)

6. Critics of an earlier draft have, at this point, raised the problem of aesthetic as compared with moral or intellectual superiority. They have suggested that a person may adjudge his colleague who has 'bad taste' comparably to the colleague who is 'in error' or who 'has not seen the light'. My argument with such critics can only be resolved empirically. The implicit hypothesis of this chapter, which reflects my general position, is that persons tolerate wide divergencies in tastes or preferences much more readily than divergencies in beliefs.

7. The behaviour of leaders and followers within cult relationships, where something like slavery emerges from a conversion process, is considered to be abnormal and even bizarre. The general public attitude toward such cults corroborates my central theme.

8. For a general discussion of this point, *see* Geoffrey Brennan and James Buchanan, *The Reason of Rules* (Cambridge University Press, forthcoming), Ch. 1.

9. Cf. John Rawls, *A Theory of Justice* (Cambridge, Mass.: Harvard University Press, 1971); James M. Buchanan and Gordon Tullock, *The Calculus of*

Consent (Ann Arbor: University of Michigan Press, 1962).

10.   My reference here is to individuals who participate in ordinary markets as they confront exchange opportunities. If we extend the interaction examined to include the activities of entrepreneurs, who can be described as seeking out potential exchange opportunities that have not been previously foreseen, the model of the scientist becomes more acceptable. In this context the reality sought is the valuations of persons, and the generalization of beliefs about such reality is reflected in the tendency for any newly discovered profit opportunities to be dissipated quickly.

For a discussion of the entrepreneurial role, *see* Israel Kirzner, *Competition and Entrepreneurship* (Chicago: University of Chicago Press, 1973).

11.   *See*, for example, Paul Johnson, *Modern Times* (New York: Harper & Row, 1983).

12.   'Salvation by Science' was the title of one of the most devastating of Frank Knight's review articles. *See* Frank H. Knight, 'Salvation by Science: The Gospel According to Professor Lundberg', *Journal of Political Economy*, LV (Dec. 1947); reprinted in Frank H. Knight, *On the History and Method of Economics* (Chicago: University of Chicago Press, Phoenix Books, 1956), pp. 227–50.

13.   *See* T. W. Hutchison, *The Politics and Philosophy of Economics* (Oxford: Blackwell, 1981), p. vii.

6   Sources of Opposition to Constitutional Reform[1]

I. INTRODUCTION

In this chapter I seek to examine the sources of opposition to constitutional reform, independently of the specific form or direction of proposals for change.[2] For me this task is difficult because the constructivist-contractarian-constitutionalist position has always seemed sufficiently self-evident to make methodological defence unnecessary. I continue to be surprised when I encounter persons, whose intellectual stature commands respect and attention, who explicitly take an anti-constitutionalist stance. What are the sources of their ideas? How do they conceptualize socio-political order? How do they model their own roles in social interaction?

It is necessary at the outset to clarify an important distinction between straightforward opposition to general constitutional change, as such, and opposition that stems from what may be called a genuine anti-constitutionalist mentality or mind-set. The sources of opposition discussed in sections II and III need not reflect anti-constitutionalism in some conceptual sense. In section IV, I examine a particular position that is broadly summarized under the term 'majoritarian.' Section V introduces what I call a 'rights' position, which embodies constitutionalist elements while at the same time reflecting anti-constitutionalism in political argument. In section VI, I examine the fundamental element of the anti-constitutionalist mind set, that which involves conceptualization of democratic process. Finally, section VII represents my attempt to collect the several strands of the argument into a coherent summary that may offer some basis for elaboration.

II. CONSTITUTIONAL REFORM AND THE CONSTITUTIONAL PERSPECTIVE

The constitutional perspective embodies as a necessary element a two-stage (or multi-stage) conceptual model of behaviour, whether the acting entity is the person, the voluntary association, or the inclusive collectivity. Decisions or choices over alternative *outcomes* or end-states are made within the constraints of well-defined operating *rules* (institutions). In the deliberations over choices of outcomes, the rules are provisionally fixed. But decisions or choices may also be made over alternative rules or processes, which define constraints within which subsequent choices over outcomes may be made.[3]

It is possible to make the constitutional distinction between rules or processes within which post-constitutional or within-rules choices are made and the actions made within such rules without, at the same time, accepting the possibility, and hence the desirability, of making changes in the rules in any explicitly chosen sense. That is to say, a person may respect the importance of established rules and institutions but reject the full constitutionalist position, if the latter is interpreted in a constructivist manner. I do not want to quibble about labels here; whether or not the non-constructivist who does respect processes can appropriately be called a constitutionalist is not important for my argument. It will suffice to say that, in my own interpretation of the constitutionalist perspective, rules and institutions of social order are treated as variables subject to modification, but at a very different stage from the within-rules decisions over end-states.

Opposition will arise to almost any conceivable proposal for change in socio-political arrangements. Some persons are by nature conservative in their subconscious evaluation of change. They will acquiesce in institutional change that emerges without deliberative decision; but their reaction to history is passive. They refuse to acknowledge man's power to make his own history, and they explicitly reject the notion that observed institutions of interaction are, in themselves, 'products' of intended human action. I shall postpone discussion of the evolutionist version of this perspective until section III. My concern at this point is with the unthinking conservative stance that does not inquire into the origins of institutional change, that simply accepts that set of rules in existence and evaluates this set as 'good' only because such a set exists and has endured. In a somewhat bizarre use of the term, such a position might be called one of 'extreme constitutionalism' because of its elevation of the status quo to sacredness. But, as noted above, it should not be classified as such in my perspective.

As proponents of this position are observed, however, they are difficult to separate from persons who oppose constitutional reform out of genuine constitutional illiteracy. The latter simply cannot enter into constructive dialogue and discussion about the rules for socio-economic order. They cannot be engaged by those who seek to suggest explicit changes in the rules. Such persons react only to perceived short-term benefits that are promised by this or that politician or party. It becomes impossible to ask such persons to think of their long-term interest, and certainly it remains folly to ask them to think of the interests of the more inclusive community. These individuals tend to oppose changes in basic rules because they cannot translate the benefits that changes may offer into measurable short-term gains. The status quo tends to be supported out of ignorance rather than any adherence to the principles of conservatism outlined above. Unfortunately, most of the American politics that we observe, circa 1982, seems to be based implicitly on the hypothesis that large numbers of the electorate belong to the group of persons just described.

Opposition to constitutional reform may also stem from economic self-interest in a direct sense and need not reflect more fundamental proclivities in either one of the types noted. Members of the groups to be identified below may well recognize that the basic rules (institutions) are subject to modification and change, that differing sets of rules generate differing patterns of outcomes, and that some comparative evaluation of alternative rules is possible and meaningful. Members of the groups to be mentioned here benefit or think they benefit explicitly from the operation of the status quo set of rules. I include this source of opposition to reform in my general examination because, generally speaking, the arguments advanced by members of these groups will seem indistinguishable from those that may be made by disinterested anti-constitutionalists. Members of these groups become anti-constitutionalists in debate-discussion because at a fundamental level they are indeed constitutionalists.

Included in these groups are those who administer the existing rules, the agents of the bureaucracy, who have job-specific and role-specific human capital invested in the status quo. They oppose any attempt to modify institutional structure since this amounts to erosion in the value of their own endowments. A second category includes those who think themselves to be differentially advantaged by the operation of existing rules, or to be especially well informed about the potential exploitability of such rules. Agents of political organizations as well as individual politicians may have 'learned the ropes', or think that they have done so, and hence may be reluctant to modify the rules as the game is being played. The necessary uncertainty about how any changed rule will work creates possible opposition even among persons and groups who might, if they could foresee how alternatives might work, secure differential gains.

A third and very influential category of persons who oppose reform out of economic self-interest includes the interpreters of the status quo set of rules, the constitutional lawyers, in the academy, at the bar, and on the bench. The intellectual capital of the constitutional lawyer is heavily invested in the rules that exist and that have evolved through standardized thought processes and value norms of the legal insiders. Members of this group will resist, and strongly, any effort to shift the constitutional margins by non-judicial means, including resistance that takes the form of attempts to choke off discussion of basic constitutional issues by those who are not accepted in the priesthood. The in-group of constitutional lawyers is acting in this respect precisely as any protected monopoly would act; it is seeking to preserve rents. It is not surprising, therefore, when we see how few constitutional lawyers and legal scholars advocate explicit constitutional reform.

I have identified several sources of opposition to constitutional reform in this section largely to dismiss their various arguments as irrelevant to the dialogue that I seek with the genuine anti-constitutionalists. These sources of opposition are included only because it is useful to be able to recognize the origins of the arguments advanced.

III. INSTITUTIONAL EVOLUTIONISTS

In recent years, and notably arising from interpretations of the position of Professor F. A. Hayek, prominent social scientists have advanced what I shall call here an 'evolutionist' theory of basic social institutions.[4] In this construction, the institutions that are observed to exist are those that have somehow spontaneously evolved and survived. Because they have done so, they are to be classified as 'efficient' in at least one sense. Note that this position does offer intellectual support for the more naïve conservative stance previously discussed. It does so from the presumption that it is essentially impossible to 'construct' social rules and institutions; hence, any attempt to do so is doomed to frustration. The evolutionist position necessarily embodies respect for those rules and institutions that are observed to exist, indeed even to the extent of generating an attitude of quiescence before any of the potential proposals for reform.

Fortunately, however, many of those who seem to adopt the evolutionist perspective in some generalized methodological sense do not really act in accordance with these implications. Hayek himself is a strong advocate of fundamental constitutional change, presented in terms of very specific proposals. In practice, therefore, Hayek combines the evolutionist with the constructivist-constitutionalist perspective. Appropriately constrained, more or less as it is in Hayek's usage, the evolutionist perspective on social institutions can offer helpful counters to the sometimes romantic urges of the constitutional reformers, along with romantics of all other kinds. For those who seek, through the design and the implementation of new rules, to modify the essential nature of man, as this nature has evolved culturally through the ages, it is well that they be called up short by those who insist on the non-malleability of basic elements in human motivation and behaviour.[5] There remains nonetheless the danger that the evolutionist perspective, at the same time, will dampen enthusiasm for genuinely viable reform prospects that are consistent with man as we know him, and particularly on the part of social scientists and social philosophers who might, otherwise, tend to be broadly supportive of reform proposals advanced by modern constitutionalists.

IV. MAJORITARIANISM

My discussion to this point has really been preliminary to the examination-analysis of what I consider to be more important sources of opposition to general constitutional reform, sources that can much more directly be classified as anti-constitutionalist. Why do eminent and respected social scientists and philosophers, who are not natural conservatives and who do not seem motivated by self-interest, reject, and seem to do so categorically, any argument for constitutional change?

One apparent source of an anti-constitutionalist mind-set arises from a naive commitment to 'democracy', without any underlying examination of what this terms means. Implicitly, democracy as a political-governmental form of decision-making is equated with majoritarianism, with majority voting rules being placed in a central and critical institutional role. When carefully analyzed, however, this majoritarian stance is peculiar with respect to its implied constitutional foundations. The 'will of the majority' is to be paramount, and any limits on the exercise of this will are deemed to violate territory that is sacrosanct. At the same time, strict constitutional protection is presumably required for those institutional elements that define operation of majority voting rules themselves. Simple majorities are *not* to be allowed to act so as to abolish majoritarian processes of decision-making; they are *not* allowed to prohibit new elections at periodic intervals with any view towards freezing permanently the power position of a specific coalition.

Members of majority coalitions will, quite naturally, exhibit proclivities to maintain the powers they have achieved. To prevent majoritarian abolition of majoritarian processes, constitutional guarantees presumably become legitimate, but only if these guarantees are very strictly limited to the protection of voting-electoral processes as such. Aside from these procedural guarantees, however, the 'will of the majority' to do as it pleases becomes the essence of 'democracy'.

What majority is to count? The generalized majoritarian response to this question seems highly ambiguous. There is no clearly defined relationship between majoritarianism and representation. If all adults are franchised, but if plebiscitary methods of ascertaining majority resolution of all issues is not feasible, how are persons to be represented in a legislative assembly? There is no natural bridge between majority voting under universal franchise, as an abstract ideal, and majority voting in a specifically defined legislative assembly. It is relatively easy to show with the simplest of analytical models that the 'majority will' of the legislature may not be consistent with the 'majority will' of the electorate under a very wide variety of circumstances.

Even if the problem of effective representation is neglected, there remains, of course, the familiar difficulty that arises because of possible inconsistency in majority decisions. In the presence of voting cycles, there is no majority will, which then prompts the question of when voting should stop?

Quite apart from the questions raised above, and even if we assume that somehow these might be satisfactorily answered, any simplistic majoritarian position founders on the shoals of limits. Almost all of those persons who explicitly or implicitly argue that the exercise of the will of the majority in duly elected legislative assemblies should not be restricted, do so only with reference to potential changes at the margin of current political order. That is to say, few persons, whether they be scholars or laymen, can be found who will openly and avowedly defend the 'rights' of legislative or electoral majorities to do whatever they please to do, even within the constitutional guarantees of the majoritarian process itself. Would it not be legitimate for a duly elected and constituted majority coalition in a legislature to make speech or publication illegal? To make association unlawful? To take valued goods from members of a political minority in a discriminatory way? To jail opponents for their political opinions?

Almost all announced majoritarians will invoke *constitutional* protections and guarantees as the appropriate means of checking or limiting the unconstrained will of majority coalitions. In so doing, however, have not the majoritarians really emerged from what seems to be an anti-constitutional stance? If constitutional protections for both electoral-majoritarian institutions and basic 'human rights' are acknowledged to be necessary and legitimate, what is there left in the standard majoritarian opposition to constitutional dialogue, other than possibly pragmatic disagreement concerning the location of the constitutionally protected margins? And need these margins correspond with some historically determined status quo?

V. THE DOMAIN OF CONSTITUTIONAL RIGHTS

We do not normally associate what can roughly be called a 'rights' position with anti-constitutionalism, generally considered. There would seem to be relatively little intersection between the sometimes intense discussion among political philosophers about rights and the reactions of that set of economists, political scientists, and lawyers who reject contemporary proposals for constitutional reform for general rather than specific reasons. It is possible, nonetheless, to assign to some members of the second group what seems to be a strongly held, even if not explicitly stated, rights position. If we take this step, it becomes possible to explain this group's seemingly contradictory stance on constitutionalism on the one hand and rights-imposed limits on the exercise of majoritarian democracry on the other.

The set of basic freedoms—to speech, press, assembly, and franchise—are not, in the mind-set suggested here, constitutionally protected or guaranteed *for the same reasons* that justify constitutional limits to the constitutionalist-cum-contractarian. The rights position does not derive those protected spheres of individual activity, even at the most abstract conceptual level of consideration, from generalized consensus or agreement among members of the polity. There is no agreement, or pseudo-agreement, even metaphorically, among freely negotiating parties located in some original position and behind some appropriately defined veil of ignorance or uncertainty. In other words, there is no *constitutional choice*, as such, that is conceived to have been made. The basic personal liberties that are to be constitutionally protected are 'natural rights', which are presumed to be known to all persons and which are also 'naturally' beyond the boundaries for the exercise of majoritarian discretion. In this rights perspective there is no rational basis for constitutional limits as such.

The fundamental liberties are constitutionally protected, and legitimately so, because these liberties represent 'rights' that are self-evident to all who seek wisdom and truth. Persons have rights to free speech, transcendently defined 'natural rights', that governments, whether majoritarian or otherwise, dare not abridge. The argument for the protection of such liberties is *moral* rather than rational. In this view it is immoral for a legislative majority to restrict speech; it is equally immoral for a military junta to do the same thing. There is no widely accepted rational basis for morality, however, and once the argument has been shifted to moral grounds, effective dialogue with the contractarian-cum-constitutionalist may become impossible.

The constitutional moralist, whose attitudes are under examination here, need feel no tension between his sometimes extreme opposition to proposals to restrict or expand the exercise of majoritarian powers over areas of social and economic behaviour and his sometimes equally passionate defence-support of a specified range of human liberties against any and all governmental intrusions. There is no inner psychological conflict, because the constitutional moralist does not treat the line between the protected and the non-protected spheres of human activity to be subject to analysis and discussion. This line is given externally, by God as it were, and who is to so much as to question its location?

In so far as the moralist interprets existing constitutional rules as embodying basic rights, he may make a sharp and indeed categorical distinction between these rights and ordinary political activity that goes on within the unprotected spheres. In this limited sense, the rights advocate may seem constitutionalist in many of his overt arguments. As Bernard

Siegan has demonstrated, however, the set of rights that are deemed to deserve legal protection may shift dramatically over time.[6] The Lockean notion of rights to property dominated our legal history for decades, and these rights were accorded constitutional protection. However, the protection was based on a perspective that included property rights as morally deserving of legal protection. Rights to property were not derived from a conceptualized contractarian process in which individuals make rationally informed constitutional choices. In other words, the status of economic rights in the early years of this century in the United States was evaluated on essentially the same grounds that is now accorded to 'human rights'. As we know all too well, this rights-based support of economic liberties proved to be unsustainable in the shifted moral climate of the mid-century. It seems plausible to suggest that a genuinely derived constitutionalist argument for these economic liberties might have fared somewhat better. It could hardly have fared worse.

VI. THE CONCEPTUALIZATION OF POLITICS

The argument that is based on rights, as this argument is used to oppose constitutional change on general grounds, does explain important parts of the dialogue that we now observe. The moral precepts of the late twentieth century do not include economic liberties in the empirically accepted set of rights that warrant constitutional-legal protection. Hence, those who interpret the legitimately protected spheres of activity to be those that are coincident with morally based rights cannot, by the nature of their thought processes, become enthusiasts for constitutional reform arguments. At best they may become pragmatic supporters for specific reforms, which they may reluctantly treat as constitutional.

To those who adhere to the rights position, however, the set of proposed restrictions on the powers of government and on the range of activities over which majorities may exercise their wills, does nothing to violate the basic rights that are within the moral boundaries. It is far-fetched to suggest that majorities hold rights that are justified in some moral sense. The person who does acknowledge the need for constitutional protection for a morally legitimatized sphere of human activity will be neither outraged nor indignant at proposals for shifts in the margins allowed for the working of majoritarian politics. The rights advocate seems quite unlikely to classify those who do advance such proposals as fascist, whether intentional or otherwise.[7] To understand this most extreme form of anti-constitutionalism, it is necessary to examine carefully the conception of politics and government that such a position must embody.

What is there in the constitutionalist position generally, or even specifically, when its advocates advance proposals for, say, constraints on the taxing, spending, and money-issue powers of modern governments, that provokes the fascist charge? We may recognize, of course, that 'fascist' is an emotionally loaded scare word and that its usage might simplistically be explained by the inability of its users to make a coherent response to constitutionalist arguments. But there is a serious question to be answered here. Why does any person, whose views deserve respect and attention, feel it necessary to reduce his discussion to such non-dialogue? What is it in the constitutionalist reform position that generates the apparently genuinely felt fear and loathing? The various elements of anti-constitutionalism previously discussed in this paper cannot possibly provide the basis for the emotional intensity that seems to be aroused.

My hypothesis is that the anti-constitutionalist mentality or mind-set from which the intense reaction emerges embodies an inability to enter, even vicariously, into a conceptual political dialogue in which all persons are assigned equal values. This position does not, and cannot, locate the ultimate source of values in individuals who make up the polity with separate persons counted as equally weighted units. In this very real sense, the position I am describing here is anti-democratic and anti-liberal.

In its crudest formulation the position seems avowedly elitist. If persons are not to be given equal weights in some ultimate constitutional discussions concerning the rules under which they must live, some persons must count for more than others. Discrimination and differentiation among persons is necessary, and the straightforward elitist simply assigns differentially higher weights to the values of his own group.

Unfortunately, the elementary elitist model is not sufficiently explanatory for the position I am trying to analyze here. At a meaningful level of self-consciousness, the anti-constitutionalist need not think that he or she is assigning higher weights to his or her own values than to those of others in the community. Unless this step is taken, however, what is the origin of the observed reluctance to allow all values to count equally in some individualist-democratic-constitutionalist perspective?

My secondary hypothesis is that the basic difference lies in the conceptualization of what politics is all about. The anti-constitutionalist, whose attitude I am trying to understand and explain in this section, does not (cannot) think of political-collective interaction in an exchange or contractarian paradigm. That is to say, individuals are not modelled, even conceptually, as forming and maintaining a polity analogously to entering a complex set of exchange arrangements aimed at securing mutually demanded and jointly consumed 'goods'.[8] The political-governmental process is conceptually divorced from human *interaction* as such.

Politics is instead conceived as an institutional process or experience through which those in designated roles search for 'truth', which, when found, comes to be embodied in 'solutions' for the body politic, as a community. The whole institutional apparatus (elections, politicians, parties, bureaucrats, legislatures, agencies, etc.) may or may not be 'efficient' in discovering or in implementing the 'true' or the 'right' results. Nonetheless, such uniquely 'true' or 'right' results exist, out there waiting to be found, and the never-ending quest of politics, as an activity, is one of coming closer to the desired objective reality (see Ch. 5).

In this idealist conceptualization of politics, individual evaluations are useful only in so far as they offer a means for arriving at a 'truth judgement'. Individual evaluations are not incorporated as value weights that count because they represent persons' own values or opinions or interests. In this conceptualization, 'truth' is not located by counting heads, and agreement itself is not a criterion for the 'truth' or the 'rightness' of an outcome.

I can perhaps best illustrate the profound differences in the two opposing conceptualizations of politics by introducing the contrasting examples of the jury and the market. Consider, first, the decision process of those individuals who find themselves on a jury assigned the task of determining the guilt or innocence of a person charged with a specific crime. These individuals, as jurors, are chosen because they are disinterested in the result; overt conflict of interest would tend to disqualify anyone from jury duty. The jurors are directed to find the truth, to ascertain the correct either-or answer to the question of guilt or innocence. The presence of several persons on the panel, rather than a single person, reflects an understanding that such an institutional arrangement offers a more desirable means of securing correct results than alternative structures, because this arrangement provides protection against biased insights and because, historically, it has been held to assure disinterestedness. Similarly, the voting rule used by the jury, whether this be unanimity, qualified, or simple majority, is evaluated solely in terms of its efficacy in generating patterns of outcomes that are independently defined to be desirable.

By contrast, consider a simple two-person, two-commodity exchange. Persons A and B enter into potential trade with separately owned endowments of apples and oranges. Trade takes place. When trade ceases, the final imputation of apples and oranges differs from the initial or pre-trade imputation. It would seem highly unusual, indeed inappropriate, to classify the post-trading set of endowments, the results of trade, as 'true' or 'right'. On the other hand, the results may be classified to be 'efficient' in economists' terminology, provided only that the trade was seen to be voluntary on the part of both parties and provided that no fraud was seen to be present. The results here are classified by criteria applied to the *process*. In the jury example, by contrast, the process is evaluated by criteria applied to the *results*.

These examples allow me to illustrate the profound difference in the two conceptualizations of politics. The constitutionalist-contractarian interprets the political process as a *generalization of the market*.[9] The anti-constitutionalist, truth-judgement conceptualist interprets politics *as a generalization of the jury*.[10]

My purpose is not to discuss in depth the implications of these dramatically differing conceptualizations of politics. I introduce the difference here only to explain the intensity of anti-constitutionalist argument as it seems to be encountered when proposals for reform are presented. For the persons whose mind-set embodies the truth-judgement conceptualization, *any* overt limits on politics as an activity must serve only to close off preselected avenues of possible exploration and discovery. To such persons, politics as an activity or experience to be constrained within rationally chosen rules makes no sense. From this perspective there follows naturally the view that those advocates who seek to impose limits on the exercise of political authority must proceed from some motive aimed at preventing 'true' judgements from being allowed to emerge. Constitution-alists, viewed in this light, are basically immoral, since they stand opposed to 'truth' and 'right'.[11]

Additional insight may be gained here if we think of the social scientist or social philosopher who adheres either explicitly or implicitly to the truth-judgement conceptualization of politics, as he examines his own role. In such an intellectual setting, the scholar does not, and indeed cannot, model himself directly in a participatory capacity. The activity of politics, as such, is clearly one to be carried out by professional politicians and bureaucrats, who are necessarily modelled as disinterested seekers after solutions to political problems as these emerge. These persons are not agents, or even representatives, who act on behalf of franchised citizens as such, and the observing scholar does not treat his own interests to be relevant in some indirectly participatory sense. Almost by necessity, the truth-judgement perspective requires the social scientist to model his behaviour as that of a disinterested adviser or consultant to those who are the active participants. Like the professionals, the observing consultant scholar seeks only to promote truth through politics.

The scholar I am here describing remains almost totally immune to Wicksell's charge that he behaves as if he is proffering advice to a benevolent despot. If he cannot model politics in some ultimate exchange paradigm, in which outcomes necessarily must reflect some amalgamation of separate individual and group interests and values, there is simply no way that the scholar can envisage a role for himself other than that of the disinterested scientist whose evaluation of truth may be somewhat more heavily weighted than that of the ordinary citizen.[12] This perception necessarily rules out any search for a compromise among separate interests and makes the scientist-scholar unwilling to look closely at processes as means of placing judgements indirectly on outcomes.

If he assumes the advisory role noted, the scientist-philosopher must oppose suggestions for constitutional reform if these involve additional limits on the exercise of political authority. For the same reasons, he should support suggestions for relaxing existing constitutional barriers on political action. Any restriction on political authority directly impinges on the scholar's freedom of choice once removed. In his idealized search for political truth, such a scientist-philosopher needs to roam the universe of potentially feasible political space. His possibility set must remain as inclusive as observed environmental parameters allow. He must be concerned especially about the emergence of unforseen events and about the ability of political authority to respond effectively to such events unconstrained by previously imposed constitutional limits, always on the presupposition that such authority, if unconstrained, can indeed locate and implement the 'right' action.

VII. CONCLUDING HYMNAL NOTES IN PRAISE OF POLITICAL PHILOSOPHY

In preceding sections of this paper I have tried to uncover several elements of what I have called the anti-constitutionalist mentality. These various elements may be, but need not be, combined in the attitudes of particular persons. It seems quite possible that the truth-judgement conception of politics may be overlaid on a rights position, especially if the latter remains largely implicit. A truth-judgement conception is not totally congruent with majoritarianism; the truth-in-politics adherent can scarcely applaud the populist strains of majority rule where each man does seem to count as one. On the other hand, majoritarianism is broadly consistent with a rights position so long as majority coalitions work their will along the peripheries appropriate to the stage of cultural history and well outside the range of rights deemed appropriate for protection. Neither majoritarianism nor rights advocacy is fully consistent with the evolutionist perspective on institutional change. But there may be congruence between the latter and the truth-judgement conceptualization.

Even to list the possible sources of opposition to constitutional reform that are generally based and not specific to the proposals advanced, suggests the magnitude of the challenge that the constitutionalist faces, even at the most fundamental level of ideas. I now think that many of us, myself included, who have tried to advance practical suggestions for constitutional change, have been guilty of oversight and/or neglect of challenges at the more basic level. We have been negligent because of an implicit assumption that the constitutional-post-constitutional distinction is widely and readily understood, and that arguments are concentrated on the particular proposals for change.

We have been successful in gaining a few adherents, both in the academies of the United States and among those whose political influences are closer to the realities of practical affairs. But we are likely to remain unsuccessful in the large until and unless we win more converts in the continuing battle of basic ideas. (It seems appropriate to use 'battle of ideas' rather than the more familiar 'market for ideas'. Since we are referring to mutually exclusive options, the first metaphor seems more descriptive than the second.)

As I hope that the analysis of this chapter has suggested, it is in the realms of political philosophy that the struggle must be waged. At base, what is at issue here is how persons conceive themselves with respect to their interactions one with another and with respect to the collectivities that attempt to command their loyalties. As of any chosen moment in time and space, with a national history and with a geographic identification, a people's attitudes in these respects may be empirically described. There are no universal constraints in such descriptions, temporally or locationally. Ideas may be changed, however, and ideas that persons have about their own positions in the social order may be influenced by articulated statements of the alternatives.

The United States citizenry has surely come closer to an embodiment of a set of constitutional attitudes than any other people in the history of the world. I have often noticed and remarked about the clearly observed differences between the acceptance of constitutionalism by Americans and non-Americans. My admonition here is that the 'constitutional mentality' that so many of our fellow citizens possess almost unthinkingly is a precious heritage that we must do everything within our powers to preserve. At the sheer level of prediction, I am not at all hopeful in this respect.

Let us never disparage the sometimes tedious and often repetitive discourse of the political philosophers among us. In the ontology of politics there are no revelations of 'science'. There are only visions of ourselves that may be either sustained or destroyed by a continued flow of argument. Failure to tend the intellectual fires may ultimately produce the non-renewable ashes of Western civilization.

The constitutionalist vision suggests that free men and women may impose constraints upon themselves and live within these constraints, both in their private and in their political capacities. This is indeed a noble vision, but those of us who hold it will be the fools of history if we fail to recognize that the vision is neither natural to the human psyche nor universally accepted as part of our modern culture. Frank Knight often asked the question: Was (is) the free society an accident in history? He did not answer his own question. I might ask: Is (was) the constitutionalist mentality an accidental time-place constrained framework for ideas that shows little evidence of staying power? I do not answer my own question, but, to me, the two questions are the same.

NOTES

1. Material in this chapter was initially presented at a conference on 'Constitutional Economics' in Washington, D.C., in November 1982. The conference was sponsored by the Heritage Foundation and organized by Professor Richard McKenzie. The paper was published in the conference volume, *Constitutional Economics*, ed. Richard McKenzie (Lexington: Lexington Books, 1984), pp. 21–34. I appreciate the permission to republish the paper in this volume, and I want to thank both Professor McKenzie and the Heritage Foundation.

    I am indebted to Peter Bernholz, Geoffrey Brennan, and Viktor Vanberg for helpful comments on earlier drafts.

2. The important debates between proponents and opponents of this or that proposal for constitutional reform are outside the scope of this paper. Arguments may, of course, be advanced in opposition to particular proposals for constitutional reform while remaining within the general constitutionalist perspective.

3. For an early discussion, *see* James M. Buchanan and Gordon Tullock, *The Calculus of Consent* (Ann Arbor: University of Michigan Press, 1962).

4. My treatment of this subject matter here can be limited because, both elsewhere in this book and in other publications, I have discussed these ideas in some detail. *See* Ch. 8 below and my paper 'Law and the Invisible Hand', in my book, *Freedom in Constitutional Contract* (College Station: Texas A & M University Press, 1977), pp. 25–39.

    For a statement of Hayek's position, *see* the 'Epilogue' to his *The Political Order of a Free People*, Vol. III of *Law, Legislation and Liberty* (Chicago: University of Chicago Press, 1979), pp. 153–76.

5. For an attempt to reconcile Hayek's perspective with my own along essentially the lines suggested here, *see* Viktor Vanberg, *Liberaler Evolutionismus oder Vertragstheoretischer Konstitutionalismus?* (Tubingen: J. C. B. Mohr, 1981), an Eucken Institute monograph.

6. Bernard Siegan, *Economic Liberties and the Constitution* (Chicago: University of Chicago Press, 1980).

7. I have, personally, both in print and in discussion, been so classified, at least indirectly. *See* John Foster, Review Note, *Economic Journal*, 91 (Dec. 1981), 1105; In discussion I was called an 'intellectual fascist' by an anonymous participant after a lecture at University of York, England, in April 1982

    In a more general context, and without personal reference, even so distinguished a scholar as Paul Samuelson has introduced the fascist epithet in discussing proposals for constitutional change. *See* Paul A. Samuelson, 'The World Economy at Century's End', *Bulletin of the American Academy of Arts and Sciences*, 34 (May 1981), 35–44, especially p. 44.

8. It is ironic that Paul A. Samuelson, in particular, should be among the anti-constitutionalists discussed here, since the modern normative theory of 'public' or 'collective' goods owes so much to his seminal papers of the 1950s.

As these papers and subsequent writings indicated, however, Samuelson was never interested in the processes of decision-making as such, but rather in the formally defined properties of outcomes or end-states. *See* Paul A. Samuelson, 'The Pure Theory of Public Expenditure,' *Review of Economics and Statistics*, 36 (Nov. 1954), 387–89; 'Diagrammatic Exposition of a Theory of Public Expenditure,' *Review of Economics and Statistics*, 37 (Nov. 1955), 350–56.

9. My colleague Geoffrey Brennan has objected to my treatment of the constitutionalist as necessarily contractarian. As noted earlier, there is a sense in which the distinction between rules and politics within rules can be appreciated without at the same time accepting the notion that rules are themselves subject to explicit change. In this variant, contractual origins of rules may be rejected, while at the same time politics within rules can be modelled in an exchange paradigm. It is difficult for me to define a coherent position that would model within-rule politics as a generalization of exchange and constitutional politics in a truth-judgement perspective. At best, therefore, the Brennan critique would seem to suggest that all those who reject the exchange paradigm for constitutional politics need not be classified as within the group that adheres to the truth-judgement paradigm.

10. The general attractiveness of the second interpretation is enhanced because, in the conception of many scholars, it fits descriptively with the development of science. Even with science, however, the interpretation may be seriously misleading, and the extension that models politics as science is surely misplaced. On all these issues, *see* my 'Politics and Science,' *Ethics*, 77 (July 1967), 303–10; reprinted in my *Freedom in Constitutional Contract* (College Station: Texas A & M University Press, 1977), pp. 64–80; also, *see* Ch. 5 of the present work.

11. For a paper that deals with related issues, *see* Geoffrey Brennan and James Buchanan, 'Is Public Choice Immoral?', presented at the March 1982 meetings of the Public Choice Society (mimeographed: Center for Study of Public Choice, George Mason University).

12. The long-continuing tension in the social choice literature, and one of the features of this subject matter that seems to attract scholars, lies precisely in the opposing pulls of the two disparate conceptualizations of politics discussed here. The social choice theorist wants simultaneously to array social outcomes in some relationship to individual evaluations of those outcomes and to be able to evaluate those outcomes that are so arrayed in accordance with some non-process criteria.

Part Two
The Emergence of Order

7 Order Defined in the Process of Its Emergence[1]

Norman Barry at one point in his essay 'The Tradition of Spontaneous Order' states that the patterns of spontaneous order emerging in a market economy 'appear to be a product of some omniscient designing mind' (p. 8). Almost everyone who has tried to explain the central principle of elementary economics has at one time or another made some similar statement. In making such statements, however, even the proponents of spontaneous market order may have inadvertently 'given the game away' and, at the same time, made their didactic task more difficult.

I want to argue that the 'order' of the market emerges *only* from the *process* of voluntary exchange among participating individuals. The 'order' is itself defined as the outcome of the *process* that generates it. The 'it', the allocation-distribution result, does not, and cannot, exist independently of the trading process. Absent this process, there is and can be no 'order'.

What, then, does Norman Barry mean (and others who make similar statements), when the order generated by market interaction is made comparable to that order which might emerge from an omniscient, designing single mind? If pushed on this question, economists would say that if the designer could somehow know the utility functions of all participants, along with the resource, technological, and institutional constraints, such a mind could, by fiat, duplicate precisely the results that would emerge from the process of market adjustment. By implication, individuals are presumed to carry around with them fully determined utility functions, and in the market they act always to maximize utilities subject to the constraints they confront. As I have noted elsewhere, however, in this presumed setting there is no genuine choice behaviour on the part of anyone. In this model of market process, the relative efficiency of institutional arrangements allowing for spontaneous adjustment stems solely from the *informational* aspects.

This emphasis is misleading. Individuals do not act so as to maximize utilities described in *independently existing functions*. They confront genuine choices, and the sequence of decisions taken may be conceptualized, *ex post*, in terms of 'as if' functions that are maximized. But these 'as if' functions are themselves generated in the choosing process, not separately from such process. If viewed in this perspective, there is no means by which even the most idealized omniscient designer could duplicate the results of voluntary interchange. The potential participants *do not know until they enter the process* what their own choices will be. From this it follows that it is *logically impossible* for an omniscient designer to know, unless, of course, we are to preclude individual freedom of will.

The point I seek to make in this note is at the same time simple and subtle. It reduces to the distinction between *process* and *end-state* criteria, between consequentialist and nonconsequentialist, *teleological* and *deontological* principles. Although they may not agree with my argument, philosophers should recognize and understand the distinction more readily than economists. In economics, even among many of those who remain strong advocates of market and market-like organization, the 'efficiency' that such arrangements produce is independently conceptualized. Market arrangements then become 'means', which may or may not be relatively best. Until and unless this teleological element is fully exorcised from basic economic theory, economists are likely to remain confused and their discourse confusing.

NOTE

1.   A note stimulated by reading Norman Barry, 'The Tradition of Spontaneous Order,' *Literature of Liberty*, 5 (Summer 1982), 7–58.
      This note was initially published in *Literature of Liberty*, 5 (Winter 1982). I am grateful to the Institute of Humane Studies for permission to reprint the note here, with only minor revision.

8 Cultural Evolution and Institutional Reform[1]

I. INTRODUCTION

In his widely and justly acclaimed treatise *Knowledge and Decisions* (1980),[2] Thomas Sowell explicitly acknowledges his indebtedness to F. A. Hayek, and the book may be intepreted as variations on and applications of Hayekian themes. Sowell's primary stress is on the diffusion of localized knowledge among all participants in social interaction and upon the possible benefits achievable by an appropriate matching of the informational and institutional structures. The mismatch between the hierarchically organized decision-making institutions that presume and require a centralization of knowledge that simply does not exist is an identifiable and reformable source of inefficiency.

The Hayekian emphasis on the diffusion of knowledge or information is corollary to a second major Hayekian theme, one that has eighteenth-century origins, a theme that stresses the spontaneous coordination of the results that emerge from the operation of decentralized institutional structures (the market). This theme is of course encapsulated in the principle of the invisible hand, perhaps the major intellectual discovery in the whole history of economics, and upon which the normative precept of *laissez-faire* was constructed and defended.

The coordination emerges as an unintended consequence of human actions that are motivated by divergent localized purposes. An understanding of the principle of such coordination enables the economist to shed the vulgar prejudice towards 'constructed' or 'planned' integration and to suggest that *laissez-faire* not only maximizes liberty but also the wealth of the nation. This principle of spontaneous order, 'the logic of liberty,' to introduce Michael Polanyi's felicitous designation, becomes the Lakatosian hard core for the economist, around which and from which his research programme emerges.

I endorse fully both of the Hayek-Sowell central themes noted, and I yield to no one in my admiration for Hayek's insightful contributions and for Sowell's imaginative applications. However, there is a third theme that has become increasingly important in Hayek's recent writings, and which is not wholly absent from Sowell's treatise, that does give me concern. This theme involves the extension of the principle of spontaneous order, in its *normative* implications, to the emergence of institutional structure itself. As applied to the market economy, that which emerges is defined by its very emergence to be that which is efficient. And this result implies, in its turn, a policy precept of non-intervention, properly so. There is no need to evaluate (indeed there is no possibility of evaluating) the efficiency of observed outcomes independently of the process; there exists no external criterion that allows efficiency to be defined in objectively measurable dimensions. If this logic is extended to the structure of institutions (including laws) that have emerged in some historical evolutionary process, the implication seems clear that that set which we observe necessarily embodies institutional or structural 'efficiency'. From this it follows, as before, that a policy of non-intervention in the process of emergence is dictated. There is no room left for the political economist, or for anyone else who seeks to reform social structures, to *change* laws and rules, with an aim of securing increased efficiency in the large. Any attempt to design, construct, and to change institutions must, within this logical setting strictly interpreted, introduce inefficiency. Any 'constructively rational' interferences with the 'natural' processes of history are therefore to be studiously avoided. The message seems clear: relax before the slow sweep of history. Shades of the Hegelian mysteries!

In some parts of his recent writings Hayek has come close to the counsel of despair sketched out above.[3] In yet other parts of his work, however, Hayek himself seems clearly to be a 'constructive rationalist', or a 'rational constructivist' since he does not shy away at all from advancing specific proposals for institutional-constitutional reform. Two examples are provided in his widely discussed proposal for the denationalization of money issue[4] and in his proposal for changes in the division of functions as between two separate elected assemblies.[5]

My aim in this chapter is to reconcile the Hayek critique of constructive rationalism with his advocacy of institutional reform. In an earlier paper I criticized Hayek's extension of the principle of emergent and spontaneous order to institutional and legal structures.[6] In that paper I presented the Hayek stance as being internally contradictory; I made no attempt to remove or resolve the contradiction. My effort at reconciliation in this chapter is prompted specifically by an initial and highly stimulating paper by Professor Viktor Vanberg, who sought not only to reconcile the contradiction within Hayek's own work but also to reconcile Hayek's approach with my own, which Vanberg called that of the 'contractarian constitutionalist'.[7] The ideas that I present in this chapter are fully consistent with Vanberg's argument, and in a sense reflect little more than my own variations, as initially developed in a prefatory note designed to accompany the ultimate publication of his paper in monograph form.

II. MARKET ORDER AND NATURAL SELECTION

Economists who understand and appreciate the spontaneous order generated by a competitive market process are aesthetically attracted to the theory of natural selection expounded by their colleagues in biology. There are evident similarities between the selection process that takes place as a market functions to reward the efficient and to drive out the inefficient and biological evolution that accomplishes what seem to be comparable results. Observed survival becomes the test for efficiency in either case.

The differences may be more important than the similarities, however, and these differences tend to be too readily overlooked by economists. The selection process of the market is guided by self-seeking actions of persons who explicitly try to improve their own positions, by entrepreneurs who quite deliberately do things differently than they are being done on the basis of a vision of potential reality that might be but is not. Some entrepreneurs succeed; others fail. But it becomes difficult, if not impossible, to model a market interaction process analogously to natural selection. In an economy without entrepreneurs, how could measurable change occur? Biological man, if dependent on mutational shifts, would be foredoomed to remain at or near the level of animal subsistence if, indeed, he could survive at all. Is there any evidence that man, considered solely as a reacting rather than as a choosing animal, could survive in the evolutionary chain?

Having long since moved beyond the level of animal subsistence, man is dependent on his entrepreneurial talents, his wit, his intelligence, and his explicitly directed adaptability to changing circumstances. At some stage of human history, some man 'invented' rules for interacting with his fellows, and then convinced (by force or by persuasion) these fellows to abide by these rules. Some of these rules (institutions, conventions, mores) survived; others did not. The critical question for my purposes here concerns the equation between survival and efficiency, as applied to institutions themselves.

The level of existence for man in civil society remains much above that level that would characterize minimum survival as a species. Hence, there exists a very large 'cushion' between where we are and where we might be pushed to before species survival might be threatened. If we take our whole complex structure of social institutions (rules) as a unit, therefore, the mere fact of survival tells us nothing at all concerning whether or not this structure, as a whole, is efficient by comparison with alternative structures. We might be able to do much, much better, as well as much, much worse than we do by living within the particular institutional structure that we have inherited.

The fact is that we do not have the opportunity to try out alternative institutional structures; there is no close analogue to the selection process in a many-product, many-service competitive economy. In the latter, selection proceeds by the substitutability of 'better' for 'worse' in a setting where persons face alternatives that may be simultaneously observed and valued. In an institutional context, by contrast, persons face one structure at a time; alternatives may only be imagined, not 'tasted'; alternative rules describe that which might be rather than that which is.

To the extent that differing institutional structures exist simultaneously in different communities (nations), something more akin to market selection may be present. Individuals do observe across community limits, and countries do build walls to prevent the competitive selection process from working its way. But even those who adhere most strongly to an evolutionist perspective with regard to institutions would not place much reliance on international migrations to ensure efficiency in institutional form.

They seem, instead, to rely on some sort of piecemeal, pragmatic adjustment process that generates gradual improvement in institutional structure through time without attention being paid by anyone to the overall design or pattern of coordination or discoordination. Emphasis is placed on the unintended consequences of limited-vision actions, with an implicit faith that these consequences will be benign. It is as if the many entrepreneurial choices, in the small, act always to push the institutional frontier toward efficiency, in the small *and* in the large. The analogy with the developments of English common law joins with that of the market economy.

There are, of course, logical reasons for accepting the notion that imaginative persons will seek always to improve the rules under which they operate, given the limited informational perspective that they must necessarily adopt. Institutions that embody major inefficiency presumably do not exist, when inefficiency is strictly measured by the presence of potential for improvements in the small. The critical question concerns the possible coincidence of this efficiency in the small and efficiency in the large, or rather as applied to the order of the whole institutional structure. Is it not possible that those very changes that may well reflect movement towards local optima can shift the whole system away from rather than towards some global optima? If this possibility is admitted, what rules out the legitimacy of extending entrepreneurial effort to effect changes in the large, to act as 'rational constructivists', and to discuss alternatives grand designs for the whole set of rules that exist?

At this point it is useful specifically to recall the central logic behind the conclusion that the market process generates coordinated results that are, indeed, likely to be more 'efficient' than any alternative organizational structure for delivering ordinary goods and services. The market accomplishes this 'miracle' because self-seeking individuals, who are presumably made secure in their persons and properties by the legal framework, carry out exchanges largely if not exclusively in *separation* or *isolation* from spill-over effects on other individuals who are not directly parties to the exchanges in question. In somewhat different and perhaps more familiar terms, the results of efficiency-seeking in the small, guarantee efficiency in the large because Pareto-relevant *externalities* are either absent or insignificant. The institutions of property and contract are presumed to be such that third-party or neighbourhood effects are minimized.

But we cannot simply extend such logic backwards, so to speak, and presume that, for the organization of 'institutional exchanges' any such separability exists. Almost by definition, an institution or rule constrains the behaviour of many parties in a relevant interaction. In a very real sense, 'publicness' necessarily enters which, in turn, ensures that 'exchanges' must be complex in the sense of including all affected parties if they are to meet any efficiency test analogous to the market. This publicness of institutions suggests that any correspondence between efficiency in the small and efficiency in the large vanishes. Entrepreneurial efforts applied at the institutional margins, in the small, may represent efficiency gains, in the small, but there is no implication that these, taken separately, enhance efficiency in the large since, by definition, all parties affected are not brought into the agreed 'exchanges' that are made.

Hayek seems to raise his objections against any attempts to look and suggest improvement in the whole structure of institutions, referring to such activity as dangerous 'rational constructivism'. At the same time, however, Hayek proposes basic changes in the institutional-constitutional structure of the social order. He remains quite unwilling to adopt a *laissez-faire* stance towards institutions, the stance that would seem to be dictated by his critique of rational constructivism.

III. HAYEK ON CULTURAL EVOLUTION

Hayek is a sophisticated rather than a naïve evolutionist. He does not fall into the absurdity that models the evolution of social institutions on strict biological foundations. He recognizes explicitly that, biologically, the whole epoch of recorded history is well below the minimal time required for any effective adaptation of the human species to environmental changes. Hayek is a cultural, not a biological, evolutionist. Within historically comprehended time, the ages of civil man, patterns of behaviour have emerged, have adapted to changing environmental circumstances. 'Human nature' has been modified within the more inclusive biological limits of animal man. Cultural evolution has produced or generated abstract rules for behaviour that are not instinctual but which we live by without understanding. These rules explicitly counter the instinctual proclivities that man carries always with him, but they do so in ways that we cannot appreciate and understand at the personal level germane to individual choices.

Hayek's strictures against the rational constructivists are directed at those putative scholar-reformers who would ignore the boundaries established by these culturally evolved abstract rules for behaviour, who would, quite literally, seek to make 'new men', who would overturn the eighteenth-century discovery of the essential uniformities of human nature upon which any understanding of, and hence prospect for reform of, social interaction must rest.

IV. RULES FOR HUMAN BEHAVIOUR: INSTITUTIONS WITHIN WHICH BEHAVIOUR DESCRIBED BY SUCH RULES FOR BEHAVIOUR CAN TAKE PLACE

The central, indeed the only, point of emphasis in this chapter lies in my suggestion that we distinguish categorically between culturally evolved rules for behaviour, which we do not understand and which cannot be explicitly ('constructively') modified, which act as ever-present constraints on our ability to act, and the set of institutions within which we may act, always within these rules for behaviour. The culturally evolved rules for behaviour clearly impose constraints on this set of institutions, but they need not define a unique and specific institutional structure.[8] There are many possible structures within which men may behave, and these structures (sets of institutions) may be normatively evaluated one against the other. The discussion of institutional structures that are inconsistent with the nature of man as he exists is properly subjected to Hayek's contempt. Such discussion charitably interpreted may seem little more than romanticizing about unrealizable Utopias. But, when taken seriously, the romantic delusions wreak havoc on constructive dialogue.

As among those alternative sets of institutions that do not place unduly severe demands on man's behaviour in accordance with the culturally evolved rules, there are clearly 'better' and 'worse' adjectives and adverbs to be assigned, given sound analysis along with defensible evaluative standards. Hayek's proposals for constitutional-institutional reform can be interpreted as suggestions that existing institutions are indeed 'worse' than that set which he proposes in their turn. His effort in presenting these reform proposals can be interpreted as rational constructivism in the sense that he is examining the whole complex network of interaction in recognition of the inherent publicness embodied in rules-institutions. In advancing these proposals for change, Hayek is *not* directly relying on the processes of institutional selection in any analogue to natural selection to generate efficiency in the large. He is not expressing confidence that entrepreneurial efforts by limited-vision participants exerted on the margins of institutional change will ensure movement towards the ideal society. In this respect, Hayek's position seems to be quite different from that expressed by other economists who do indeed reflect some such confidence.[9]

Hayek's advocacy of institutional-constitutional reform is not to be classified as the work of a rational constructivist, however, if by this term we refer to the modelling of interaction structures that neglect or ignore the culturally evolved rules for human behaviour that constrain the set of institutional alternatives while not, at the same time, generating uniqueness in results. Hayek is rationally constructivist, within the limits of a human nature as culturally evolved, a stance that allows his position to be made both internally consistent and also consistent with that taken by those of us who, as contractarians, may be classified somewhat more readily as constructivists. This reconciliation is along the lines suggested by Vanberg in the paper noted above.

V. THE UNDERGROUND ECONOMY: AN EXAMPLE

It will be useful to bring this overly abstruse discussion down to earth through resort to a simple and familiar example. In almost all Western countries, increasing concern was expressed about the growth of the underground or non-taxed sector of the economy in the 1970s, stimulated by very high marginal rates of tax, especially as non-indexed in an inflationary setting. As persons locally adjust to high rates, new institutions emerge that are designed to facilitate further adjustments; new loopholes are located by tax entrepreneurs and taxpayers move to exploit these as they are discovered.

The persons who act as tax entrepreneurs, along with the persons who respond by taking advantages of the loopholes, are acting to improve their own positions. Such an expansion of the underground or non-taxed sector of the economy reflects a shift towards increased efficiency in the small; those who are directly involved in the new institutions of adjustment shift toward a local optimum, given the tax structure as it exists. Continued expansion of the underground sector might ultimately lead to a shift in the tax structure itself. Interestingly enough, however, this ultimate reform would in this case be produced because efficiency in the large is reduced rather than increased by entrepreneurial efforts to increase profits in the small.

The point here seems worth some elaboration in detail. Consider a setting in which an individual earns a pre-tax return of $10 on an asset, and faces a 50 per cent marginal tax rate. The government collects $5; the taxpayer retains $5. A loophole is now discovered which allows income from the capital that the asset represents to escape tax. The new tax exempt investment yields a gross return of $6, all of which is now retained by the taxpayer. There is a net loss of value of $4 in the economy, despite the gain to the taxpayer. In an overall or global sense, the economy is less efficient than it was before the discovery of the loophole.[10]

As more and more taxpayers learn of the new tax-exempt options, the economy becomes less and less efficient until, at some point, it may seem evident to all concerned, including governmental decision-makers, that structural changes in the tax code are required. Institutional reform may then emerge that will tend to enhance efficiency in the large, to shift the economy towards some sort of global optimum.

In a sense, of course, such institutional reform can be interpreted as being produced by the responses of persons to the increasing 'badness' of the situations that they confront. But there are dramatic differences between this path of institutional change and the selection process that characterizes the competitive market economy. In the latter—that is, in the market—entrepreneurial effort that is successful displaces values by *higher* values. That is to say, a successful entrepreneur makes a profit on his venture; he increases localized efficiency. He may also create bankruptcy (losses in capital values) on the part of his competitors. But the gains in value to the entrepreneur, along with the owners of scarce inputs and consumers generally, will more than offset the losses incurred by those persons who are damaged. The efficiency of the economy as a whole, in the large, is increased, not decreased, as a result of each and every successful entrepreneurial venture.

As the tax-adjustment example shows clearly, however, comparable entrepreneurial effort decreases overall efficiency, or at least may do so. Ultimate institutional reform that may reverse this localized draft towards inefficiency in the large is postulated only because of some faith that a developing generalized recognition of the need for more basic structural change will emerge. Here there is no direct correspondence between the decentralized, localized responses to the limited-information settings in which persons separately find themselves and the efficiency-enhancing results on the economy considered as an integrated whole.

A second dramatic difference between the process of efficiency-enhancing institutional adjustment traced out in the example and the selection process in the market lies in the implied necessity for decision-makers, at some point in the sequence, to consider structural-constitutional change, to shift their attention to changes in the rules that affect all persons in the community, *to look beyond the localized, individualized settings, and to do so explicitly.*

The world in which all persons act only as tax entrepreneurs and taxpayers responding to the potential advantages offered in a specified tax code could never achieve basic changes in the code itself. *Constitutions, as such, cannot emerge in a process of simultaneous coordination* analogous to that which allows us to classify the market as efficient or which characterizes natural selection. Criticisms of efforts aimed at genuine constitutional change that are based on mistaken notions about the superior efficacy of some sort of 'natural selection' or 'natural emergence' of institutions that meet overall efficiency criteria are simply misguided.

VI. CONSTITUTIONAL REFORM AND HUMAN NATURE

The critique advanced by the example is aimed less at Hayek and Sowell than at those economists who do, indeed, counsel a position of relaxation before the slow history of institutional evolution. As noted earlier in this chapter, Hayek does not stand still before the observed drift of institutional change, which he sees as going in the wrong direction. He explicitly advocates constitutional reform while at the same time he continues to castigate those who adopt the rational constructivist stance. As noted earlier, reconciliation is possible between these apparently contradictory attitudes if we limit the range of institutional reform proposals to those which are consistent with man's own behavioural capacities, as these are shaped in part by the culturally evolved rules that he does not understand. We may accept, with Hayek, that such behavioural rules probably do emerge slowly in a process that is in many respects analogous to natural selection.

The question to be addressed in this section is one that was answered by assertion and not analyzed in section IV above, and it concerns the size of the allowable set of institutional-constitutional reform proposals. How confining are the culturally evolved rules for behaviour that we find ourselves to be saddled with, for better or for worse? If 'human nature' is, indeed, a 'relatively absolute absolute', for purposes of analyzing institutional-constitutional alternatives, does not this imply, also, that there is a relatively narrow, and perhaps even unique, set of such alternatives that will meet 'efficiency' criteria?

To this point I have been able to avoid defining 'efficiency' in the overall sense of application to an economy or a polity. It is no longer possible to do this since the answer to the questions posed immediately above depends critically on the definition that is adopted. If 'efficiency' is defined in terms of an objectively measurable and objectively identifiable value indicator, there would be a *unique* set of institutions for economic-political interaction that would maximize the indicator, given the relatively absolute absolute rule for behaviour that describe the reaction-responses of individuals to their circumstances. In such a setting, the suggested distinction between the restrictions imposed by 'human nature' and those that might be imposed by institutional constraints loses most, if not all, of its usefulness. Hayek could have, in this sort of setting, reserved his criticism for those who might seek other objectives than maximization of the relevant value indicator (which need not of course be limited to simple economic value as ordinarily measured). There would have been little or no reason to talk about those constructivists who disregard the limits of man as he exists.

The distinction here takes on more usefulness, however, when the existence of such a value indicator that objectively measures efficiency of the economy-polity is categorically rejected. The alternative definition for efficiency relies in no way on the existence of such a measure. Instead, 'efficiency' is defined as 'that which tends to emerge from the voluntary agreement among persons in the relevant group'. This definition becomes the only one possible unless it is presumed that the subjective evaluation of individuals are objectively known to external observers or that the evaluations relevant to efficiency are to be divorced from individual evaluations altogether. Once we define efficiency by voluntary agreement, however, we must allow for the non-uniqueness of the set of rules and institutions that may satisfy 'efficiency criteria'. Since that which is efficient is that which emerges from agreement, and not vice versa, we cannot restrict or limit the range of agreement to a unique outcome.

This point is so simple that it is often overlooked. Consider two traders, each initially endowed with a stock of a single 'good', one with apples, the other with oranges. There is no *unique* result of the trading process that can be objectively identified as such. A whole set of outcomes will satisfy the efficiency criterion. In orthodox economic theory, the outcome can be shown to approach uniqueness in the limit as the numbers of traders on both sides of the exchange approach infinity. But for purposes of the analysis of 'exchange agreements' on institutional changes, this general-equilibrium emphasis on uniqueness tends to be seriously misleading. As noted earlier, 'publicness' is necessarily embodied in institutions. Hence, if efficiency criteria are to incorporate individual evaluations, all individuals must be brought into the relevant 'exchange', and agreeement among all these must be the only meaningful conceptual test.

Hayek's criticism of the rational constructivist can be interpreted in this light as an appeal to restrict proposals for institutional-constitutional changes to those that are possible, given the limits of human nature as it exists. To participate in the ongoing dialogue-discussion of constitutional alternatives and to advance proposals that fail to recognize man for what he is, this participation becomes equivalent to proposing that we transcend ordinary laws of logic or science. The difference lies in the immediacy of feedback in the latter cases, a feedback that may only occur after disastrous social experimentation in the former. The fools are not nearly so readily exposed, and it remains always possible that agreement will be reached (at least among a relevant decision-making group) on the introduction of social changes that would require some being other than ordinary man in order to generate the outcomes that are promised.

Tragedy of major proportions has, of course, been the result of such experiments throughout history. But political man especially remains the romantic fool, as Frank Knight emphasized, and we need the essential wisdom of the scholars like Hayek and Sowell to warn us against our own romanticism. But on balance it would surely have been more accurate for Hayek to have warned us all against the 'romantic constructivist', since, properly interpreted, a 'rational constructivist' stance must be taken if institutional reform, even within the relatively narrowed Hayekian limits, is to be seriously examined.

NOTES

1. This chapter was initially presented as a paper in a Liberty Fund Conference in Savannah, Georgia in March 1982. I acknowledge permission of Liberty Fund and Professor Karen Vaughn, organizer of the conference, for permission to publish the paper in this book.
2. Thomas Sowell, *Knowledge and Decisions* (New York: Basic Books, 1980).
3. *See* especially *Rules and Order*, Vol. 1 of *Law, Legislation and Liberty* (Chicago: University of Chicago Press, 1973).
4. *See* F. A. Hayek, *Denationalization of Money*, Hobart Paper 70 (London: Institute of Economic Affairs, 1976).
5. *See The Political Order of a Free People*, Vol. 3, *Law, Legislation and Liberty* (Chicago: University of Chicago Press, 1979).
6. *See* James M. Buchanan, 'Law and the Invisible Hand', in Buchanan, *Freedom in Constitutional Contract* (College Station: Texas A & M University Press, 1977), pp. 25–39.
7. Viktor Vanberg, 'Libertarian Evolutionism, Constructivist Rationalism, and Contractarian Constitutionalism—The Issue of Constitutional Reform', presented at Liberty Fund Conference on Economic and Philosophical Foundations of Capitalism, Freiburg, Germany, February 1981. A revised version of this paper is published as a Walter Eucken Institute monograph, *Liberaler Evolutionismus oder Vertragstheoretischer Konstitutionalismus?* (Tubingen: J. C. B. Mohr, 1981).
8. On this point, *see* below, section VI.
9. The work of Demsetz immediately comes to mind, with his early and much-cited reference to the emergence of private property rights among the

Labrador Indians. *See* Harold Demsetz, 'Toward a Theory of Property Rights', *American Economic Review*, 57 (May 1964), 347–59; *see also*, S. Pejovich, 'Towards an Economic Theory of the Creation and Speculation of Property Rights,' *Review of Social Economy*, 30 (Sept. 1972), 309–25. More recently, Andrew Schotter has attempted to model a formal theory of institutional emergence, using game theory constructions; *see* Andrew Schotter, *An Economic Theory of Social Institutions* (Cambridge: Cambridge University Press, 1981).

10.   The illustration is, of course, oversimplified and the conclusion depends on the satisfaction of some conditions. If the $5 collected by the government should be *totally* wasted, the discovery of the loophole would then increase rather than decrease efficiency. If, however, as much as $1 is spent productively, even on pure transfers, the conclusion holds.

9 Notes on Politics as Process[1]

In Chapter 3, entitled 'The Public Choice Perspective', I distinguished two related components that set public choice aside from orthodox approaches to politics. One is the extension of the economists' utility-maximizing framework to the behaviour of persons in various public-choosing roles. The second is the idealized conceptualization of politics as complex exchange. In this conceptualization the political process and the market process are analogous. In each process, individuals seek to further *their own* purposes, whatever these may be, by engaging in social interaction. There exists no purpose or objective over and beyond those of participating individuals. In the public choice perspective, properly understood, there simply are no such things as 'social objectives', 'national goals', or 'social welfare functions'.

This much is surely familiar ground to any modern public choice scholar. In these preliminary notes, however, I want to explore some of the implications of the politics-as-exchange conceptualization more thoroughly. I want to look closely at 'politics as process'.

The relationship to the Austrian and near-Austrian perspective on economics should be evident. For economists it is surely necessary to interpret the social interaction summarized as 'the market' as a process before we can so much as commence to interpret politics similarly. If, by contrast, the market is viewed as a 'mechanism', 'device', or 'instrument' for the furtherance of some independently existing objective—whether this be 'efficiency', 'social justice' or the 'glory of God'—there is no point in extending the argument prematurely to politics. That is to say, the required paradigm shift must have already occurred with respect to the conceptualization and understanding of the market before constructive dialogue can begin about politics.

Before getting into such dialogue, therefore, let me stay with the 'market as process' and summarize what I mean and what I think that the Austrians mean, or should mean, when they make such reference. The market is an institutional process within which individuals interact, one with another, in pursuit of their separate individual objectives, whatever these may be. The great discovery of the eighteenth-century philosophers was that, within appropriately designed laws and institutions, separately self-interested individual behaviour in the market generates a spontaneous order, a pattern of allocational-distributional outcomes that is chosen by no one, yet which is properly classified as an order in that it reflects a maximization of the values of the participating persons. What these values are are defined only in the process itself; the individual values, as such, do not exist outside or independently of the process within which they come to be defined. In this sense, and in this sense only, can the order generated in the market process be labelled or classified as 'efficient'. Economists who presume some inherent ability to define that which is 'efficient' independently from the behaviour of persons in the market process itself, a definition that is then utilized to evaluate the performance of the market as an institution, these economists presume an arrogance that simply should not be countenanced.

Now let me return to two statements made above. I said that the market is an institutional process within which individuals interact, one with another, in pursuit of their separate individual objectives, whatever these may be and that the great discovery of the eighteenth-century philosophers was that, *within appropriately designed laws and institutions*, separately self-interested behaviour in the market generates a spontaneous order. I then went on to say that this order reflects a maximization of individuals values as these values are revealed in the process itself. What I want to emphasize here is that, without the appropriate laws and institutions, which would include defined private property rights that are respected and/or enforced and procedures for guaranteeing enforcement of contracts, the market would not generate a spontaneous order embodying 'efficiency' in any value maximization sense, if indeed we could refer to 'a market' at all. The spontaneous order of Hobbesian anarchy would not maximize individual values and presumably would come closer to value minimization. The point to be made here is that the behaviour of persons in any social interaction always takes place within a tension between at least two separately directed motivational pulls: between the furtherance of narrowly defined and short-term self-interest on the one hand and enlightened and long-term self-interest on the other, with the second behaviour described as embodying respect for the equal rights of others in the interaction process. (I shall leave other possible motivations, such as genuine altruism, out of account here.) That is to say, in any trade or exchange, the individual participant has a self-interested motivation to dissemble, to cheat, to defraud, and to default. Laws, customs, traditions, moral precepts — these are all designed and/or evolve to limit or control the exercise of such short-term self-interest. And the spontaneous order emergent from the market process maximizes separately conceived individual values *only* if these institutional constraints operate successfully.

Let me now turn to 'politics as process' after the tour through what should have been familiar intellectual territory. The central point I want to make is that the complex exchange process of politics requires a much less familiar but precisely analogous set of institutional and/or moral constraints if the order emergent from such a process can be described as embodying any tendency at all towards the maximization of separately derived individual values. To think about this, return to the ever-present tension between narrow short-term self-interest and the enlightened self-interest that embodies respect for the rights of other participants in the interaction or exchange. Our ethos is such that the internal and external constraints on 'deviant' self-interested behaviour in market exchange seem both natural and necessary. Honesty, as an attribute of exchange, is a quality that we acknowledge to be appropriately encouraged by internally applicable moral codes and by externally imposed legal sanctions. There is no comparable encouragement of a quality in political 'exchange' that corresponds to 'honesty' in market dealings. To be sure, there are both moral and legal sanctions against overt bribery and corruption, but these activities are miniscule in relation to the departures from what we might call 'honesty' in political exchange in a sense at all comparable to that summarized under this rubric in connection with market behaviour. Many of the activities that are, by common interpretation, acceptable within the range of modern politics would be classified as predatory if carried out in markets.

In the market I respect the ownership rights of the person with whom I trade, and vice versa. I do not defraud my exchange partner, and I do not default on my contractual obligations. My exchange partner behaves reciprocally. At least this pattern of behaviour describes the idealization of the market process that we spend our time analyzing. In politics, as we observe it, ownership rights are not respected, if indeed such rights can be said to be defined at all. In certain conceptualizations of politics, the polity, the state, seems to lay claim to all values nominally held by its citizens, and, particularly, this putative claim is held to be 'legitimate' if all citizens are somehow allowed access to equal voices in the ultimate determination of state decisions.

In Hobbesian anarchy there is no 'mine and thine'; there are neither moral nor legal sanctions against my taking from you that value which I have the physical power to take. How is the modern state empirically any different? As envisaged by most modern political scholars as well as by practising politicians, there would be no discernible distinctions at this level. In such conceptualization, politics is not a complex exchange process, even in its most idealized perception.

Let me be clear that my concern here is not with politics as it operates as an observed institutional reality. My concern is with the idealization of politics, the basic model from which the empirical reality may be conceptually derived. What would be required if politics is to be appropriately conceived as complex exchange analogous to that which takes place in the idealized market?

Clearly, it is possible to conceptualize a contractual process in which many separate persons, each endowed with a set of valued claims (to person and property) that is acknowledged by all others in the group, enter into agreement to establish a political community, the agency of which will be charged with the task of enforcing the terms of the contract along with other contractually designated functions. As I tried to trace out in my book, *The Limits of Liberty* (1975), each person gains in such a contractual process.[2] There are mutual gains from trade fully analogous to those emergent in the idealized market. And, indeed, some such political contract is a necessary precondition for the establishment of the constraining laws and institutions without which the market process itself cannot function.

In this most fundamental idealization, therefore, *politics is a complex exchange process* fully analogous to the market. But both as it is observed to operate and as it is justified in modern political discourse, politics is not constrained to ensure that mutual gains emerge from the exchange. There are no well-recognized limits to behaviour in politics that act to ensure that individual values are separately maximized.

Even if the requirement for such constraints should be fully recognized, however, designing them is not the straightforward task it may seem. To ensure mutuality of advantage over all parties to the complex exchange of politics, a Wicksellian rule of unanimity would seem necessary. But such an inclusive decision rule would of course make political action almost impossible. Some departure from unanimity must be accepted, by all contracting parties, as the Buchanan-Tullock analysis in *The Calculus of Consent* (1962) was designed to demonstrate.[3] Once such a departure is in place, however, there is necessarily an opportunity offered to those who would use politics for predation, who would leap outside of any boundaries defined by the range of mutuality of advantage. The only means of keeping the potentially exploitative polity from following its natural tendency in this respect lies in contractual-constitutional constraints that restrict sharply the range of state activities and functions. Politics that is confined to a few and well-defined tasks cannot be seriously predatory.

The American founders seemed to recognize this simple truth. Modern political scholars do not. Through their continuing refusal and reluctance to conceptualize politics as a complex exchange process, even in its ideal form, modern political scholars offer varying apologies, justifications, or rationalizations for the predatory politics that we all observe. Such predation tends to be obscured by all discourse that interprets politics teleologically, as if, in some ideal image, politics is aimed at the furtherance of some transcendant, extra-individual purpose or objective, whether this be 'truth', 'efficiency', 'goodness', 'social justice', or 'the glory of God' (see Ch. 5).

The Austrian insight of the market as process tends to undermine the teleological interpretation of economic interaction, although many who call themselves modern Austrians do not seem to have totally recognized the normative implications of the process interpretation. Public choice, in its Wicksellian-contractarian-constitutionalist variant or component that idealizes politics as a complex exchange process, tends necessarily to undermine any teleological interpretation of political interaction, although many public choice economists do not seem to have totally recognized the normative implications of the process interpretation.

NOTES

1. Material in this chapter was initially presented in a panel discussion at the Public Choice Society meeting in Savannah, Georgia in March 1983.
2. James M. Buchanan, *The Limits of Liberty* (Chicago: Chicago University Press, 1975).
3. James M. Buchanan and Gordon Tullock, *The Calculus of Consent* (Ann Arbor: University of Michigan Press, 1962).

10 Rights, Efficiency, and Exchange: The Irrelevance of Transactions Cost[1]

I. INTRODUCTION

Economists commence analysis with utility functions and production functions as defining attributes of choosing-acting entities. Interdependencies among utility and production functions of separate persons and units provide the origins of exchanges, which become the central subject matter for economists' attention. Interdependencies that remain outside exchanges—uncompensated transfers of positive and negative values—become externalities in the economists' lexicon. One of the contributions of the property-rights, law-economics research of the last three decades has been the focus of economists' attention on the necessity of including legal-institutional constraints along with resource constraints in any analysis of economic interaction.

Lawyers commence analysis with legal rights assignments as defining attributes of potential litigants. Differential evaluation of rights by separate persons and units give rise, in the legal setting for analysis, to exchanges in rights, which are equivalent to the exchanges that the economists analyze. Predation or invasion of rights, whether actual or potential, give rise to appeals to the protective capacity of the state, or, with uncertainty in rights definition, to potential litigation.

Note that the economists' conception of externalities bears no direct relation to the legal invasion of rights. Persons may impose economic harm or benefit, without payment or exaction of compensation, while confining behaviour within spheres of legally defined rights. Lawyers, as well as economists, have come to recognize, however, that well-defined rights can facilitate exchanges.[2]

Ambiguity remains on the question as to whether or not legally permissible impositions of harm (and/or benefit) of a person (persons) on another (others) generate inefficiency in resource utilization in a setting where rights are well defined and contracts are enforced and in which all persons can enter into voluntary exchanges. In such a setting, *will resources necessarily move towards their most highly valued uses*?

The central argument in Coase's seminal 1960 paper, 'The Problem of

Social Cost', is that voluntary exchange in well-defined rights provides a sufficient condition for allocative efficiency.[3] Coase amended this central proposition by what has been widely interpreted as a 'zero transactions costs' qualifier, which, as I shall demonstrate, weakened the force of his argument.[4] Robert Cooter raised the question explicitly in his 1982 paper, 'The Cost of Coase'.[5] He argued that allocative efficiency is guaranteed by voluntary exchanges of rights only in fully competitive environments, and that strategic bargaining behaviour will emerge as a source of potential resource wastage in non-competitive interactions. In the absence of some externally imposed rule for dividing the purely distributional gains, there is no assurance that exchanges in rights will shift the economy towards the Pareto efficiency frontier and maintain a position on the frontier once reached.

My purpose in this paper is to exorcise the ambiguity here, an ambiguity that emerges from confusion on elementary conceptual principles, and a confusion that is shared, at least to some degree, by the Coasians as well as their critics. I shall demonstrate that consistent application of a *subjectivist-contractarian* perspective offers genuine clarification along several dimensions of the law-economics intersection.[6]

II. A CONTRACTARIAN RECONSTRUCTION OF THE COASE THEOREM

Coase was primarily interested in showing, through a series of both hypothetical and historical examples, that freedom of exchange and contract will ensure that resources are allocated to their most highly valued uses, that if the assignment of rights is clear, parties involved in actual or potential interdependence will have incentives to negotiate among themselves and exchange rights to the disposition over resources so long as differential evaluations are placed on those rights of disposition. Put in externality language, Coase was essentially arguing that all Pareto-relevant externalities would tend to be eliminated in the process of free exchange-contract among affected parties.[7]

It is unfortunate that Coase presented his argument (through the examples) largely in terms of presumably objectively measurable and independently determined harm and benefit relationships. In his formulation these relationships become *identical* in the perception of all parties to any potential exchange of rights.[8] Hence, the unique 'efficient' (benefit-maximizing or loss-minimizing) allocation of resources exists and becomes determinate conceptually to any external observer. The efficacy of free exchange or rights in attaining the objectively determined 'efficient' outcome becomes subject to testing by observation. The exchange process, in this perspective, is itself evaluated in terms of criteria applied to the outcomes that the process is observed to produce. There are values inherent in allocations that exist quite independently of the means through which these allocations are generated.

Despite his own earlier contribution to what may be called the subjectivist theory of opportunity cost,[9] Coase's position on the independent determinacy and existence of an 'efficient' allocation of resources is not clear. Both his use of the numerical examples and his introduction of the transactions-costs proviso suggest that Coase was indeed applying outcome criteria to results of the exchange process rather than limiting his attention to the process itself. To the extent that Coase does apply outcome criteria for allocative efficiency, however, his whole analysis, along with that of his many favourable interpreters, becomes vulnerable to the critique mounted by Cooter and others, who suggest that elements of confusion have been introduced by thinking that transactions costs involve only communication-information difficulties. In fact, parties to bargains in small-number settings with distributive as well as allocative implications have strategic reasons for concealing their preferences and, in large-number settings, all parties may have free-rider motivations, independently of any communication-information failures. In both of the latter cases, voluntary exchange would not seem to guarantee the attainment of the Pareto efficiency frontier, and for reasons not well defined within the transactions-costs rubric. Interpreted in terms of satisfying outcome criteria for efficiency, the Coase theorem fails in non-competitive settings; free exchange and contract among parties does not necessarily generate an allocation of resources to their most highly valued uses. 'Social value' is not necessarily maximized; 'externalities' that are Pareto-relevant may remain in full trading equilibrium.

The Coasian, who remains at the same time an objectivist for whom an 'efficient' resource allocation exists independently of the process of its generation, will have difficulty responding satisfactorily to the critique advanced by Cooter and others who make similar arguments. Parties to potential exchanges who are rational maximizers of expected utilities may fail to reach the presumed objectifiable Pareto efficiency frontier. 'Gains from trade' may remain after the parties conclude their bargaining sessions; resources may remain in uses that yield relatively lower values than they might yield in alternative uses.

If, however, the whole Coase analysis is interpreted in subjectivist-contractarian (or, if preferred, Austrian-Wicksellian) terms, the critique can be shown to be without substance. If the only source of valuation of assets or resource claims is the revealed choice behaviour of parties to potential exchanges, there is no means through which an external observer can determine whether or not trade, as observed, stops short of some idealized norms. If a person A is observed to refuse an offer of $ X for asset T, then person A must be presumed to place a value on T in excess of $X. That asset, in A's usage, must be yielding a value or benefit more than $X. The fact that some portion of the imputed subjective value of T, to the current owner, A, may be based on his estimates as to the real preferences (valuations) of B, the potential purchaser, is totally irrelevant. In the institutional setting implicitly postulated here, in which A and B are isolated parties to potential exchange, the absence of a consummated exchange of the asset T demonstrates that this asset remains in its most highly valued use. 'Efficiency' in resource use, *given the institutional setting*, is ensured so long as A and B remain free to make the exchange or to refuse to make it.

Note that the invariance version of the Coase theorem is *not* valid in this perspective. The contractarian approach suggests that free exchange among parties will guarantee that resources remain in their most highly valued uses, but it does imply that the ownership or liability patterns, the assignment of legal rights, may affect the allocation that emerges in small-number settings, and quite apart from the acknowledged relevance of income effects. A switch in the assignments of ownership rights in my example, from A to B with respect to the initial ownership of the asset T, may well result in the retention of the asset by B and, therefore, in a usage different from that to which A might have put the asset with the earlier ownership assignment.

III. IS WHAT IS ALWAYS EFFICIENT?

The contractarian reconstruction of the Coase theorem outlined in section II may seem at the outset vulnerable to the charge that, so interpreted, the theory becomes a tautology.[10] If there is no objective criterion for resource use that can be applied to outcomes, as a means of indirectly testing the efficacy of the exchange process, then so long as exchange remains open and so long as force and fraud are not observed, that upon which agreement is reached is, by definition, that which can be classified to be efficient.[11] In this construction, how can inefficiency possibly emerge?

In an early paper, published initially in 1959, I suggested that agreement is the only ultimate test for efficiency, but that the test need not be confined in application to the allocative results or outcomes generated under explicitly existing or defined institutional-structural rules.[12] The agreement test for efficiency may be elevated or moved upwards to the stage of institutions or rules as such. Agreement on a change in the rules within which exchanges are allowed to take place would be a signal that patterns of outcomes reached or predicted under the previously existing set of rules are less preferred or valued than the patterns expected to be generated under the rule-as-changed. Hence, the new rule is deemed more efficient than the old. The discussion and agreement on the change in the rules here is analogous to the trade that takes place between ordinary traders in the simple exchanges made under postulated rules.

With a change in the rule or institution, however, the pattern of outcomes reached through within-rule trades or exchanges would be expected to be different from that attained under the rules that existed prior to the change. This suggests only that any allocation of resources that is to be classified as 'efficient' depends necessarily on the institutional structure within which resource utilization-valuation decisions are made.[13] This implication creates no difficulty for the subjectivist-contractarian who does not acknowledge the uniqueness of the resource allocation that is properly classified to be efficient.

The position I am advancing here may be clarified by reference to the familiar prisoners' dilemma. The contractarian is not put in the role of denying that such dilemmas exist. Indeed, his diagnosis may suggest that such dilemmas characterize many areas of social interaction. Consider, then, how the contractarian-subjectivist would approach the prisoners' dilemma. Take the most familiar and original example, where there are two prisoners presented with the classic alternatives and allowed no communication with each other. Here, the outcome predicted, and possibly observed, to emerge may be classified as 'presumably inefficient' for the set of prisoners considered as a group because they are not allowed to make explicit exchanges. If they are instead allowed to communicate, one with another, and to make *binding-enforceable contracts*, they would never remain in the 'both confess' trap. They would exchange binding commitments not to confess, and this result, as observed, would be classified properly as 'efficient', again for the set of prisoners treated as the relevant group.

The dilemma, as such, may, however, be an efficient institution for forcing prisoners to confess. That is to say, the subset of the population made up of prisoners only may not be the set relevant for a political-collective evaluation of the institution. In the more inclusive community, the test for whether or not that institution which removes the option of binding contracts among prisoners is efficient would depend on the attainment or non-attainment of community-wide consensus on change to some alternative institution.

IV. TRANSACTIONS COSTS

I have not introduced transactions costs as a possible barrier to the attainment of allocative efficiency through voluntary exchanges anywhere in the above discussion. And, as I noted earlier, the thrust of Coase's argument is weakened by the insertion of the transactions costs qualification. There is no meaning of the term 'allocative efficiency' in an idealized zero-transactions costs setting under the subjectivist-contractarian perspective. Such 'efficiency' assumes meaning only if an objectivist conceptualization of resource use is implicitly postulated. Resources will, of course, be differently allocated by voluntary exchanges of rights in differing institutional settings, as noted above, but to say this is to do nothing more than to say that persons will behave differently under differing constraints.

To the extent that trade is free to all parties in an interaction, and all parties have well-defined rights, resources will move towards their most highly valued uses without qualification. To the extent that potential traders are coerced, either by prohibitions on their ability to make enforceable contracts or by the imposition of non-compensated transfers, no conclusion about value-maximizing resource use can be drawn because the rules permit no test.[14] The only criterion available, that of prior agreement on the transfers of value, is explicitly replaced as a decision rule, although it remains as the valid test.

In this section, I propose to discuss three broadly defined categories of problems that are often placed in the transactions costs rubric, and I shall show how these putative barriers to allocative efficiency are readily incorporated into a coherent subjectivist-contractarian argument.

Information-Communication Constraints. Transactions costs are perhaps most familiarly discussed as arising from some failure of parties to potential exchange to attain access to information on proffered terms of trade or to communicate their own offers effectively to other traders. Hence, or so the orthodox argument might run, if potential traders could be better informed and be made better able to communicate one with another, now-unconsummated trades might be worked out, generating increments in value, ensuring greater efficiency in resource use. If 'efficiency' is defined as that pattern of resource use reached through voluntary exchanges *after* the new information-communication setting is in place, then, of course, the prior-existing allocation is *now* 'inefficient'. But in the postulated initial setting, there was a different information-communication environment. Given the then-existent constraints under which traders behaved, the prior allocation was 'efficient'.

Whether or not a shift in information-communication constraints is in itself an efficient or Pareto-superior change can be determined only by applying some criterion that remains *internal* to the set of potential traders. If the initial constraints are deemed to be 'inefficient', potential traders will, themselves, find it advantageous to invest resources in efforts to shift them.

Consider a simple example. There are two totally isolated villages, Adam and Smith, with no communication with each other. In one village, two deer exchange for one beaver. In the other, two beaver exchange for one deer. In the setting of isolation, the allocative results are efficient provided that trade is free in each village. If the isolation between the villages is not itself efficient, it will be to the advantage of a trading entrepreneur in one village or the other to seek out means of breaking the trading barrier. Profits from arbitrage will attract such behaviour as will be required to remove differentials in the terms of trade and to generate differing patterns of resource use, if the shift is such as to confer net benefits. It is misleading to suggest that the initial setting of isolation prevented efficient resource utilization because of the transactions cost barrier. Voluntary exchange must be defined to include entrepreneurial trading effort which will emerge to ensure that all gains-from-trade in breaking down information-communication constraints are exhausted.

To the extent that the constraints that exist are *artificially* imposed, via the auspices of political-governmental agency, the activities of entre-preneurial traders that might otherwise generate an optimal breakdown of barriers may be prevented or inhibited. In the presence of observed artificial constraints, the allocative patterns can be labelled as 'presumably inefficient', since trade is not allowed to take place.

Free Rider Constraints. The question of the possible efficacy of removing existing governmental-political constraints, or of imposing new ones, shifts analysis to the second familiar source of alleged barriers to resource utilization, a source that is is often swept within the transactions-cost qualification, but is more specifically discussed under the 'free rider' rubric. In large-number settings, the individual participant has little or no incentive to initiate action designed to yield benefits for all members of the community, to secure information about alternatives, and to be concerned about enforcement of community-wide agreements. There may exist complex exchanges that might be agreed to by all participants, but it is to the advantage of no single person or small group to assume the leadership role in the design and implementation of such potential agreements.

This setting differs from that discussed under the information-communication rubric in that individual entrepreneurial efforts cannot here be depended on to search out productive shifts in institutional arrangements due to the absence of residual claimancy. In my 1959 paper I suggested that the proper role for the normative political economist was that of discovering potential rules changes that might yield general benefits and then of presenting these changes as *hypotheses* subject to the Wicksellian contractual-censensus test. If, when presented a suggested change in rules, agreement among all potentially interacting parties is forthcoming, the hypothesis is corroborated. The previously existing rule is proven inefficient. If disagreement emerges on the proposed rules change, the hypothesis is falsified. The existing rule is classified as Pareto-efficient. And, given this institutional setting, any outcomes attained under free and open exchange processes are to be classified as efficient.

It is useful at this point to introduce the classic externality case from welfare economics, the setting in which ordinary economic activity within well-defined legal rights impose non-compensated damages on a sufficiently large number of persons so as to ensure failure of a bargained solution due to free-rider motivation.[15] Can 'uncorrected' outcomes in this setting be labelled to be efficient? Consistent application of the contractarian perspective must attach the efficiency label here, so long as all members of the relevant community remain free to make intervening offers and bids to those traders whose activity is alleged to generate the spill-over harm. There is no overtly coercive overriding of individual claims. The fact that, given the institutional structure postulated, outcomes are reached through an exchange-contract process open to all entrants is the criterion for efficiency of those outcomes, the only one that is available without resort to some objectivist standard.

Note, however, that this classification of such 'non-corrected' outcomes in the alleged large-number externality situation as 'efficient' is not equivalent to taking some Panglossian attitude towards the set of arrangements that generates such outcomes. The institutional structure may *not* be efficient, and the political economist may hypothesize that general agreement can be secured on some realignment of rights (including required compensations to those who might be asked to give up valued claims) that will allow potentially damaged parties in the interaction to possess rights of veto over specified in-market activity of the ordinary sort.

In the contractarian perspective, to say that free and open exchange tends to ensure that resources flow to their most highly valued uses means only that such uses are relevant to the institutional structure in being. It is not to say that the unfettered market under any and all assignments of rights is the most 'efficient' institution. These are two wholly different propositions that have become confused because of the failure to make the distinction between the objectivist and the subjectivist perspective on allocative processes.

It is necessary to distinguish carefully between agreement or unanimity as a *test* for an 'efficiency-enhancing trade' and unanimity as a *decision rule*. This distinction tends to be neglected in analyses of simple exchanges organized through market processes, largely because the decision rule that effectively operates coincides with the ultimate test for the results of that rule. Within a specific legal order, if entry is free, market exchanges are made under an implicit rule of unanimity.[16] If A and B voluntarily agree to an exchange, and if C remains free to offer possibly differing terms to either party, there is no outcome that does not pass the consensus test. The outcome attained can be classified as 'efficient' because it reflects agreement among all parties, and the decision rule or institution that allows such outcome patterns to be generated can be classified to be 'efficient' if there is no consensus to be reached on any possible change.

With 'public good' or 'public goods' in the standard meaning, however, it may be impossible that market exchanges, made voluntarily within well-defined assignment of rights, will generate patterns of results that are preferred by participants. Given the assignment of rights, and given the institution of exchange, the outcomes reached may still be classified as 'efficient'. But the institution of voluntary exchange, as ordinarily understood, may not in this case be 'efficient', because there may emerge general agreement upon a change in institutional structure. Explicit political or governmental decision rules may be accepted by all parties as being preferred to the decision rules of the market. That political-governmental decision rule upon which agreement is reached, however, may *not* require consent of all parties to reach particular outcomes, either explicitly or implicitly. That is to say, the 'efficient' decision rule may be such that specific outcomes need not meet the consensus test.[17]

Consider an example. Suppose that there is general agreement upon a constitutional rule that specifies that police services shall be politicized and that decisions on the organization and financing of these services shall be made by majority voting rules in an elected legislature. By the fact of general agreement, this *institution* is efficient. There is no change upon which everyone affected might agree. Within the operation of the rule or institution, however, there is no basis for presuming that particular outcomes are 'efficient' in the contractarian perspective. A majority coalition may impose its preferences on the members of the minority. And, given the legal order which may prohibit side payments, resources may well be allocated to uses that are valued less highly than they might be in alternative uses. There is simply no means of making the required test for efficiency or inefficiency within the rule or institution as it operates.

The majority-rule setting here is analogous to that discussed earlier under the prisoners' dilemma. For the inclusive community, a rule that places captured prisoners in isolation and prevents binding contracts may be 'efficient', despite its evident presumed inefficiency for the subset of prisoners themselves. With majority rule, or any less than unanimity rule, for political-governmental decisions, the decision structure may itself be 'efficient' while at the same time the particular outcomes attained under the structure may be presumed inefficient, at least in some situations, for those who are directly coerced. To introduce 'transactions costs' as a barrier to the attainment of efficiency in this generalized free-rider context seems to confuse rather than to clarify the complex set of issues involved.

Strategic Behaviour. The third source of alleged inefficiency in resource utilization, also sometimes included in the broadly defined transactions-costs basket, is summarized under the rubric *strategic behaviour*. Cooter concentrated his critique of the Coase theorem on this element, in the sense previously noted.

The strategic-behaviour setting differs from the two previously analyzed. As Cooter correctly indicates, the alleged barrier to possible agreement among potential traders or bargainers arises in small-number, non-competitive settings, not necessarily from any necessary informational or communication failure that might be profitably eliminated by arbitrage. And, since the numbers of potential interacting parties are small, there is no free-rider motivation for behaviour. In this setting, how can criteria for improvement be derived internally from the parties?

Here there is a direct analogue to the large-number setting in the sense that any modification of the structure of interaction becomes a 'public good' for all parties. Hence, in a strict two-person interaction where both parties expect to engage in a whole sequence of similar potential interactions, they may acknowledge the wastefulness of investment in strategic bargaining. In such a case, they would agree on an arbitration procedure or rule which might take the form of the appointment of an external or third-party adjudicator along with a commitment to accept the terms laid down. Again, as in all other settings, the test for efficiency in the institutional rule is agreement among affected parties.

In a more inclusive context, if all members of the relevant political community recognize that many of them will be placed in small-number bargaining settings on occasion, as either buyer or seller in potential exchanges, there may possibly emerge some general agreement on political-legal rules that reduce the potential profitability of strategic investment. Such rules may involve the promotion of competitive environments for exchanges of rights since competition, actual and potential, dramatically restricts the scope for strategic behaviour. Note, however, that such an agreement would not be based putatively on any perception that competition produces an objectifiably meaningful efficient allocation of resources. The agreement itself becomes the test as to whether or not competitive arrangements are more 'efficient' than the alternative arrangements in being.

VI. COMPETITION AS A DEVICE OR AS A DETERMINANT

As the last remarks suggest, there are two profoundly different conceptions of competition and the competitive process that emerge from the objectivist perspective on the one hand and from the subjectivist-contractarian perspective on the other. In the former there exists an efficient allocation of resources independently of any process through which it is generated. From this supposition it follows that institutional arrangements may be directly evaluated in terms of their relative success or failure in attaining the desired pattern of resource use. Normative argument in support of competitive institutions emerge, in this perspective, only because such institutions are judged to be relatively superior 'devices', 'instruments', or 'mechanisms' in generating independently derived results. Where competitive institutions do not seem to exist, as defined by some independently derived structural criteria (e.g. number of firms in an industry, concentration ratios, etc.), there emerges a normative argument for direct intervention with voluntary exchange process as a means of moving results towards the externally derived allocative norm or ideal. Small-number bargaining settings (bilateral monopoly, isolated exchanges, locationally specific assets) necessarily fail to guarantee efficiency due to the presence of incentives for strategic behaviour. Governmental action in monitoring the bargains struck in all such settings seems a normative consequence of the analysis.

In the subjectivist-contractarian perspective, 'efficiency' cannot be said to exist except as determined by the process through which results are generated, and criteria for evaluating patterns of results must be applied only to processes. In this perspective, voluntary exchanges among persons within a competitive constraints structure generate efficient resource usage, which is determined only as the exchanges are made. Competitive institutions, in this perspective, are not instruments to be used to generate efficiency; they are, instead, possible structures, possible rules or sets of rules, that may emerge from generalized agreement. If such institutions do not emerge from a consensus operating via politically orchestrated exchanges, those alternative arrangements that may be observed to persevere must themselves be judged to be 'efficient', and, within these structures, patterns of voluntary exchange outcomes may also be so classified.[18] The role of the political order, of law, or government, is to facilitate agreement on institutional arrangements and to police rights assigned under such agreements. There is no role for specific governmental monitoring of bargains anywhere in the picture.

I should acknowledge at this point that it is difficult for anyone trained in economics in this century to hold consistently to the perspective that I have laid out in this paper. What is government's role, for example, in the case of natural monopoly, which operates 'inefficiently' under the orthodox perspective and thereby seems to warrant political-governmental intrusion into the exchanges that might be made between the monopolist and his potential customers? No such normative inference can follow from a consistent application of the contractarian perspective. At best the hypothesis may be advanced to the effect that consensus should emerge on a scheme to 'buy out' existing owners of such monopolized resources (opportunities) and to replace their operation with governmental-political management, based on some cost-based pricing rules. But the subjectivist will also acknowledge that costs are not independently determinate, in which case such operating rules become absurd. At best the hypothesis must be for a scheme that would compensate the monopoly owners and replace them with governmental agents. Modern public choice theory has put the nod to 'public interest' idealizations of the behaviour of such agents. In some final analaysis the subjectivist-contractarian must be hypothetically pragmatic in all those cases that seem to have been the bread-and-butter of conventional normative political economy, welfare economics, and, now, law-and-economics. He may, with little fear of analytical ambiguity, strongly urge that alternative sets of rules be presented and tested in the political exchange process. And he may of course utilize his specialist talents in the design and predicted operation of such alternative arrangements. He should not, however, ever be allowed to take the arrogant stance of suggesting that this or that set of institutions is or is not more 'efficient'.[19]

VII. CONCLUSIONS

In this chapter, I have tried to support the following propositions:
1. Given the institutions within which behaviour is constrained, voluntary exchanges among traders in a legal market order tend to ensure that resources flow to and remain in their most highly valued uses.
2. The most highly valued uses of resources depend on the institutional setting within which voluntary exchanges take place.
3. Institutions are themselves variables subject to change, and agreement among persons who operate within institutional constraints is fully analogous to voluntary exchange within established rules.
4. The several so-called 'transactions costs' barriers to 'efficiency' in resource allocation can be more appropriately analyzed in the context of hypotheses about institutional reform.
5. The ultimate test for institutional reform remains that of agreement among affected parties.

I have shown that these propositions follow consistently from a subjectivist-contractarian perspective on the behaviour of persons within well-defined institutional structures as well as on their behaviour in modifying such structures. The perspective allows a functional role for the political economist to be well defined. The propositions place the now-famous Coase theorem in a position that renders it much less vulnerable to its objectivist critics. At the same time, however, the implication that what is is always efficient is avoided.

Analysis must be based squarely on the recognition that persons are simultaneously 'trading' at several levels. They are considering voluntary exchanges within institutional rules that they treat, for purposes of such within-rule calculus, as fixed. Given the institutions of the market or private sector, resources tend to be flowing to their most highly valued uses, although care should be taken here to state this proposition in terms of the continuously equilibrating properties of the system rather than in terms of any achieved equilibrium. At the same time, however, the same persons are engaged in non-market or political 'trades', within the defined political order that exists. In this set of interactions, economic resources need *not* be moving towards their most highly valued uses because, under the decision rules of the political order, persons may be permitted to effectuate resource transfers without the voluntary agreement, explicit or implicit, of all affected parties. The political decision rule, as contrasted with the market decision rule, offers no test of the results that it acts to generate.

At the same time that they act within defined market and political rules, persons are considering 'trades' that may involve changes in these decision rules, or institutional structures, themselves. There will be, at this level, forces generated by utility maximizing considerations that move the rules-structure towards that which is 'efficient'. The patterns of resource use generated under less-than-unanimity decision rules in the political order, which embody no presumption of value maximization for the reasons noted, may offer reasons for considering shifts towards the market order, which does generate results that may be presumed to be value-maximizing. However, other reasons may well dominate any such comparative institutional calculus. Consistency requires that the contractarian apply the same criterion for institutional efficiency that he applies to allocative efficiency within institutions. That which is efficient is that upon which all potentially affected parties agree, explicitly or implicitly. While the absence of the unanimity rule in politics does give some basis for the generalized hypothesis that where they are substitutes, individuals would agree to replace politicized arrangements with market-like arrangements, this must remain strictly a hypothesis subject to the agreement test.

My whole analysis in this paper has been based on the presupposition that in both the market and the political order, rights are well defined. With reference to constitutional reform in particular, however, basic uncertainties in the assignment of rights may inhibit agreement on rules changes. Persons who remain uncertain as to just what rights they do possess in a politicized economy cannot consider rationally based plans for exchanges in these rights. Those members of politically organized groups who seem politically advantaged under existing rules will not agree to constitutional reform without compensation, and those who might otherwise be willing to pay such compensation may not do so because they do not acknowledge the rights of those to whom such payments would have to be made. It is in this whole area of potential political-constitutional 'exchange' that the problems of modern Western societies are acute, and it is to the analyses of these problems that scholars in the broadly defined law-economics, property-rights, public-choice subdisciplines should turn increasing attention.

NOTES

1. This chapter was initially presented as a paper for a plenary session of the *Verein für Socialpolitik* at a meeting in Basel, Switzerland, in September 1983. It was published in the conference volume, *Ansprüche, Eigentums, und Verfügungsrechte* (Berlin: Duncker & Humblot, 1984), pp. 9–24. I acknowledge permission to republish the paper here, with minor revisions.

    I am indebted to A. J. Culyer, David Levy, Viktor Vanberg, and Karen Vaughn for helpful comments on an earlier draft.

2. A by-product of law-economics analysis has been the proposition that the definition of rights 'should' reflect some underlying economic efficiency norm. I shall not discuss this norm here, but my analysis suggests that the norm enters the analysis quite differently under the conception of efficiency herein advanced.

3. R. H. Coase, 'The Problem of Social Cost', *Journal of Law and Economics*, III (Oct. 1960), 1–44.

4. Coase did not refer to transactions costs, as such. The qualifying statement that has been interpreted in zero-transactions cost terms is as follows: 'and the pricing system works smoothly (strictly this means that the operation of a pricing system is without cost)' (*ibid.*, p. 2).

5. Robert Cooter, 'The Cost of Coase', *Journal of Legal Studies*, XI (Jan. 1982), 1–34.

6. I have elaborated this perspective in earlier writings. *See* in particular James M. Buchanan, *Freedom in Constitutional Contract* (College Station: Texas A & M University Press, 1978).

7. This sentence summarizes the central argument made in James M. Buchanan and Wm. Craig Stubblebine, 'Externality', *Economica*, XXIX (Nov. 1962), 371–84. In writing that paper, Stubblebine and I considered ourselves to be developing an argument that was wholly consistent with Coase's, even if we also recognized that our approach was basically contractarian, whereas his was not explicitly defined. Coase, who had been a colleague at the University of Virginia, did not, however, like the Buchanan-Stubblebine paper, presumably because he strenuously objected to any usage of the term 'externality'. Also, his objection may have stemmed from the ambiguity in perspective that I emphasize in this paper.

8. For an analysis of a setting in which potential traders differ in their evaluation of benefits and/or harms, *see* James M. Buchanan and Roger L. Faith, 'Entrepreneurship and the Internalization of Externality', *Journal of Law and Economics* (Mar. 1981), 95–111.

9. *See* R. H. Coase, 'Business Organization and the Accountant,' in *L.S.E.*

Essays on Cost, ed. James M. Buchanan and G. F. Thirlby (New York: New York University Press, 1981), pp. 95–134; revised version of materials written and published initially in 1938.

10.   Cooter, *op. cit.*, pp. 14–15.
11.   Note that this statement does not require any presumption about the knowledge possessed by potential participants in the interaction process. An alternative formulation of the Coasian perspective may be advanced in which the presumption of shared knowledge of institutional results is critical to the allegedly tautological character of the Coasian propositions. In his interesting paper, which ties together several strands of modern theory, T. K. Rymes seems to advance this alternative formulation. *See* T. K. Rymes, 'Money, Efficiency, and Knowledge', *Canadian Journal of Economics* (Nov. 1979), 575–89.
12.   *See* James M. Buchanan 'Positive Economics, Welfare Economics, and Political Economy', *Journal of Law and Economics*, II (Oct. 1959), 124–38; reprinted in Buchanan, *Fiscal Theory and Political Economy* (Chapel Hill: University of North Carolina Press, 1960), pp. 105–24.

       For recent papers that deal with the general topic under discussion in this section, *see*: David Levy, 'Is Observed Monopoly Always Efficient?' (Mimeographed: Center for Study of Public Choice, 1982); A. J. Culyer, 'The Quest for Efficiency in the Public Sector: Economists versus Dr Pangloes' (Mimeographed: University of York, Sept. 1982).
13.   On this point, *see* W. C. Stubblebine, 'On Property Rights and Institutions', in *Explorations in the Theory of Anarchy*, ed. Gordon Tullock (Blacksburg: Center for Study of Public Choice, 1972), pp. 39–50. Also, *see* James M. Buchanan, 'The Relevance of Pareto Optimality', *Journal of Conflict Resolution*, VI (Dec. 1962), 341–54; reprinted in Buchanan, *Freedom in Constitutional Contract*, *op. cit.*, pp. 215–34.
14.   Interpreted in these terms, the Coase qualifying statement, cited in note 4 above, should have been 'the pricing (exchange) system works *without interference*'.
15.   For an analysis of this setting in a more general context, *see* James M. Buchanan, 'The Institutional Structure of Externality', *Public Choice*, XIV (Spring 1973), 69–82.
16.   On this point, *see* James M. Buchanan, 'Individual Choice in Voting and the Market', *Journal of Political Economy*, LXII (Aug. 1954), 334–43; reprinted in Buchanan, *Fiscal Theory and Political Economy* (Chapel Hill: University of North Carolina Press, 1960), pp. 90–104.

       Also, *see* Ludwig von Mises, *Human Action* (New Haven: Yale University Press, 1949), p. 312.
17.   For elaboration, *see* James M. Buchanan and Gordon Tullock, *The Calculus of Consent* (Ann Arbor: University of Michigan Press, 1962).
18.   I seek no quarrel at this point with the evolutionists who argue that institutions emerge from the historical process of development without any explicit constitutional-political agreement having been made. So long as rights are well defined and enforced, the institutional evolution meets the criterion of implicit unanimity analogously to the market process more narrowly defined. And the continued acceptance of institutional forms itself suggests the presumption that these forms meet the efficiency test.

       Wegenhenkel has specifically related the process of evolutionary change in an economy to the transactions-costs discussion. While accepting the orthodox meaning of the Coase theorem, Wegenhenkel argues that the evolutionary process, generated by entrepreneurial effort, pushes the economy continually in the direction of transactions-costs reduction. *See* Lothar Wegenhenkel, *Gleichgewicht, Transaktionskosten und Evolution* (Tübingen: Mohr, 1981).

19.   It should be evident from my argument that there is no justification at all for *judicial* introduction of the putative efficiency norm, presumably to be imposed independently of the political process. On this, *see* James M. Buchanan, 'Good Economics—Bad Law', *Virginia Law Review*, 60 (Spring, 1974), 483–92; reprinted in Buchanan, *Freedom in Constitutional Contract, op. cit.*, pp. 40–9.

11 Moral Community, Moral Order, or Moral Anarchy[1]

I. INTRODUCTION

In this chapter I shall discuss the 'ties that bind' persons with each other in society and the instruments and attitudes that may break those ties that exist. I am concerned with the ways that persons act and feel towards one another. For this reason, I have inserted the adjective 'moral' before each of the nouns in my title. 'Community, Order, or Anarchy', standing alone, would not convey my desired emphasis on personal interaction. To forestall misunderstanding at the outset, however, I should note that there is no explicitly moral content in the chapter, if the word 'moral' is interpreted in some normative sense.

My diagnosis of American society is informed by the notion that we are living during a period of erosion of the 'social capital' that provides the basic framework for our culture, our economy, and our polity—a framework within which the 'free society' in the classically liberal ideal perhaps came closest to realization in all of history. My efforts have been directed at trying to identify and to isolate the failures and breakdowns in institutions that are responsible for this erosion.[2]

My discussion here will be exclusively conducted in terms of the three abstract models or forms of interaction listed in my title: (I) moral community, (II) moral order, and (III) moral anarchy. Any society may be described empirically as embodying some mix among these three forms or elements. A society is held together by some combination of moral community and moral order. Its cohesion is reduced by the extent to which moral anarchy exists among its members. The precise mix among the three forms or elements will therefore determine the observed 'orderliness' of any society, along with the degree of governmental coercion reflected in the pattern that is observed to exist. The need for governance as well as the difficulty of governing are directly related to the mix among the three elements.

II. MORAL COMMUNITY

I shall commence by defining the three abstract models or forms of interaction. A *moral community* exists among a set of persons to the extent that individual members of the group identify with a collective unit, a community, rather than conceive themselves to be independent, isolated individuals. In one sense, of course, moral community always exists. No person is totally autonomous, and no one really thinks exclusively of himself as a solitary unit of consciousness. Each person will to some extent identify with some community (or communities) whether this be with the nuclear family, the extended family, the clan or tribe, a set of locational, ethnic, racial, or religious cohorts, the trade union, the business firm, the social class, or, finally, with the nation-state. Most persons will identify simultaneously and with varying degrees of loyalties with several communities of varying sizes, types, and sources of valuation. The set of communities and the value or loyalty weights assigned to the members of the set will of course differ from person to person. I suggest, however, that it is possible to characterize different societies in terms of the relative importance of *moral community* as an element of social cohesion among persons within those societies. It is possible to classify societies as more or less communitarian (collectivistic)—as less or more individualistic.

III. MORAL ORDER

A *moral order* exists when participants in social interaction treat each other as moral reciprocals, but do so without any sense of shared loyalties to a group or community. Each person treats other persons with moral indifference, but at the same time respects their equal freedoms with his own. Mutual respect, which is an alternative way of stating the relationship here, does not require moral community in any sense of personal identification with a collectivity or community. Each person thinks about and acts towards other persons as if they are autonomous individuals, independently of whom they might be in terms of some group or community classification scheme. In a moral order it is possible for a person to deal with other persons who are not members of his own community if both persons have agreed, explicitly or implicitly, to abide by the behavioural precepts required for reciprocal trust and confidence.

The emergence of the abstract rules of behaviour describing moral order had the effect of expanding dramatically the range of possible interpersonal dealings. Once rules embodying reciprocal trust came to be established, it was no longer necessary that both parties to a contract identify themselves with the same moral community of shared values and loyalties. There was no longer any requirement that trading partners claim membership in the same kinship group.[3] Under the rules of a moral order it is conceptually possible for a genuinely autonomous individual to remain a viable entity, whereas no such existence would be possible in a structure characterized solely by moral community.

I suggest that different societies may be classified in terms of the relative importance of the rules of moral order in describing the observed relationships among the persons within each society. These rules may either supplement the sense of moral community as a source of social cohesion where the latter exists, or these rules may substitute for moral community to the extent of rendering it unnecessary.

IV. MORAL ANARCHY

Moral anarchy exists in a society (if it can remain a society) when individuals do not consider other persons to be within their moral communities and when they do not accept the minimal requirements for behaviour in a moral order. In moral anarchy, each person treats other persons exclusively as means to further his own ends or objectives. He does not consider other persons to be his fellows (brothers) in some community of shared purpose (as would be the case in moral community), or to be deserving of reciprocal mutual respect and trust as autonomous individuals (as would be the case in moral order).

In a real sense, moral anarchy becomes the negation of both moral community and moral order. It is a setting within which persons violate the basic Kantian moral precept that human beings are to be treated as ends not as means. It is perhaps more difficult to conceptualize moral anarchy as a general model of human interaction than the two alternative models already discussed. Moral anarchy seems somehow less descriptive of the behaviour that we observe around us. For my purposes, however, I want to employ the model in the same way as the others. I suggest that it is possible to classify different societies in terms of the relative significance of moral anarchy in describing the attitudes and behaviour of their members, one to another.

V. IMPLICATIONS FOR SOCIAL STABILITY AND GOVERNABILITY: MORAL ANARCHY

I shall now employ the three basic models or elements of interaction in order to discuss problems of social viability and, indirectly, problems of governability in a society. It will be useful to take extreme examples in which one of the three models is primarily descriptive rather than some undefined mix among the three. It will also be useful to change the order of discussion from that which was used in defining the three elements. I shall first take up moral anarchy, then moral order, and, finally, moral community.

Consider first, then, a setting in which many persons behave as moral anarchists. In this setting, life for the individual is 'poore, nasty, brutish, and short', to employ the colourful language of Thomas Hobbes. Men who neither feel a sense of community with others nor respect others as individuals in their own right, must be ruled. Individuals will sacrifice their liberties to the coercive sovereign government that can effectively ensure order and personal security. But those persons who act on behalf of the sovereign government may also be moral anarchists. There would seem to be no reason to anticipate that persons who secure powers of governance would be less likely to behave as moral anarchists than their fellows; indeed, the opposite conclusion seems the more plausible here. Social stability is purchased by individuals at the price of a coercive state regime. Repressive government may emerge as a necessary condition in a society with many moral anarchists.

VI. IMPLICATIONS FOR SOCIAL STABILITY AND GOVERNABILITY: MORAL ORDER

In sharp contrast with the setting discussed above, now consider a setting where many persons adhere to the precepts and behavioural rules of a moral order. Each individual treats other persons as deserving of mutual respect and tolerance, even though there exists no necessary sense of belonging to a community or collectivity of shared values and loyalties. In this setting, individuals may be secure in their persons and property; social stability may exist, and the needs for governance may be minimized. Correspondingly, the liberties of individuals are maximized.

In the extreme case where, literally, all persons behave in accordance with the rules of moral order, there would be no need for government at all. 'Orderly anarchy' would be produced by the universalized adherence to rules of mutual respect among persons. In a more plausibly realistic setting, where most but not necessarily all persons are expected to follow the precepts of moral order, government, as such, may be restricted to a minimal, night-watchman or protective state role.[4] The government need only protect personal and property rights and enforce contracts among persons. In more general terms, the government may be limited to enforcing the laws. It need not do more. In one sense there is no need for 'governing' as such.

VII. IMPLICATIONS FOR SOCIAL STABILITY AND GOVERNABILITY: MORAL COMMUNITY

I have relegated moral community to third position here because this model is much the more difficult of the three to discuss in terms of the implications for overall social stability and for the needs for governance. The difficulties arise because of the many possible moral communities that may exist within a single society simultaneously, communities that may carry with them quite differing implications for the viability of social order. At one limit, if all persons should identify with the community that is coincident in membership with the inclusive political unit, the nation-state, the implications are relatively straightforward. In such a setting as this, all persons act as if they share the same objectives, as members of the national collectivity, including those persons who act on behalf of the government. Vis-à-vis other nations, this model of society might be a source of nationalistic adventure. Or, to put the same point in a different perspective, when the national unit is threatened by external enemies, the sense of national community is more likely to emerge as a real force. Since all persons tend to share the same objectives, governance becomes easy. Persons 'obey' the sovereign because they feel themselves to be part of the larger unit; conversely, the sovereign also behaves as persons would have it behave. Persons, ruled or rulers, do not behave towards each other as separate interacting individuals. They do not really consider themselves to be autonomous units.

At the other limit there may exist no sense of moral community, no shared values, over the whole membership of the inclusive political unit, the nation-state, while at the same time all or substantially all persons may express and act upon loyalties to collective units, subnationally classified. Persons may identify with specific communities (ethnic, racial, religious, regional, occupational, employment, class, etc.) while sensing no identification with or loyalty to the national unit. This sort of society will have some of the characteristics of that which contains only moral anarchists. The difference here is that the relevant entities are themselves collectives rather than individuals. Persons may in this society exhibit sharply divergent behaviour patterns as between treatment of members of the relevant community and persons who do not qualify for membership. Social conflict will tend to emerge between the relevant communities or between persons who are members of differing communities. Because of the prevalence of such conflicts, there will be a need for governance, and possibly by a coercive sovereign. Without such force, the Hobbesian war of each against all may apply to the separate collectivities rather than to individuals.

In effect, moral community as a concept can satisfactorily be discussed only in two-dimensional terms. The first dimension involves the general *individualism-communitarianism* spectrum, discussed initially. The second dimension involves what we may call the *nationalized-localized* spectrum, described in the two examples immediately above. A simple two-dimensional diagram (Fig. 11.1) will be helpful here.

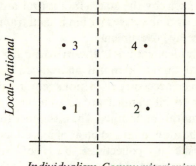

Individualism-Communitarianism

Figure 11.1

A society located at Point 1 of the diagram is largely individualistic, with little sense of moral community but with what there is limited to localized groupings (perhaps family or business firm ties). A society located at Point 2 would be, in contrast, largely communitarian but also with the loyalties of persons largely limited to localized collectivities and with little or no sense of national community. A society at Point 3 would remain largely *individualistic*, like that at Point 1, but in this society there does exist some sense of national community. At Point 4 the society is largely *communitarian*, but also the personal loyalties are largely concentrated on the national collectivity; there is little sense of localized community.

If we restrict analysis to the more basic concept, *moral community*, without reference to the national–local dimension, we can classify societies along the left–right dimension of Figure 11.1 only. Any society classified to fall on the right side of the matrix would exhibit moral community as a relatively predominant characteristic.

VIII. MORAL COMMUNITY, MORAL ORDER AND THE RANGE AND SCOPE FOR GOVERNMENTAL ACTION

In this section I shall compare the two forces for potential social cohesion, moral community and moral order, in terms of the specific implications for the range and scope for governmental actions. I shall largely ignore the considerations raised in section VII concerning the existence of moral communities of subnational memberships. I shall restrict discussion to the sense of moral community that exists among all members of a polity. As noted, in such a setting persons share the same national objectives and need not be 'directed', as such, by the state. In a moral order, as noted above, persons further their own objectives within a legal framework that requires no active interference by government.

As we part from the idealizations of these two models, however, and as we allow for a potential threat of moral anarchy in each case, important differences emerge. The necessary conditions required for the maintenance of tolerably effective social stability are considerably more constrained in moral order than in moral community. The difference to be emphasized here lies in that between the individualized basis of any effective moral order and the non-individualistic or collectivist basis of any effective moral community. In the former, individuals are bound together in adherence to a set of abstract rules or laws which are fundamentally impersonal and which are grounded in the generalized recognition that all persons are cooperating moral equals. The moral requirements placed on persons in such an order are minimal. The individual need not feel himself to be part of some inclusive collectivity. He need not exhibit feelings of benevolence or altruism towards any other persons, whether these be his neighbours or strangers. On the other hand, if he is expected to abide by the minimal behavioural precepts for such an order, to refrain from lapsing into the role of moral anarchist, he must think that the framework rules of the legal-political order are themselves 'fair' in the sense that all persons are effectively required to play by the same rules.

In an effective moral order, a government that discriminates among persons in its treatment, that violates elementary precepts for fairness in dealing with separate individuals, will immediately face resentment and must ultimately expect rebellion. This predicted reaction follows from the very autonomy of individuals; each person remains a person and as such can claim entitlement to uniform treatment by those who administer the law. There exists no overriding 'community interest' within which individual interests are subsumed.

This setting may be contrasted with one properly described as moral community coincident in membership with the national political unit. Here government may discriminate among persons without necessarily generating negative feedbacks in citizen discontent provided only that the discrimination is justified, explained, or legitimized in terms of the wider interest of the inclusive national community, an interest that exists by definition of the community, as such, and which is, also by definition, shared by everyone. Since the individual person in such a setting thinks of himself as a member of this community rather than as an individual, he will more readily acquiesce in what would seem overtly unfair treatment under a moral order. In the setting best described as moral community, therefore, the whole set of issues involving 'justice' or 'fairness' in governmental dealings with separate persons does not arise with nearly the same degree of intensity as they do in a moral order. It follows that government in a society described by national moral community will possess a wider range of options in taking actions than would government operating within a comparable moral order.

The range and scope for governmental action is more limited in a society that locates its source of social cohesion largely in moral order rather than moral community. At the same time, however, such a society (one based on moral order) can allow for greater flexibility and change in the attitudes and behaviour of its individual members. As noted, in an effective moral order, individuals need not share common purposes; they need only respect each other as individuals. From this it follows that individual attitudes and behaviour may be widely varying and may accordingly change within wide limits, still within the minimal requirement for productive interpersonal interchanges. Individuals are free to select their own private purposes in this setting, a freedom that is necessarily absent in moral community.

The range and scope for governmental action is more extensive in a society that locates its sources of social cohesion in moral community rather than in adherence to the rules of moral order. On the other hand, the society largely held together by moral community is necessarily more vulnerable to shifts in the attitudes and the behaviour patterns that might reflect individual departures from the shared purposes of the community. Persons are tied, one to another, by their common identification with the collective, with their shared sense of nationhood, race, class, or ideology. The loss of this identification may involve an unavoidable plunge into moral anarchy. Persons are not free to 'do their own thing', within limits, as they might be in a society organized on the principles of moral order, principles that are mutually acknowledged to generate general benefits to all adherents.

IX. THE UNITED STATES IN THE 1980s

To this point my discussion has been confined to a generalized analysis of the three abstract models or forms of social interaction: moral community, moral order, and moral anarchy. Any historically observed society will embody elements of each one of these models. Nonetheless, the mix may vary significantly among separate societies, and these differences may be important. In the next two sections I shall apply the analysis to real-world societies. In this section I shall discuss the United States in the 1980s in terms of the three models of interaction. In section X, I shall briefly discuss modern Japan for purposes of comparison and contrast with the United States.

In the United States of the 1980s there is little moral community that extends to the limits of the inclusive national unit, the nation-state, as such, and which embodies the central instrument of the polity, the federal government in all of its arms and agencies. There is relatively little sense of shared purpose among the 230 million persons in the nation. Individuals tend instead to relate to and to identify with communities larger than themselves and their immediate families, but these communities tend to be of subnational sizes of membership, both geographically and numerically. The central government, therefore, is unable to call upon or to exploit a strong sense of genuine 'national interest' or 'national purpose', although, of course, such an 'interest' might be called into being in the face of a demonstrated and well-understood external threat. Further, and importantly, those persons who themselves serve as 'governors' possess little sense of 'national interest', and they are not seen to possess such interest by those who are 'governed'. Those persons in positions of political power, like their cohorts who are outside governmental office, identify with various subnational groupings, if indeed they adhere to moral community at all in any relevant way.

The United States, as a single society, does not depend primarily or critically on the presence of national moral community among its citizens. By historical tradition, the society has been made viable because its citizens have adhered behaviourally to the precepts of a moral order. There has existed a tradition of respect for adherence to the rule of law, for general rules, for promise-keeping, for honesty in trading even of the most complex types. Voluntary adherence to the rules and regulations laid down by government remains widespread, including the voluntary payment of income taxes. With relatively few exceptions, government has not needed to become repressive.

For several decades, however, our moral order has been in the process of erosion. Larger and larger numbers of persons seem to become moral anarchists; they seem to be losing a sense of mutual respect one for another along with any feeling of obligation to abide by generalizable rules and codes of conduct. To the extent that such erosion continues and/or accelerates, the internal social stability of the United States must deteriorate. If confronted with this apparent breakdown in the internal cohesion of the social structure, more and more persons who are not themselves moral anarchists will turn to the arms and agencies of government for more direct protection than seems to be currently provided. The problem is explicitly exemplified in observed increases, in criminal activity, which must, after some time lag, result in an increase in governmental coercion on all persons, the lawful and the unlawful alike. The voluntary limits on behaviour that have worked in the past but which now seem to fail must be replaced by governmentally imposed restrictions. Government necessarily will move towards repression in the society as moral anarchy becomes more and more descriptive of the relationships among persons.

Government itself is partially responsible for the erosion of the traditional moral order in America. As the national government sought to take on a more comprehensive role in this century, and a role that is necessarily coincident with the presence or presumed presence of some 'national interest', it has been unable to find moral support in the communitarian sense discussed above. Those who have promoted the extension of government's role under the folly that some national interest exists have, perhaps unwittingly, aided in the breakdown of effective moral order. As laws and regulations have multiplied, competing group interests have been promoted. And persons selected for governmental office have exploited their positions to advance their own private interests under the guise of non-existent 'national purpose'. Observing this, citizens have become more disillusioned with governmental processes and are more and more attracted to assume roles as moral anarchists. Confronted with a government that imposes rules that seem to command little or no respect, individuals quite naturally come to question other long-standing rules that have traditionally solicited voluntary adherence. Restoration of moral order, or even a stop to the erosion process, requires a roll-back of governmental intrusions into the lives of citizens, while, at the same time, the growth in moral anarchy suggests, for the reasons noted above, an expanded governmental role in maintaining social stability.

Somewhat paradoxically, as our traditional moral order loses its ability to ensure social stability, the United States becomes increasingly ungovernable even while the share of resources commanded politically continues to increase and as governmental interferences with the lives of ordinary citizens expand.

X. JAPAN: COMPARISON AND CONTRAST

I shall now discuss modern Japanese society for purposes of drawing comparisons and contrasts with the United States. I do this not because I claim any expert knowledge of Japan and its people but because my initial reflections on the subject matter of this chapter were prompted by an assignment to examine the 'governability' of the Japanese.

There is widespread agreement, both among modern Japanese

themselves and among external observers, that there is a relatively strong sense of identification of persons with moral communities beyond themselves, or, in terms of my three models, that Japan is clearly less individualistic and more communitarian than the United States. Disputes may arise concerning the relative importance of national and localized moral communities in modern Japan. To a degree, of course, the communitarian sense is limited to subnational groups and notably to the employing firms. But, nonetheless, for many reasons, it remains evident that there does also exist a relevant national moral community. The Japanese, as Japanese, share a set of values that affects their behaviour as individuals. There is genuine meaning in the term 'Japan, Incorporated'.

As I have noted, this relationship between the individual and his fellow citizens in the inclusive national community allows the Japanese government greater freedom in the formulation and administration of laws and regulations than would be the case in a society more critically dependent on moral order. However, and also for the reasons discussed above, the continuing stability of the society may be dependent on the maintenance of the shared loyalties that now exist. From this it seems to follow that Japan may possibly be more vulnerable to shifts in attitudes and behaviour patterns on the part of individuals and groups who somehow lose their identification with the nation. If such identification should be lost, such individuals may lapse directly into roles of moral anarchists.

If this scenario should unfold, there might exist no apparent means through which Japan could recapture its sense of national moral community short of possible international adventure. If my diagnosis is at all suggestive here, the question that emerges is whether or not a nation like the Japanese, faced with a possible erosion in their shared sense of moral community, could adopt essentially Western notions of moral order before moral anarchy assumes predominant importance and generates a breakdown in social structure. Can the Japanese citizen, circa the year 2000 or 2050, who may have lost his identity with the nation as a community, as an entity that commands his loyalty and respect, can he come to understand, appreciate, and live by the behavioural precepts of moral order, precepts that require him to grant fellow citizens mutual respect as moral equivalents and which give him criteria for evaluating governmental rules in some personal and non-communitarian way? Can Japanese governments, in their own right, keep within the limits of power that will allow a functioning moral order to evolve, and, further, can Japanese governments hold this stance as Western nations, themselves, are observed to sink further into the collectively dominated moral anarchy that now seems their fate?

XI. PROSPECTS FOR CONSTRUCTIVE REFORM

F. A. Hayek has stressed that modern man's behavioural instincts are those that characterize what I have here called moral community and which evolved over the ages in essentially tribal settings. He suggests that Western man very slowly evolved patterns of adherence to abstract rules that he does not understand, the rules of moral order, and which really run counter to his instinctual proclivities.[5] Professor Hayek's response to the first question posed for the Japanese society above would presumably be negative. The behavioural rules of effective moral order cannot be 'laid on'; cultural evolution cannot be directed. I am somewhat less evolutionist and more constructivist than Hayek, but my concern here is not primarily with what the Japanese society may face in future decades. My concern is with the prospects for constructive reform in the social order of the United States, and I should stress that reform need not depend exclusively on changes in rules for behaviour.

I have suggested that those who have promoted the extension of Western national governments have done so in their failure to recognize that the moral order, described as voluntary adherence to abstract rules of behaviour, carries implications for the reach of governance. Accordingly, these governments have been allowed to grow far beyond the limits that might sustain and reinforce effective moral order, while, at the same time, they have failed to generate effective moral community as a replacement force that might in turn legitimate such extended governance. Indeed, the moral anarchists among us have used the instruments of governance to subvert both moral community and moral order as necessary to advance their own ends.

Even in the 1980s, however, relatively few Americans are moral anarchists; most Americans continue to treat their fellows with mutual respect and abide by the rules of moral order. Most Americans also maintain a limited sense of moral community, a sense that could be maximally exploited with appropriate devolution and decentralization of governmental authority. Constructive reform is possible provided that the institutions of social order are so modified as to make them consistent with the *empirical realities* of modern man as he is rather than man as the naïve reformers of decades past have hoped he might become.

Institutional and constitutional reforms are not equivalent to behavioural reforms, and they need not depend critically on changing 'man's nature'. In economists' terminology, institutional-constitutional change operates upon the constraints within which persons maximize their own utilities; such change does not require that there be major shifts in the utility functions themselves.

NOTES

1. This chapter was initially published as *The Abbot Memorial Lecture No. 17* by Colorado College, Colorado Springs, Colorado, 1981. The lecture itself was presented on 6 May 1981. I am indebted to Professor Timothy Fuller and to Colorado College for permission to reprint the lecture, substantially without change.

2. For earlier works that provide some indication of the development of the ideas presented in this chapter, *see: The Limits of Liberty* (Chicago: University of Chicago Press, 1975); 'Markets, States, and the Extent of Morals', *American Economic Review*, 68 (May 1978), 364–8; 'Moral Community and Moral Order: The Intensive and Extensive Limits of Interaction', in *Ethics and Animals*, ed. Harlan Miller and W. Williams (Clifton, N. J.: Humana Press, 1983), pp. 95–102; 'A Governable Country', in *Japan Speaks*, 1981 (Osaka, Japan: Suntory Foundation, 1981) III, pp. 1–12.

3. F. A. Hayek has stressed the emergence of these abstract rules of behaviour through some proces of cultural evolution, rules that man does not and cannot understand and which run counter to those instinctual bases of behaviour which find their sources in the primitive sense of moral community. *See* F. A. Hayek, *Law, Legislation, and Liberty*, Vol. III, *The Political Order of a Free People* (Chicago: University of Chicago Press, 1979), especially 'Epilogue', pp. 153–76.

4. The term 'minimal state' is used by Robert Nozick in his *Anarchy, State and Utopia* (New York: Basic Books, 1974). I used the term 'protective state' in my *The Limits of Liberty* (Chicago: The University of Chicago Press, 1975). The nineteenth-century writers often used the term 'night-watchman state'.

5. *See* Hayek, *op. cit.*

Part Three
Explorations in the Theory of Justice

12 Rules for a Fair Game: Contractarian Notes on Distributive Justice[1]

I. INTRODUCTION

In this and the following chapter I shall make an effort to clarify my own ideas on a topic or subject area that I have often chosen deliberately to neglect or to put aside. In my book *The Limits of Liberty* I discussed distribution at some length, but I did not explicitly raise issues of 'justice'.[2] Several critics have interpreted my efforts as supporting the 'justice' of the distributional results that emerged from my analysis, but I did not, at least in any conscious sense, consider myself to be offering any such argument. My primary concern in that book was to show that contractarian agreement, at some initial and pre-legal stage, might emerge that would involve the definition, the guarantee, and the enforcement of a distribution of rights and claims (endowments) among persons in a community. I was concerned to show that such a distribution of rights and claims is necessarily prior to the simple as well as the complex exchanges that a market economic process embodies, the process which, finally, determines a distribution of end-items or product values, final goods and services, upon which attention tends to be directed when we talk loosely about 'distribution'.

My analysis was essentially positive rather than normative, but there are direct implications for the methodology of discussing matters of distributive justice. My whole argument suggested that the focus of attention should be on the distribution of rights and claims prior to or antecedent to the market process itself rather than on some final distribution of social product.

I shall return to this central point later in this chapter, but let me now plunge directly into the assigned topic and ask the personalized question: Are the nominal claims to income and wealth that I now hold 'just'? Am I 'entitled' to these claims which allow me to translate values into measured quantities of goods, services, and real assets produced by others in the economy?

123

II. RELATIONAL ASPECTS OF JUSTICE IN HOLDINGS

Let me first point to some considerations that must be reckoned with in any answer. Perhaps the most important of these to keep in mind is the *relative* or *relational* characteristic of 'justice in holdings' or 'entitlements'. Are the nominal claims that I now hold 'just'? Now let me pose the question differently. Is there anyone else 'more entitled' to these holdings than I am? And, even more specifically, are you more 'entitled' to my nominal holdings, to the cash in my wallet or in my bank accounts, than I am? If you choose, you may include everyone in the 'you' in thinking about this question. Would a revised distribution, with you holding the cash or claims rather than me be more 'just'? Or is the 'state' or the 'government' somehow more entitled to them? If so, what is 'the state'? Who is 'the government'? Who is 'entitled to act as governor'?

As you can surmise, it becomes very easy to translate all such questions into those familiar from the oldest and deepest issues in political, moral, and legal philosophy. And, of course, the reason that such issues are the oldest and the deepest is because they are the hardest to resolve satisfactorily.

III. PROSPECTS FOR DISAGREEMENT

The second consideration, already suggested by the first, involves the prospect of disagreement among persons. Let us suppose, provisionally, that I believe that my entitlement to my holdings is at least as strong, in a moral sense, as that of anyone else. If you accept this judgement—that is, if you acknowledge my relative claim—then we really do not need to argue further about the larger issues of the 'moral-ethical' supports for such claims. It is critically important here to recognize that most of our ordinary economic dealing proceeds on the basis of just such a mutual acknowledgment of the justice of the holdings that exist in the status quo. I can go to the university bookstore and buy a book with relatively minor transactions costs because I fully acknowledge the bookstore's claim to ownership of the book before I buy it, while at the same time the bookstore accepts my claim to the cash in my wallet. Neither of us need be concerned at all about 'justice' in the large. (I should add a digression at this point to say that I am leaving off the adjective 'distributive' before 'justice', but I am exclusively discussing 'distributive justice' here as opposed to 'commutative justice'. The latter is of course important in its own right. We can attribute 'injustice' to any institution or rule that would prevent the bookstore and me from making mutually advantageous trades.)

Serious issues arise only when disagreement emerges. Let us suppose that

I believe that I am more entitled to my holdings than you are, but that you do not agree with me. You think that you are really more 'entitled' to the cash in my wallet than I am.

If you act out your beliefs, you will simply take my wallet if you have the power to do so, and I will at the same time exert every effort to prevent you from so doing. We fight unless one of us is protected in our claims by the force of law, of the state. In my example, if you attempt to take my wallet, I can call the local policeman and he will arrest you. In the foreknowledge of this probable scenario, you may refrain from attempting to take the wallet by force; that is, you may be observed to acquiesce in my holdings while at the same time you may continue to think that you remain more 'entitled' to these holdings than me. In this case you may then seek to modify the existing set of claims by political action that would involve the government levying a tax on me while at the same time making cash transfers to you. If you succeed, I may then acquiesce in the tax and transfer programme, but I shall do so only because I am unable to violate the tax law without probable penalty. The basic conflict remains. We continue to fight by political rather than by more direct means.

In any such fight or conflict, questions of 'justice' necessarily get mixed up and intermingled with pure self-interest. You may want to take my wallet simply because you want the money, quite independently from any consideration of entitlement or justice in holdings. If you cannot take the holdings directly, you may be quite willing to let the agency of government do it for you. I may want to keep my holdings because I want to keep them, and I may be quite happy to allow government to prevent you taking these by force. 'Justice' need not enter at all, on either side of the potential conflict. Your utility function may dictate that you would like my money under any conceivable distribution; but you may be constrained from taking these holdings by law. If, however, the law is not effective, either directly or indirectly, you will take the money unless additional constraints are present. And among these additional constraints are your attitudes towards the 'justice' of my holdings. (Let me add a clarification at this point concerning the indirect constraint that law may exercise on behaviour. You may be constrained, not by the law directly, but by the fact of law itself. You may consider it unethical to violate law, not because the law is just in its object but simply because it is law.)

We come back, therefore, to agreement. What are the conditions or characteristics that determine whether or not you agree that my holdings are 'just', that my entitlements to these holdings are superior to anyone else's? There are of course many ways of getting at this question, but I want to concentrate on what we may call the contractarian response.

IV. GAMES WITH FAIR RULES

This response may be summarized in the subsidiary question: Can my claims to holdings be interpreted and understood as one component in the outcome of what we might agree is a *fair game*? This question, in its turn, raises several subsidiary ones. What is a fair game? What is fairness? Is the game analogy appropriate for interpreting the economic interaction process?

I shall deal with the last question very briefly here. The contractarian position is distinguished from its alternatives by its dependence on criteria that are internal to the individuals who are participants in the interaction. It becomes illegitimate to invoke external criteria for evaluating either processes or end-states. Once this is recognized, the game analogy emerges almost necessarily, with the qualifications as noted in the discussion to follow. For those who do not accept the basic contractarian logic and who want to invoke external norms for evalution, there is little to be said.

Let me therefore return to the other questions concerning the nature of 'a fair game' and the meaning of 'fairness'. The contractarian response, not surprisingly, comes back again to agreement. A 'fair rule' is one that is agreed to by the players in advance of play itself, before the particularized positions of the players come to be identified. Note carefully what this definition says: a rule is fair if players agree to it. It does not say that players agree because a rule is fair. That is to say, fairness is defined by agreement; agreement does not converge at some objectively determined fairness.

One way of proceeding from this point would be to discuss the derivation of what we might call 'ideally fair rules' or even 'plausibly fair rules'. This is essentially the approach taken by John Rawls in *A Theory of Justice*.[3] While I have considerable affinity with Rawls, this method of proceeding would take me too far afield for my purposes. I find it useful to commence with an existing or even an abstracted status quo and to try to use the fairness criteria to determine the possible correspondence between the results, actually or potentially observed, and personal attitudes toward the 'justice' of these results. To return to my personal example, could my claims, my current holdings, have emerged as one outcome of a game that we might agree has been carried out under tolerably fair rules?

V. STOCHASTIC ELEMENTS IN DISTRIBUTIONAL RESULTS

It is first necessary to look at the factors that might determine distributional results, under real or imagined institutional structures. Anyone who would argue that a person's holdings are 'unjust' or indeed that they are 'just', by fairness criteria, must presume genuinely monumental knowledge of both economic analysis and statistical interpretation. Too often our academic colleagues in economics and other disciplines, as well as commentators outside the academy, are unwilling to undertake the chore work of understanding how distributional patterns actually might emerge under differing sets of rules. They tend instead to stand ready and willing to 'jump' directly into evaluative-normative judgements about existing distributions of holdings, and hence about particular personal holdings within these distributions, before they really know what they are talking about. This point is made emphatically by my former colleague at the University of Virginia, Professor Rutledge Vining. He has for a long time argued that students of distributions (of any kind) should be forced to understand stochastic patterns, should be thoroughly grounded in the elementary principles of probability theory, before they are allowed to advance evaluative diagnoses.[4]

It is evident that if we take Vining's admonition strictly, none of us could say much of anything about income and wealth distribution, and I could not write several chapters on justice here. I think that we can, however, take the Vining admonition as a warning to temper all of our efforts at discussing distribution. Here, as elsewhere in economic policy analysis, we must be careful to remain with relevant comparisons. We can start to lay out the factors that determine the distribution of claims to economic value in differing institutional settings, in different games, under differing rules.

VI. THE MARKET ECONOMY ABSTRACTED FROM THE POLITICIZED MIXED ECONOMY

In the United States economy of the 1980s, the institutional setting is one that combines markets and politics in an extremely complex web of intersecting and often conflicting relationships. To attempt to model this structure, this game, in any plausibly acceptable manner, even when allowing for highly abstracted models, is beyond my competence. I propose, instead, to abstract from the politics, from the manifold governmental influences on distributional patterns in the economy that we observe, and to look directly at the market process and at the distributional patterns it might generate in the absence of governmental intervention. That is to say, I want to look at a relatively pure market structure, a relatively pure market game, a game operating within a legal-political framework that is limited to the protection of life and property and to the enforcement of contract. For labels here, we can say I shall be discussing distribution in the market economy in a minimal or protective state.

As noted above, this model is not at all realistic, but by examining the distributional patterns that might be predicted to emerge from it, we may begin to get some feel for what we mean by the terms 'justice' or 'injustice' applied to distributive results, again with both terms interpreted within fairness conceptions.

VII. BIRTH, LUCK, EFFORT, AND CHOICE

One way of avoiding the pitfall that Vining warns against is to forego discussion of 'distributions', as such, and to stick with the simple personal example introduced earlier. Take a single person—take me. What are the elements or factors that have determined my relative share in the status quo claims to economic value, or rather would have determined my share in these claims in the relatively pure market economy, as defined? (Since I earn my salary from a governmental institution, I cannot really be sure that my claims would be meaningful in a pure market economy.)

At this point let me call on my own professor, Frank Knight of the University of Chicago, who said that in a market economy, claims are determined by 'birth, luck, and effort' and 'the least of these is effort'. Knight's three determinants offer us a good starting point for discussion, but let me add only one additional determinant, 'choice'. As you can already envisage, there are interdependencies among these elements. Let me take these four determinants in the following order: choice, luck, effort, and birth. Consider choice.

Choice. Surely my own choices have in part influenced the value of my current claims on economic product, or more generally, my current holdings. It must, I think, be readily acknowledged that any person's claims have been influenced by his own choices, of course with varying degrees of importance. With the proviso noted above, take my own personal history. I chose, deliberately, to undertake an academic career at a time shortly prior to the academic boom of the late 1950s, the 1960s, and early 1970s. That is to say, I chose to enter an industry that was shortly to experience extremely rapid growth, with the predictable consequences for the income levels of its participants. Even before I made this occupational choice, however, I had chosen to continue with my education, even at the cost of foregone earnings (which admittedly were pretty dismal in the late 1930s). I do not of course suggest that my various choices along the way were fully informed. I was personally lucky in these choices, and as I noted above, we cannot really separate some of the determinants I have separately listed. Persons necessarily choose under conditions of great uncertainty, and I could have chosen a declining industry rather than an expanding one, in which case the consequences for my relative income-wealth position would have been quite different.

My purpose is not, however, to discuss in detail the influence of choice on individual or family shares in the claims to total economic value. I want only to suggest here that in so far as personal differentials in the relative sizes of such claims can be attributed to choices freely made, there is no legitimate argument for assessing such differentials as being 'unfair' or 'unjust'. The wino in Chicago who 'might have been' a success had he chosen differently may, it seem to me, appeal to the compassion of his fellows; but he cannot, and should not be allowed to, appeal to their innate sense of 'fairness', which has in no way been violated in his own situation.

Luck Choice merges with and intersects with luck, fortune, or chance as an element that influences the distribution of claims. A person may not have deliberately and explicitly chosen to do this or that, and yet his share in the claims to value may have been shifted unexpectedly and dramatically upwards or downwards. The farmer who tills the family farm in the standard manner did not choose to have oil discovered under his land. He was simply lucky. Others may be unlucky and see their holdings vanish into nothing by flood, fire, or pestilence. Again, I do not propose to discuss the relative significance of luck in the total imputation of claims to value in the United States economy of the 1980s or anywhere else. My point, once again, is to suggest that to the extent that luck is the acknowledged causal influence, and provided all persons 'could have been' in the game, so to speak, there would seem to be no violation of basic fairness precepts in observed relative differences in the sizes of claims.

Effort There need be little discussion of effort. To the extent that a person's share in claims are traceable to his own efforts, there must be near-universal agreement, on fairness or any other set of criteria, that his claims are 'just'. Indeed, we could argue that in the absence of such effort, there would have been no value existent to claim. In a very real sense, therefore, this value attributable to effort involves no opportunity cost to anyone in the community, even in the narrow context of potential value available for redistribution.

Birth We are left with birth as the remaining influence or element in determing the distribution of claims, and it is not at all surprising that most of the charges of 'injustice' and/or 'unfairness' concerning income and wealth distribution arise or are alleged to arise from this source. Few persons could say that the economic game is intrinsically unfair just because some persons are lucky or because some persons make better choices or because some persons exert more effort than others. Unfairness in the economic game described by the operation of market institutions within a legal framework of private property and contract tends to be attributed to the distribution of endowments with which persons *enter* the game in the first place, *before* choices are made, *before* luck rolls the economic dice, *before* effort is exerted.

VIII. THE EASTER EGG HUNT: A MARKET ANALOGY

I can introduce some of the issues raised indirectly by resort to an analogy, that of the Easter Egg Hunt, an analogy that I borrow from my former colleague Professor Richard Wagner, now of Florida State University. The distributive patterns in a market process are not too different in kind from those of the Easter Egg Hunt. In large part, 'finders are keepers', and the final division of product depends on the historical accidents of person, time, and place—on luck, talent, capacity, effort, discussed to some extent earlier. But as I noted in connection with effort, there is no fixed sum to be 'found'; there is no fixed quantity of total economic value to be somehow shared among all participants. The fact is that unless the hunt is properly organized, many of the eggs will not be found at all. Product of potential value will remain 'undiscovered', 'unproduced'. The person who by luck, talent, or effort finds a cache of eggs is not necessarily 'entitled' to keep them in some basically moral sense, but surely no one else, individually or collectively, is similarly 'entitled' since, by supposition, the cache might not have been located at all by anyone else.

All of this is of course merely a way of emphasizing the positive-sum nature of the competitive economic process. But the attribution of 'justice' or 'fairness' to the rules of the finders-keepers game depends critically on the presence of one of two conditions. Either there must be 'many games in town' *or* the starting positions must be approximately equivalent. There need be little or no concern about relative starting positions if there are 'many games in town' so that any player who joins a particular game does so voluntarily and at the same time retains the option of exit from the game. If, however, there is 'only one game in town', and if everyone, willy nilly, must participate, attention is immediately drawn to relative starting positions. Before we can even begin to evaluate results in terms of justice or fairness criteria, the starting positions must be reckoned with. If there are some players endowed initially with superior capacities, which they possess through no choices on their own part, these players will be relatively advantaged in any playing of the game. Our ordinary sense of 'fairness' seems to be violated when such players are put on equal terms with those who are relatively less advantaged but who must, nonetheless, participate in the same game.

IX. HANDICAPS AS FAIR RULES

Must, therefore, an acceptable fair game embody handicaps? Many of us will recall Easter Egg hunts when older and larger children were deliberately handicapped by being placed behind the younger and smaller children, in distance or in time. Presumably, all children must have been entrants in the same hunt; the smaller children were presumed unable to have their own game, at least advantageously. In a sense, this setting offers a reasonably appropriate analogy to social process, at least for the purposes of discussion here.

If there are demonstrable and acknowledged differences in endowments, talents, and capacities, differences that are discernible at or before the effective starting point, there would seem to be persuasive arguments for discriminatory handicapping, even at a reckoned cost in lost social value. But if we postulate an idealized veil of ignorance, in which no person knows what position in the predicted array of initial endowments, talents, and capacities he or she might occupy, expected value is maximized only in the absence of handicaps. Social product is largest by allowing the market process to operate without redistributional encumbrances, and if each person has the same opportunity to secure each share in product value, rationality precepts, defined on expected values, seem to reject any discriminatory handicapping at all.

Expected value will not, however, be the only criterion. If the predicted distribution of starting points—defined by endowments, talents, and capacities to produce value—extends over a wide range, then variance matters. Empirical estimates concerning actual as well as perceived differences among persons become important in determining possible departures from expected value maximization. If we agree with Adam Smith about the absence of natural differences between philosophers and porters, the starting-position problem becomes immensely more tractable than it is if we agree with Plato about inherent natural differences. In addition, the relative importance of differentials in starting positions in influencing final shares in consumption value will of course affect the attitudes towards possible adjustments in starting positions. That is to say, if choice, luck, and effort dominate birth in the determination of any person's actual command over economic value, the fairness issue in the possible distribution of starting points may be of relatively little import.

I shall discuss this point in considerably more detail, even if indirectly, in Chapter 13. But the point is, I think, important enough to warrant some elaboration here. The sources of the observed and the imagined differences in command over final product values, at the potential consumption stage, are relevant for any attribution of 'justice' or 'injustice' to the economic game. Consider a simple two-person example. Suppose, first, that the incomes of A and B are exclusively determined by their initial endowments, which for A is double that for B. Hence, A's income is two times that of B. Contrast this setting with one in which initial endowments remain as before, with A's being double B's. Assume now, however, that income shares also depend on choice, luck, and effort. Before these additional determinants enter, the expected value of A's income share will exceed that for B. In observed results, however, B's income share may well exceed that of A. In this setting, there will tend to be less concern about the disparity in initial endowments than in the first.

Two further points need to be made. In the political-economic 'game', the inequalities in starting positions that become relevant for considerations of 'justice' are inequalities among the opportunities to produce whatever is deemed to be 'valuable' for social order and stability. These values need not, and normally would not and should not, include all observed differences among persons in preferences, talents, and endowments. This recognition of the multiplicity of values is closely related to a second point. In the extremely complex 'game' that modern social order must represent, capabilities to produce value take on many different forms. In effect, there are many sub-games on simultaneously within the larger 'game', each one of which might require a somewhat different mix of endowments and talents for success. 'Equality of starting position', even as an ideal, surely does not imply that each person be qualified to enter each and every sub-game on all fours with everyone else. Properly interpreted, 'equality of opportunity', even as an ideal, must be defined as some rough and possibly immeasurable absence of major differences in the ability produce values in whatever 'game' is most appropriate for the particular situation for the person who participates.

X. THE PROBLEM OF IMPLEMENTATION

With all the qualifications and provisos, however, rules of fairness would seem to suggest some imposition of what we may call handicaps so as to allow an approach to, if not an attainment of, something that might be called equality in starting positions, or, more familiarly, equality of opportunity. Before this implication of 'justice as fairness' is accepted too readily, however, we must ask and try to answer the awesome question of who is to do the handicapping? There is no external agent or overlord or benevolent despot who can spot the differences among the players in advance and adjust starting positions. Indeed, the individual who conceives himself to be in some original position behind the Rawlsian veil of ignorance would be foolhardy to turn the handicapping task over to that subset of persons who might be temporarily or permanently assigned powers of political governance over their fellow citizens. Genuinely fair rules might include some equalization of starting positions, but if some of the players are also allowed to serve as umpires, it may well be best to leave off consideration of such rules altogether.

The implementation of handicapping rules, even those upon which conceptual agreement might be reached most easily, presents any community with a formidable institutional dilemma. If those persons who are to be assigned powers of governance are not to be, and cannot be, trusted to use their own discretion in carrying out the rules that are given to them because of some fear that they will exploit these rules for their own self-interest, how can 'equality of opportunity' be promoted, even in a limited and proximate sense?[5]

Some resolution of this dilemma may be secured by resort to *constitutional* order, to the selection of institutional rules that are chosen independently of in-period political strife and conflict and which are designed to be quasi-permanent constraints on the behaviour of governments as well as private parties. Constitutional rules may be laid down that establish institutional structures within which some equalization of starting positions may be encouraged. If this constitutional as opposed to the political route towards implementation is taken, however, the inability to accomplish any 'fine tuning' as among possibly widely disparate opportunities must be acknowledged. At best, constitutional design might allow for institutions that take some of the more apparent rough edges off gross inequalities in starting positions. I shall discuss two such institutions in the next two sections.

XI. THE TAXATION OF TRANSFERS

Could a polity that allows intergenerational transfers of assets to proceed unencumbered pass any test of fairness? Such intergenerational transfers are perhaps the most blatant and most overt devices that are seen to create *inequalities* in starting positions and hence to run directly counter to any objective of equalization. Even when the above-mentioned difficulties of implementation are recognized, some system of taxation of asset transfers would almost surely emerge from any agreement on a set of fair rules. Some such tax structure would seem to be almost a necessary part of any set of starting-position adjustments.

This conclusion is not affected by the various arguments that may be, and have often been, advanced against transfer taxation. It may be fully acknowledged that such taxes are Pareto-inefficient, that saving, capital formation, and economic growth are adversely affected, and that such taxes necessarily interfere with the liberties of those persons who are potential accumulators of wealth and potential donors to their heirs. These arguments do suggest the relevance of some trade-offs between the requirements for fairness in the rules and the objectives for economic efficiency and growth. But they do not imply that the latter objectives somehow dominate or modify those for fairness. They imply only that the fairness objective be tempered by a recognition of the costs of achieving it. Nor does a second and possibly much more important set of arguments modify the basic role of transfer taxation in a 'fair' society. These arguments are based, first, on the substitutability between wealth in potentially taxable and non-taxable forms and, second, on the inherent nontaxability of endowments in human capital, endowments that may be transferred genetically. Such non-taxable endowments may well be more significant in determining ultimate command over product value than potentially taxable endowments. If this should be the case, what is the moral-ethical basis for taxing the transfer of non-human assets?

As I have noted above, one such reason lies in the blatancy or overtness of such transfers; there is a fundamental ethical difference between non-human and human capital, even if modern economists can treat these two elements of endowments equally for their analytical purposes at hand. A second reason lies in the potential taxability itself. To an extent, such taxation, no matter how limited it might be in ultimate effect, represents a movement towards the objective of equality in starting points. The fact that the non-taxable elements in the transfer of endowments exist so as to make this objective ultimately unattainable should lend support rather than opposition to faltering efforts to go as far as is feasible, given the trade-off with other objectives.

XII. PUBLICLY FINANCED EDUCATION

A second institution that seems justified on basic fairness criteria, and still within the objective of equalizing starting positions, is publicly or governmentally financed education. It might be predicted that this institution would emerge from conceptualized contractual agreement, even in recognition of the difficulties of implementation already noted.

The second set of arguments against transfer taxation noted in the preceding section is also applicable here. Natural differentials, in part genetically determined, in human capacities cannot of course be offset in their effects by education, even if instruction should somehow be organized with idealized 'efficiency', whatever this might mean. But the availability of education serves to reduce rather than to increase the effects of such differences in starting positions in determining relative commands over economic value. In this sense, education acts similarly to transfer taxation.

Economists, and public-finance economists in particular, may have shifted attention away from the central issues when they classify education as a 'public' or 'collective consumption' service in the formal Samuelsonian sense. In such a schemata, public or governmental financing tends to be justified only to the extent that the benefits spill over or are external to the child that is educated and its immediate family. The whole public-goods approach, however, presumes that persons are 'already in the game'. A conceptually different justification for publicly financed education emerges when we look at potential adjustments in starting positions, at handicaps aimed at making the game 'fair'. Note that in this context the argument over governmental financing is not at all affected by the extent of spill-overs or external economies, at least in the ordinary usage of these terms.

(I should add a necessary proviso to the discussion at this point concerning the argument for public or governmental *financing* of education as opposed to the more complex extension of a possible argument for governmental provision and organization of education. I do not propose to discuss such an extension here; I should say only that there are very strong efficiency-based arguments for limiting government's role to financing, although some 'fairness' arguments may be adduced for governmental provision.)

XIII. FAIR CHANCES TO PLAY

As I have emphasized, the taxation of transfers and publicly financed education are not capable of equalizing starting positions even in some proximate manner. Inequalities will remain; opportunities will remain different for different persons. Nonetheless, these two basic institutions can reduce the impact of differences, and they can be seen to accomplish this result. To such an extent, the 'game' will be seen to embody criteria of 'fairness' in its rules.

What else might be done from fairness criteria at the starting position level? In Chapter 13, I want to concentrate attention on additional aspects of the problem; specifically, I want to discuss institutions aimed at ensuring reasonably 'fair chances to play'. Even if persons may recognize that starting positions can never be equalized, steps can be taken that allow all persons to have the same opportunities to participate. In terms of an example, the child of a sharecropper can never possess an equal opportunity to become the president with that of the child of a billionaire, but institutions can be organized so that the child of the sharecropper is not overtly *excluded* from the game. And if he is so much as allowed to play, and by the same rules, there remains at least some chance that he can win. In Chapter 13, I shall discuss these aspects of 'economic justice' in considerable detail. 'Hope' is an extremely important component of any social order that lays claim to being 'just'.

XIV. DIVISION OF THE PRODUCT

In the remainder of this chapter, I want to shift from the starting-position problem and examine more carefully possible redistributive adjustments in results or end-states, in income shares after the economic game is played. Using the same basic precepts of fairness, what scope for redistributive income transfers exists?

In order to concentrate on end-states, let us provisionally assume that starting positions, inequalities in opportunities, have been satisfactorily mitigated. Nonetheless, the interdependence between the two stages of potential application of fairness criteria should be kept in mind. To the extent that starting positions are satisfactorily adjusted, that the game is appropriately handicapped, there is surely less persuasive argument for any operation of redistributive transfer among results, and vice versa.

I have previously noted that if differences in results, in relative income shares, can be attributed to choice, luck, or effort, elementary precepts for *ex ante* fairness are not violated. So long as all players enter the game on proximately equal terms, and have the chance to play by the same rules, the rules are 'fair' in a very fundamental and basic sense. The predicted and observed results may, however, exhibit wide differentials in the shares assigned to separate persons. The efficiency of the 'finders, keepers' rules in maximizing total product value may be acknowledged. But fairness precepts, more extensively interpreted, may suggest some post-production *redistribution*. That is to say, even if the expected values of all income shares should be equal *ex ante*, the actual distribution of shares, *ex post*, may exhibit such variance as to command rejection on contractarian grounds.

The issues here are in part empirical. As noted earlier, the contractarian logic labels that rule as fair upon which general agreement is reached. Prospects for agreement depend critically on the expected or predicted pattern of results. With genuine equality of opportunity, what form would the actual distribution of income shares in a market economy take? I do not think any of us here can really answer this hypothetical question, and we are reminded again of the Vining admonition discussed above.

The prospects for agreement on any set of rules also depend upon the potential acceptability of alternatives. The generalized finders-keepers rules that are embodied in the market may not meet first-best criteria of 'justice', at least in the attitudes of most persons, but unless alternative rules exist upon which more agreement may be secured, these rules may remain superior in some consensual context. That is to say, the distributive rules of the market may represent some sort of Schelling-point outcome of the conceptualized contractual process; there may be no alternative set of rules upon which agreement can be attained. This 'defence' of the distributional results of market order has been advanced by Frank Knight and, more recently, by Dan Usher.[6]

There would seem, however, to be no convincing logical argument to demonstrate that distributive rules of the competitive market would *necessarily* emerge from generalized contractarian agreement among potential participants, even under the presumption that starting positions are equalized. The market rules *might* emerge from this postulated setting, but these are only one set of rules from among a larger number of sets. Plausible arguments could be made to the effect that some post-trading, post-production adjustments in income shares would be embodied in any contractual agreement, at least if the difficulties of implementation should be neglected. The rough edges of market-share distribution might be tempered, so to speak, with some guarantees for those persons whose luck turns sour, even at the expense of those persons who are more fortunate.

XV. COMPETITIVE MARKETS, PRE-MARKET POSITIONS, AND POST-MARKET DISTRIBUTION

For my own part, both in a positive prediction sense and a normatively preferred sense, I should remain relatively undisturbed about the distributional results of competitive market process if rough fairness in the distribution of initial endowments and capacities could be guaranteed. Much of the socialist-inspired criticism of the market economic order has been misdirected. The institutions of the market have been criticized for their failure to produce distributive results that meet stated normative objectives when, in fact, these results are more closely related to disparities in pre-market endowments and capacities.

Consider a very simple oranges-and-apples example. Suppose that, as a post-trading result, we observe that Tizio has sixteen oranges and fourteen apples, whereas Caio has only three oranges and two apples. This post-market imputation, taken alone, however, tells us nothing at all about the pre-market imputation of endowments. If, before trade, Tizio should have had nineteen oranges and thirteen apples, while Caio had no oranges and three apples, the trade of one apple for three oranges by Caio has surely improved his position, as well as that of Tizio. The distributional impact of this trade is dwarfed in significance by the pre-market disparity in endowments.

The market rules are rarely put to the test in situations where differences among pre-market endowments and capacities can be neutralized or isolated. If the distinction between the distribution of value potential in pre-market positions and the distributional effects of trade, as such, is recognized, several principles command acceptance, whether on fairness or other criteria. Attempts to mitigate distributional inequalities or injustice that may be due largely to pre-market inequalities should not take the form of interferences with the market process. Minimum-wage laws are perhaps the best example. Such restrictions harm those whom they are designed to benefit. In this, as in many other cases, the distributive justice of Adam Smith's system of natural liberty should be acknowledged and emphasized. Attempts to modify distributional results should be directed at the sources of the undesired consequences, which is the distribution of pre-market power to create economic values.

XVI. FAIRNESS IN POLITICAL RULES

It is necessary to return to the question posed earlier. Who is to do the adjusting? Who is to impose the handicaps? Precisely because the redistributional arrangements must be chosen and implemented by persons internal to the community involved, the contractarian-constitutional ethic seems to offer the only available standard for evaluation. The 'laws and institutions' of society provide a continuing and predictable framework within which individuals interact. It is important that these laws and institutions be seen to be fair, and to do so, they must contain features that to some extent rectify differences in opportunities, as previously noted. In this respect I have already suggested the importance of the taxation of transfers and the governmental financing of education. But, perhaps even more important, the institutions of political decision-making must also be seen to be fair and just. This critical element in any structure embodying 'economic justice' tends to be overlooked almost entirely by socialist critics of the market. If political adjustments are to be made, the political game itself must embody precepts of fairness even more stringent than those sometimes attributable to market dealings.

Political adjustments in claims to values can only be made to appear fair on contractarian grounds. That is to say, the arms and agencies of the state, the government, cannot be used directly to transfer incomes and assets from the politically weak to the politically strong under the disguise of achieving 'distributive justice' or anything else. The citizenry cannot be fooled by such empty rhetoric. Distributional adjustments that are implemented politically must, first of all, be strictly 'constitutional' in the sense that they must be embodied in permanent or quasi-permanent institutions of social order. No short-term legislative or parliamentary manipulation of distributive shares could possibly qualify by genuine fairness criteria. In terms of practical programmes, the argument here suggests that a progressive income tax might possibly emerge as one feature of an acceptable fiscal constitution, but the overtly political jiggling with the rate structure to reward political friends and to punish political enemies would, of course, violate all contractarian precepts. Similar conclusions apply to the pandering to politically dominant coalitions by jiggling expenditure programmes.

Libertarian critics of efforts to transfer incomes and wealth should concentrate their attacks on the unwarranted use of democratic decision-structures. An open society cannot survive if its government is viewed as an instrument for arbitrary transfers among its citizens. On the other hand, libertarians go too far and reduce the force of their own argument when they reject genuinely constitutional or framework arrangements that act to promote some rough equality in pre-market positions and act so as to knock off the edges of post-market extremes. The libertarian may defend the distributive role of the competitive process on standard efficiency grounds, and he may, if he chooses, also develop ethical argument in support of this rule. But this is not the same thing as defending the distributive results that might be observed in a market economy in which there is no attempt to adjust starting positions. The libertarian who fails to make the distinction between the two separate determinants of observed distributive results makes the same mistake as his socialist counterpart who attacks the market under essentially false pretences.

NOTES

1. Material contained in Chapters 12 and 13 was initially published in *New Directions in Economic Justice*, edited by Roger Skurski (South Bend, Indiana: University of Notre Dame Press, 1983), pp. 53–89. I acknowledge permission to republish this material here, with slight revision.

2. James M. Buchanan, *The Limits of Liberty* (Chicago: University of Chicago Press, 1975).

3. John Rawls, *A Theory of Justice* (Cambridge Mass.: Harvard University Press, 1971).

4. *See* Rutledge Vining, *On Appraising the Performance of an Economic System* (Cambridge: Cambridge University Press, 1984).

5. For further discussion, *see* Geoffrey Brennan and James Buchanan, *The Reason of Rules* (Cambridge: Cambridge University Press, forthcoming 1985), Ch. 8.

6. *See* Dan Usher, *The Economic Prerequisite to Democracy* (Oxford: Basil Blackwell, 1981).

13 Justice and Equal Treatment

I. INTRODUCTION

In Chapter 12 my primary emphasis was on the derivation of certain institutions aimed at equalizing opportunities to create economic value, with the derivation based on the criteria of fairness. I want to continue this emphasis in this chapter, even at some reckoned cost in a possibly extended treatment of income transfers. By implication as well as by specific assertion, I attribute much more normative significance to efforts to make the economic-political game fair in an *ex ante* than in any *ex post* sense.

In Chapter 12, I suggested that the institutions of transfer taxation (the taxation of inheritances and gifts) seemed likely to emerge in any set of agreed, fair rules, along with institutions that involve governmental financing of education. Both of these institutions are aimed at reducing inequalities in opportunities or starting positions. As I was careful to note, however, there should be no presumption that these institutions in themselves could go all the way towards guaranteeing equal opportunities, even if the latter are defined in some very rough or proximate sense. Starting positions for different players in the economic-political game will remain different, perhaps significantly so. What I want to do in this chapter is to look at additional institutions that may be required to mitigate particular forms of starting-position inequalities, always as evaluated with basic criteria for fairness.

More specifically, I want to elaborate the notion of 'fair chances' that I touched on only briefly in Chapter 12. In a fundamental but limited respect, 'fair chances' amount to 'equal opportunity'. Each person is assured that the claims to economic value assigned to him are determined by elements *within himself* and by chance factors that affect all persons *equally*. This criterion does not require equalization of expected values among all persons, evaluated at the starting positions. As suggested, the more restrictive definition of equal opportunity implied in the latter criterion could never be achieved, or even closely approached. But the 'fair chances' criterion does require the absence of effects on expected values that are exerted by elements external to the persons themselves and discriminatorily distributed among persons.

It is not easy to articulate the precise meaning of this criterion apart from examples to be introduced below, in which I think the notion becomes evident as well as familiar. Let me say at the outset, however, that I think the criterion of 'fair chances' or, in perhaps a more descriptive appellation, 'equal treatment', is vitally important in the generation of personal attitudes toward the 'justice' of any social order. (I think there is some relationship here to what the philosophers refer to as 'formal justice', but I had best not get involved with any claim to currency in modern philosophical terminology.) So long as each person considers himself to have a 'fair chance' to play the game, he can hope for a favourable outcome despite his own recognition that the expected value of the outcome for him may remain below that for other players.

II. THE DISTRIBUTION OF NATURAL TALENTS AND INFORMATION ABOUT THIS DISTRIBUTION

Consider my earlier argument to the effect that elementary precepts for *ex ante* fairness are not violated if income shares can be somehow attributed to choice, luck, or effort. To the extent that the rules allow everyone to play on equal terms, the pattern of outcomes, including the distribution of shares in command over final goods and services, cannot be adjudged to be 'unfair'. But, as I have also noted, to 'play on equal terms' could be strictly interpreted to require that all players possess equal capacities at the starting point. In this narrow interpretation, and even with the imposition of institutionally appropriate handicapping, the game can never really be labelled as 'fair'. But life in civil community means that all persons must, willy nilly, participate; so what is to be done?

To the extent that a person accepts his own lot in the genetic-cultural distribution of basic or natural capacities and talents, he can also think of this lot as his own 'luck', considered in the more inclusive pre-game sense of the term. None of us can change his or her genetic-cultural heritage (we cannot choose our own parents). We may therefore look on the heritage that we do have as our own particular 'luck in the draw of history', while at the same time we may acknowledge that this heritage may itself be of major importance in determining just where we will stand in the allocation of shares to value in the community. For better or for worse, we may accept the necessity to live with our lot, and especially as the political-economic rules of the game do not seem to operate so as to add to or to exacerbate the differences in value shares emergent from the distribution of natural talents.

In order to discuss this distribution of 'natural talents' more systematically, let me postulate, for purposes of argument, that all persons in the community make roughly the same quality of choices, have roughly the same luck within the game itself, and exert roughly the same basic effort. In this abstract setting, if the distribution of natural talents or capacities is known, and if each person can be readily identified in terms of where he or she stands in the distributional array, a distribution of expected values of claims to final values can be mapped as a direct correspondence with the initial distribution of talents-capacities-endowments. As noted earlier, to the extent that choices, luck, and effort vary among persons, this precise mapping between the distribution of starting positions and the distribution of final claims to product value breaks down. Considerable ranges for intersections and overlapping may emerge in the latter distribution as the game is actually played out. As I suggested, there will be a direct relationship between the importance of these 'non-natural' or 'non-starting point' influences and the perceived 'fairness' of the game itself.

We know, however, that persons cannot be readily identified in terms of their 'natural talents', their basic capacities to generate economic values, independently of demonstrated or proven performance in the economic game itself. In part at least, and perhaps in large part, the differences in the capacities of persons to create economic value, to produce what we may call 'social income', can only be seen in retrospect, after individuals act. To an extent, persons necessarily *enter* the game unidentified and unclassified. Unobserved differences in capacities may exist, and they may be important in determining the distribution of final claims to value, but there may be no way of judging these initial differences until the course has been commenced. The simplistic Easter Egg hunt analogy used in Chapter 12 breaks down; the 'faster runners' cannot be identified in advance.

If the distribution of assigned claims to final product value could somehow be put off or delayed until full information about comparative productivities is available, there is no particular problem created by the absence of such information during those initial periods when economic activity takes place. But in the economic-political game described by a market economy operating within a legal setting of property and contract, we must think in terms of extended calendar time. Persons could hardly be expected to wait for the length of a working life, or even a relatively small part thereof, before some shares of product value are passed out. Some payments scheme must be worked out and implemented that will assign per-period claims in the absence of full information about relative productivities. During some initial sequence of time periods, which we call a 'demonstration period', while individualized productivities are being determined, the market will tend to generate pay assignments — 'wages' —that are valued at some average for the whole group of entrants from the relevant subgroup. The calendar length of such a demonstration period will, of course, vary significantly as among different occupational groupings. For common labour the period may be so short as to be almost insignificant; for professors it may be quite long.

III. A FORMAL MODEL IN WHICH THE 'EQUAL TREATMENT' CRITERION IS SATISFIED

At this point I find it necessary to introduce somewhat more formal analysis through a set of simplified and highly abstract models. Let me first assume that there are N entrants into the working-producing force for a defined set of occupational categories. (I do not want to get into detailed discussion here about wholly 'non-competing' groups, with the distinctions among these being determined by the range of genuinely natural talents and abilities, e.g. artists and athletes.) For purposes of my argument, we may either assume that all potential entrants may enter all occupations, in which case we need not refer to groupings, or, alternatively, we may restrict analysis to the single set of occupational categories that all of the N entrants considered can enter and produce meaningful economic results.

The N entrants have identical time profiles; they enter the working-producing force at the same time, say, 1985. Let me postulate that the entrants differ in starting positions, in their basic capacities to produce economic values. If each person in the group of N entrants should make the average quality of personal career choices, if each should have roughly the same luck, and if each should exert roughly the same effort, the array of market-value productivities would follow the array of natural talents, as noted above. Such a distribution is shown in Figure 13.1, where, the abscissa measures expected values of economic productivity for the N persons and where numbers of persons are measured on the ordinate.

Let me postulate that the economy is fully competitive. Once information about individual productivities is known, individuals will be able to receive income shares commensurate with their marginal productivities. If this information is available at the outset, and *before* income shares are assigned in any period, no problem arises. Individuals will receive income shares that correspond with those capacities that are inherent in their own endowments. An individual's income share will depend in no way on the inherent capacities of others than himself.

Assume, however, that neither entrants themselves nor potential employers have any information about relative individual productivities when persons are hired. However, assume further that each employer knows that the productivities over the whole group of N entrants are distributed as indicated in Figure 13.1. Assume that information about individual productivities becomes available at the end of the demonstration period of a single-period duration, say, one year. For simplicity in exposition, assume that this information is available to individuals themselves and to *all* potential employers. There is no need to get into problems of firm-specific information or problems raised by differences in information as between employees and employers.

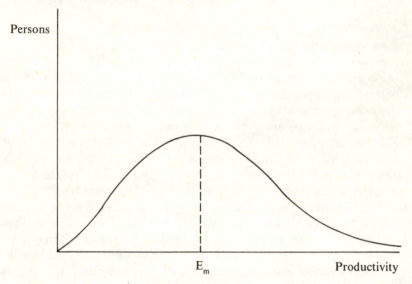

Figure 13.1

For the first period, each of the N entrants, no matter where he might stand in the distributional array, can expect to receive the mean expected value of the whole distribution, say, E_m, in Figure 13.1. At the end of this period, when full information becomes available, wages will be appropriately adjusted, and from this point in time all workers will be paid their marginal value productivities.

In this model, note that each person is *treated equally with his equals*, in terms of identification by basic natural talents and capacities. In the first period, all persons, regardless of their capacities, receive equal shares in value. After the first period, persons in each and every position on the capacity-talent scale secure the value of their own inherent contribution to value in the economy.

I want to argue that this precept or principle — equal treatment for equals — is a necessary element in any set of rules for social order in a community that makes any claim of 'fairness', and that such a principle will tend to emerge from the conceptualized contractual agreement among all persons. John Rawls did not specifically discuss this principle as such in his formulation of a theory of justice, although we may read the discussion of his criterion 'careers open to talents' as indirectly stating such a principle.[1] In one form or another, such a principle is central in normative tax theory, and it is also analogous to the more general principle of equality before the law. But the particular application of the equal treatment principle to the problems of distributive justice has not, to my knowledge, been fully worked out and analyzed.

IV. A FORMAL MODEL IN WHICH THE 'EQUAL TREATMENT' CRITERION IS VIOLATED

In the model described above, the principle is met and no further institutional adjustments are suggested. If, however, the model, as described, should obscure elements of the game as actually played, we may predict violation of the principle through the ordinary workings of the competitive market. As an alternative model, suppose, now, that the inclusive array of expected values of productivities for the N entrants is as depicted in Figure 13.1. The conditions of the model remain as before with one important exception.

Potential employers are now assumed to have *some* information about individual productivities in a probabilistic sense before persons are hired. As before, there is no information available about individuals, as individuals, but there now are assumed to exist certain identifiable characteristics that enable employers to classify persons within two roughly equal-sized sets or groupings.[2] The mean value of productivity differs as between these two sets. Further, employers are assumed to know the array of values, the distribution, for each of the two sets of potential employees. Figure 13.2 depicts the situation in this model. Note that the range of the two distributions is the same for the two sets of persons; only the mean values differ. As before, assume that the length of the demonstration period is one year and that, subsequent to this period, all employees, regardless of their initial classification, secure the full value of their marginal contributions to value.

For the initial period, employers in this setting will be forced by competitive pressures to offer different wages or incomes to workers from the two sets, A and B. All entrants from the A group will be paid a wage E_m^a for the first period, regardless of their ultimate productivity. Similarly, all workers from the B group will be paid E_m^b for the first period. It is clear that the 'equal treatment' norm is violated here by the workings of the competitive market. Workers from the A group, and identified as such, will receive a lower present value of lifetime earnings than their 'equals' in the B group, not because of something inherent in their own individualized 'luck in the draw' of natural talents and capacities but, instead, because they happen to be classified as a member of a group with lower mean productivity. To put the same result differently, an entrant from the A group who makes precisely the same choices, who has precisely the same luck in the game itself, who, for a given wage, exerts precisely the same effort, will secure over his lifetime a net claim to final product value lower than his equal from the B group. He is effectively 'penalized' by his membership in the group that happens to exhibit the lower average productivity.

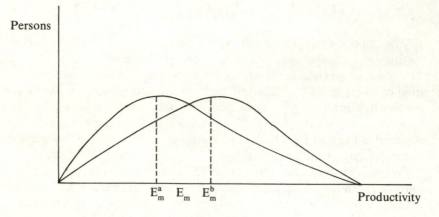

Figure 13.2

I should emphasize that the competitive market process that generates the violation of the 'equal treatment' norm is efficient, by construction. The differentials in present values between any pair of genuine equals, one from each of the two subgroups, do not reflect *market failure* in any meaningful sense of this term. In the competitive market model that I have postulated here, employers act on the basis of the information that is available to them. Their first-period information is, by assumption, limited to identification by class or group. If a single employer chose deliberately to ignore such information, and chose instead to pay all entrants the mean expected value for the whole set of N entrants, he could not hire any of the workers from the B group.[3]

Note also that there is no 'discrimination', as such, in the model. Employers are presumably interested solely and exclusively in maximizing profits, and they have no tastes or preferences as to the type of input units employed, either individually or as a mix among the two types. Similarly, employees are exclusively interested in wages and are totally indifferent as to whom their co-workers might be.

V. ECONOMIC EFFICIENCY AND ECONOMIC RENTS

Once the violation of the equal treatment principle is recognized, a question arises concerning the possible efficiency losses that any interference with the working of competitive markets designed to correct the violation might produce.

Consider the following scenario. Suppose that all potential employers should be required to hire entrants *as if* the initial classification into the A and B groups were not possible. That is to say, suppose that all employers should be constrained to 'hire blind', to deliberately throw away or to ignore information that had been of potential value to them in the setting described above. Note that in this new situation employers could do no more than pay the mean value for the whole set of N entrants for the initial or demonstration period. Despite the fact that all persons in the community, employers and workers alike, recognize that the B workers, as a set, are on average more productive than the A workers, as a set, the competitive market will force all wages during the initial period to the level E_m. All workers will be employed, as before, by assumption. Efficiency losses will emerge only to the extent that we allow workers to respond to wage-rate differences by modifying effort (e.g. through changing numbers of hours worked). If incentives of this sort are allowed, the initial market solution, with mean wages, E_a and E_b for the two classes respectively, the A-class workers will work less than they would under the uniform wage, E_m. The B-class workers, on the other hand, will work more at wage $E_b(> E_m)$ than at E_m. Since, by construction, the mean productivity of the B-class workers exceeds that of the A-class workers, there will be *some* efficiency loss involved in the shift to the arrangement where all employers pay all workers in N the uniform initial-period wage, E_m. This efficiency loss may, however, be very small.

VI. IMPLICATIONS FOR POLICY WITHIN THE SETTING OF THE MODEL

The analysis in the preceding section demonstrates that it becomes conceptually possible to secure satisfaction of the 'equal treatment for equals' or 'fair chances' criterion with little minor efficiency losses of the sort ordinarily discussed by welfare economists. There may, however, be significant gaps between conceptual possibility and practical implementation. In the model that was specifically analyzed, I simply assumed that information about individual productivities is not available until after a demonstration period is complete, a period during which some wage payments scheme must be worked out. Clearly, if potential employers could in some way secure accurate information about individual productivity before entrants are taken on as employees, there need be no violation of the equal-treatment criterion, even if the two-group identification with differing average productivities continues to hold. In such a full information setting, employers will be led by their profit-seeking behaviour to ignore averages over groups and to look exclusively at prospective individual values. Recognition of this result suggests that policy aimed directly at increasing the flow of relevant information concerning prospective employee productivity before employment commences may be of independent value in terms of promoting a basic sense of 'fair chances' in the community.

It should, however, be anticipated that some of the elements isolated by the model analyzed above will remain. The equal-treatment principle will not be fully met with improved information. How and to what extent could constraints be imposed on hiring and wage-setting behaviour in a fully competitive economy for the purpose of enhancing 'fairness'?

If constraints are to be imposed, note that efficiency in results would require that such constraints be *universally applied*. They must bear on each and every employer who faces the set of entrants into the workforce. And note that each of these employers will have a continuing private-profit motivation to use the classificatory information that we presume is available to him. To impose the hiring constraints on some employers but not on others or to impose the constraints so loosely that only some employers will be affected will guarantee net efficiency losses without accomplishing the results intended. Some minimal steps may be taken to deny the information as to class identification to employers. In this sense, legal and administrative rules that dictate that blanks for identifiable characteristics not be filled out may seem justifiable.

Care must also be taken to note precisely the nature of the constraints that would be required to prove effective in promoting genuine equal treatment for equals. A constraint that merely directs potential employers to pay all entrants *equal wages* would be disastrous for *all* entrants from the class described by the relatively low average productivity. This result emerges because, in such a setting, every employer, having the general classificatory information, will on probabilistic grounds find it in his interest to hire entrants *only* from the group with the higher average productivity. Regardless of their ultimate contribution to value, individuals from the group with relatively low average productivity will find it difficult if not impossible to find employment in this setting.

If the 'equal treatment for equals' criterion is to be satisfied, equal wages for equally productive persons will have to be paid during the initial demonstration periods as well as for all subsequent periods during which individualized contributions are fully known. But this end-result must be produced by the profit-maximizing response of potential employers within the constraint that entrants be chosen as if they are drawn from the inclusive group and not from identifiable classes within the larger set. In more specific terms, the suggested constraints must take the form of *hiring quotas*, with new entrants taken on in proportion to the relative numbers of the identifiable classes in the inclusive set. In my example, if A and B are equal in size, each being of size N/2, each employer should be required to hire equal numbers of entrants from A and from B. In this case, competition would prevent employers from paying differential wages to members of the two groups; employers will necessarily pay first-period wages equal to the average productivity expected for all entrants from N, and not from A and/or B.

The hiring quota or constraint in this model should be made to apply *only* to initial or demonstration-period hiring. By our assumption, after this period, full information is available concerning individual productivities, not only to the specific firm that employs particular persons but to other potential employees as well. Average productivities of classes or groups, even if these differ substantially by easily identifiable classes, become totally irrelevant to decisions about continuing employment and relative wage scales. Market competition will ensure universalized payment in accordance with relative marginal productivities.

In the distribution of actual productivities as indicated in Figure 13.2, the firms or industries that employ relatively more high productivity workers would be anticipated to retain relatively more B-class employees in their workforce than firms or industries that requires less productive workers. This sort of permanent 'imbalance' in the ratios between A-class and B-class employees does not imply any violation of the 'equal treatment' norm. Indeed, quite the contrary. To require that all firms and industries 'balance' the workforce as between the two classes of workers would require that the equal-treatment norm be violated, with the employees from the relatively more productive group, from B in our example, being subjected to 'unfair' treatment.

VII. THE RESTRICTIVE ASSUMPTIONS OF THE MODEL

I have tried to be careful in saying that the implications for policy outlined in the previous section depend strictly on the existence of the parameters of the model that was specified. The assumptions of this model are extremely restrictive, and it need not follow that the policy implications suggested are relevant when and if these assumptions are modified. Recall that I assumed (1) that all N entrants in the inclusive group can produce economic value in the employment categories considered; (2) that potential employers initially possess no information at all about the individual productivities to be expected from any entrant; (3) that employers do possess information that allows the N entrants to be subdivided into two readily identifiable classes, that are known to differ in average productivity; (4) that the demonstration period during which information about individual productivity comes to be available is the same for all entrants; (5) that this productivity information is known to all potential employers at the end of the demonstration period; and finally (6) that the economy is fully competitive. It is useful at this point to see just how rigid these assumptions are; how might they be relaxed without destroying the validity of the policy implications that were suggested above? The requirement for competition need not be made overly restrictive; the general competitiveness of the economy in some broadly workable sense seems all that would be necessary here. Nor need there be concern about the subdivision into only two readily identifiable classes or groups or about the uniformity of the demonstration period. These assumptions may be modified to allow for several classes with several lengths of demonstration period without changing the structure of the analysis. The assumptions that remain critical to the analytical implications are those which relate to the *absence* of information on relative individual productivities and the *presence* of information about average productivities for classes or groups smaller than the whole set of entrants prior to the workforce. These assumptions are critical because it is only on these assumptions that we get profit-seeking employers in a competitive environment differentiating among entrants on the basis of class in the complete absence of information about individual productivity. It is such differentiation that introduces the 'unfairness' in the game, that violates the equal-treatment norm, that ensures that persons who ultimately demonstrate equality with others in the 'natural draw' secure lower present values of claims to product solely because they are members of a class with relatively low average productivity.

You will of course have noticed that I have deliberately refrained from attaching labels to the classes, but you can add your own designations as you see fit, whether these be for male–female, black–white, Protestant–Catholic, short–tall, Yankee–redneck, or what have you. I should argue that in the real world where the assumptions of the formal model are not of course present, the policy implications follow generally with respect to hiring practices, provided that potential employers should be observed to make such differentiation by class, provided that those who do so are observed to survive.

Note what the analysis *does not say*. The *average* present values for claims for members of the 'less productive' class will in any case be lower than the average for the 'more productive' class. Satisfaction of the equal-treatment criterion will not modify this basic result. There is no way that a hiring quota system could or should equalize the differing average productivities of members of the various identifiable classes. A hiring quota system ideally administered should do nothing more than ensure that the individual, regardless of his ultimate productivity, is not affected in the value of the claims that he secures by factors *external to his own capacities*, that are not equally applicable to all members of the group, inclusively defined.

VIII. OBJECTIONS CONSIDERED

Objections can be raised to the policy implications and, by inference, to the analysis itself. In particular, since my whole model allows for separate individual shares in product value to be determined, in part, by 'natural capacities', and since these are acknowledged to differ among persons, why have I advanced the argument that the 'fair chances' or 'equal treatment' criterion requires blindness only with respect to one feature of a person, namely, his identification as a member of a particular class or group? If 'luck in the genetic-cultural draw' is to be accepted, and lived with, in terms of basic individual capacities to produce economic value, why should not his same 'luck in the genetic draw' be extended to cover membership in the identifiable class or group? If person A_1 is 'unlucky' in that his inherent productive capacity, when demonstrated, falls below that of the mean capacity for the community, can he not also be considered, and so consider himself, to be 'unlucky' in having been born to membership in the A group, where persons are, on average, less productive than in the B group? Perhaps to some this objection is compelling, but to me there is an element of what I should call *perverse handicapping* in the uncorrected operation of competitive markets in the setting postulated in the model. An individual member of the A group, in my example, is forced to start the race behind his equals, behind those whom he later matches in terms of demonstrated capacity. He has to catch up to be equal, which, in my set of values becomes inherently 'unfair'.

A more specific objection may be raised concerning my argument to the effect that the imposition of initial-period hiring quotas may be accompanied by relatively insignificant welfare or efficiency losses, limited essentially to the slight differences in the product value of the offsetting responses of the members of two groups in the model. In the model itself, I assumed that all of the N entrants can be employed and can produce value in the 'industry' or 'set of employment categories' considered. If for any reason some persons who might seek entry into the relevant 'industry' cannot be employed, there must be some means of rationing places. In such a setting, a legal requirement for all employers to select entrants proportionately from the A and B group may introduce an additional efficiency loss. The average productivity of persons employed will be lower than the average productivity under the encumbered operation of the competitive market.

Too much should not be made of this additional efficiency-loss emendation, provided that the market is assumed to be competitive. To the extent that entrants seek to enter occupational-employment categories, they should be able to do so and to secure employment therein if there are no barriers to entry and if wage levels are competitively determined. Problems arise only with genuinely 'non-competing' groups, where threshold differences in natural talents create sharp dividing lines between those who qualify and those who do not, and where there are no genuinely marginal employees who can readily shift into and out of such groups.

On the other hand, implementation of the equal-treatment criterion may involve significant efficiency loss in situations where, for any reason, artificial and non-market barriers to entry into occupations and employments have been established. If competitive organization is not allowed to determine the number of medical doctors, for example, there may be many more applicants for medical school than there are places. In such a setting, the introduction of quotas as among groups or classes of entrants based on some proportion to identifiable characteristics with distinguishable average productivity differentials will produce a higher fail rate (and hence higher cost) than would be the case without such quotas. This amounts to saying that 'fairness' costs less in market than in non-market settings.

A much more serious objection than any of these discussed to this point lies in the prospect that the policy implications of the whole analysis may be extended and applied to settings where the assumptions of the model are clearly violated, and notably to employment and pay structures in which information about individual productivities *is* known to employers. As noted, there is no implication in my analysis that uniform wages should be paid to all entrants, even in the initial period, save as a result of the hiring arrangements that make such uniformity a *result* rather than a specific objective. There is surely no implication that wage rates should be standardized over groups on the basis of elements other than individual productivities, when the latter are ascertained. As I suggested earlier, it is a perversion of my argument to suggest that average wages among groups with differing average productivities should somehow be forcibly equalized. Such a policy, if implemented, would violate the 'equal treatment' criterion by penalizing individual members of the group with the relatively high average productivity, a result that is no more acceptable than the opposite. Also, as noted earlier, 'equal treatment' in the initial hiring stage does not and cannot be perverted to mean the maintenance of 'balance' in employment, *after* productivities are known.

When we recognize that any projected interference with the working of the competitive market in hiring must be organized and put into being politically—that is, by persons acting on behalf of governments, persons who have their own self-interest to consider, whether this be tenure in office, electoral success, or their own idealized goal for society—the dangers that the implications derived from basically sound analysis will be perverted for use in situations where they simply do not apply, and where, if applied, will produce damage, both in terms of efficiency and of fairness, must be acknowledged.

Once again, distrust in the ordinary political arrangements suggests resort to genuinely constitutional rules that will, to an extent at least, be immune from ordinary political pressures. But courts, even if nominally bound by rules, can also get confused, and especially as the parameters of the cases at hand rarely, if ever, correspond to the conditions of the models that might have been systematically analyzed. The meanderings of the Supreme Court in the recent Bakke and Weber cases attest to this confusion. I find myself sympathetic to the Court's dilemma in both cases. This appreciation of the dilemma facing the Court would not have been present before I worked out the 'equal treatment' principle of this chapter. So, at the least, I have learned something.

APPENDIX TO CHAPTER 13

In this appendix I want to extend the basic analysis of Chapter 13 to a setting in which, for some reason, there is an arbitrary limit on the number of applicants who can secure 'employment' in an 'industry', a limit that is lower than the total number of applicants and where the competitive forces of the market are not allowed to operate. I shall develop the argument through the use of stylized models, but my aim is to isolate certain features that bear considerable relevance to policy issues.

1. Consider first a model in which there are only a hundred 'places' to be filled, but where there are a thousand applicants. Suppose that there is absolutely no information about individual capacities or productivities but that the distribution of such capacities is known to take the form depicted in Figure 13.1. How can the hundred 'best' applicants be selected? In this model it is clear that only by sampling the whole population of applicants can this objective be attained. If this sampling takes the form of a required period of demonstration, the selection process will be costly but necessary.

2. Consider, as a second model, a situation where 'entrance tests' can be administered cheaply and where there is a perfect correspondence between scores on these tests and the observed productivities in periods subsequent to the tests. In this case, the indicated policy is simply to select the hundred persons who score highest on the entrance tests. No one is excluded; the game is fair.

3. As a third model, consider a situation where nothing is known about individual capacities and where a costly demonstration period is required to determine these. Assume, however, that the set of a thousand applicants may be divided into two classes, A and B, in terms of some readily identifiable characteristic, and that the average productivities of these two classes are known to differ, as depicted in Figure 13.2. If the range of capacities is the same for both groups, all of the thousand applicants must be tested before the hundred best qualified can be chosen. Assume that if such a testing procedure is done, there will be ninety successful applicants from B and only ten from A. Note that this apparently biased result does not violate the equal-treatment criterion in any way, because at the level of initial testing, all persons are given fair chances to compete. No arbitrary exclusion based on class is involved.

In the setting of this model, however, the temptation to use the class identification information may be very strong. By testing only from the B group, known to have the relatively higher mean capacity, ninety of the hundred required applicants may be selected. The costs of locating the remaining ten applicants from the A class will be equal to the costs of getting the ninety from the B class. Further, the capacities of the ten 'best' from the A class, who might be excluded by a sampling limited to the B class, may be only slightly lower than the additional ten persons who might qualify under the more restricted testing. The benefit-cost calculus may put great pressures on decision-making authorities to sample only from the B group.

To do so, however, would clearly violate the equal-treatment criterion, as discussed in this chapter. Potential applicants, from the A class, even if they have full knowledge of the probability coefficients, can properly label the game to be unfair because they would be prohibited entry, even at the demonstration-testing stage.

4. A more complex model involves a combination of the first and second models above. Suppose that no class identification (second model) is possible and that *some* information about individual capacities can be secured from inexpensive entrance examinations but that this information will prove accurate only within rather broad probability limits. All potential applicants may be given the entrance tests, but, differently from the second model, the selection of the hundred persons with the highest entrance test scores, will not insure that the hundred 'best' persons, in terms of proven capacities, will be chosen. To determine the latter, an additional costly demonstration period must be administered. In this setting, a decision to admit more than a hundred persons for the demonstration period may well be warranted. Regardless of the number admitted to the demonstration period, however, so long as scores on the entrance test are used to determine the lower cut-off point, there is no overt violation of the equal-treatment criterion. A person who is excluded because of his low entrance test score

cannot claim unfairness; he is treated equally with his equal at this level.

5. The most complex model of all is attained by adding the possibility of class identification to the partial-information model above. In this setting there is no violation of the equal-treatment criterion *if the class identification is not used*. If applicants to be allowed to enter a demonstration or try-out period are selected purely by entrance test scores, even if it is known that these test scores are grossly imperfect predictors of ultimate capacities, those excluded cannot be justified in possible claims of unfairness.

6. This result depends, however, on the presumption that scores on the entrance test are not biased by class. Suppose, for example, that the differences in the mean test scores for A and B applicants are significantly larger than the differences in the mean values of capacities, when finally determined, although both means vary in the same way. In this situation, even though the entrance test scores may be the single best predictor of ultimate capacity, the result of the use of this score as the sole criterion to select applicants for the extended demonstration periods will tend to bias the whole selection process to the disadvantage of members of the A class, which is known to be characterized by lower mean test-scores and lower mean productivities.

There is no overt violation of the equal-treatment norm here. A person from the A group is not excluded because he or she is a member of that group. And such a person can observe members of the B group, with the same test scores as his or her own, also being excluded. However, in an indirect sense, basic unfairness can be claimed here, due to the bias in the test. With observed identical test scores, a rejected member of the A applicants will embody a somewhat higher probability of ultimate success than a member of the rejected B applicants, with an identical test score. If equals are defined by equal probabilities of success in the extended demonstration period, then identical test scores do not meet the definition. In this particular case there is a logical argument, based on fairness precepts, to put the cut-off test-score somewhat lower for the A applicants.

7. Whether or not the bias suggested exists is, of course, an empirical question to be determined. Unless it can be shown to exist, there can be no alleged unfairness in a system that relies exclusively on entrance test scores, even when everyone recognizes that these scores are imperfect predictors of ultimate capacities. In the models of this appendix, as in the body of the chapter, unfairness, in the absence of such a test bias, stems *only* from the use of class identification information.

8. The extension of the basic equal-treatment analysis summarized in this appendix are relevant to some of the problems faced by the United States Supreme Court in the Bakke and Weber cases, which were among the most important decisions made by the Court of the decade of the 1970s.[4]

Allen Bakke was successful in his particular claim that he had suffered 'reverse discrimination' in the University of California, Davis, practice of selecting medical school entrants. His evidence was that his score on an entrance test was higher than those of blacks who were admitted under a designated quota system. As the analysis above has suggested, Bakke was justified on the 'equal treatment for equals' criterion if there was no evidence of the test score bias discussed in appendix section 6 above. Even if entrance test scores could be shown to be quite imperfect predictors of success in medical school, the sole use of such scores to determine success of failure of admission does not violate the fairness precept. In such a setting there is no argument for the establishment and enforcement of racial quotas, and any attempt to introduce such quotas would violate the fairness norm for members of the relatively high mean productivity race.

Since no evidence of test score bias was explicitly introduced, the Court's support of the Bakke position seems likely to have been in accordance with applications of the equal-treatment precept. On the other hand, the apparent 'hedging' by Justice Powell on the use of race may well have been prompted by considerations of the sort discussed in appendix section 3 above. The 'low cost' way for a medical school to secure, say, a hundred entrants of reasonably high quality, given information about the mean success of persons from identifiable classes, would be to restrict persons by race or class and to use test scores only within classes. This method of operation would tend to emerge without the slightest preference on the part of anyone for racial or class preference, per se.

In the Weber case, the majority of a reduced-size Court found against Weber's claim of unfair or unequal treatment. In this case, Weber's argument was based on the fact that his employment seniority ranking was above that of the black applicant who was chosen for a training programme based on a proportionate white-black quota arrangement that had been previously negotiated between the employer and the union.

The issues raised in *Weber* were considerably more complex than those raised in *Bakke*. It will be useful to see if the basic analysis of the chapter can be applied so as to offer insights into the Court's genuine dilemma. For purposes of discussion we presume that the mean productivities of the two races, black and white, were estimated by employers to be as depicted in Figure 13.2. In this setting, and prior to any programme of affirmative action, Kaiser, the employing firm, would have presumably been willing to hire blacks initially only if they were available at lower wages (for comparable skill categories); or, if wages were equalized, at higher qualification levels for the same categories. This policy would have emerged on the assumption that uncertainty about individual productivities was necessarily present when hiring decisions were made. (No overt racial discrimination at all would have been involved in such a policy.) Union wage standardization would have presumably required equalization of wage rates across all workers in a given category. Hence, a black worker on being hired would have represented a *higher* level of qualification (on average) than his white worker counterpart. Seniority records commence, however, only from the date of initial employment, and these records could not of course reflect differential qualification levels at point of entry. It might have been argued, therefore, that a black worker was not the 'equal' of the white worker who exhibited the same seniority, and that, because of the difference, that the seniority records, standing alone, did not reflect the appropriate criterion of legal equality, for selection and advancement to a training programme. 'Equal treatment' at the level of training-programme selection, if designed to offset the initial differential in qualification on employment, might require some quota arrangement, and one that might necessarily have been inconsistent with simple seniority records.

The majority of the Court would have been on much more secure grounds in its *Weber* opinion had it chosen to use an argument like that sketched out briefly here. Unfortunately, Justice Brennan, for the majority, did not use such an argument and, instead, relied on an internally contradictory argument that seemed to reflect personally-based judicial legislation. As a result, the opinion was highly vulnerable to the scathing dissent of Justice Rehnquist. Neither the majority opinion nor the dissent recognized the potential conflict between the satisfaction of the 'equal treatment' criterion and the commitment against quotas in the discussion of the basic legislation.

NOTES

1. *See* John Rawls, *A Theory of Justice*, p. 73: (Cambridge, Mass.: Harvard University Press, 1971) '. . . those who are at the same level of talent and ability, and have the same willingness to use them, should have the same prospects of success regardless of their initial place in the social system, that, irrespective of the income class into which they are born'. In his discussion, however, Rawls seems to think that the institutions of transfer taxation and publicly financed education, both of which I discussed in the Chapter 12, will suffice to satisfy the equal chances criterion in the absence, of course, of discriminatory 'tastes'.

2. What I call identifiable characteristics are *indices* in the terminology of Michael Spence, which he defines as 'unalterably observable characteristics'; *see* Michael Spence, *Market Signaling* (Cambridge: Harvard University Press, 1974), Ch. 4.

3. Akerlof discusses the market phenomena that I have described under the heading 'statistical discrimination', which in itself is somewhat misleading since no 'discrimination', as such, is involved. In addition, although his discussion is somewhat unclear in this respect, Akerlof seems to suggest that the existence of such phenomena implies inefficiency through the generation

of what he refers to as a 'low-level equilibrium trap', one that results from the incentives exerted on the behaviour of the members of the class or group with relatively lower average qualification; cf. George Akerlof, 'The Economics of Caste and the Rat Race and Other Woeful Tales', *Quarterly Journal of Economics*, XC (Nov. 1976), 599–618.

Such incentive effects may, of course, be present, and this would imply inefficiency. In my model, however, I have explicitly eliminated these effects to ensure that there is no inefficiency in the competitive solution.

In his earlier treatment, Kenneth Arrow refers to the differences in perceived qualifications, based on perceived differences in averages, as one explanation for observed differences in wages among differing racial groups. Arrow's whole analysis is marred, however, by his apparent commitment to the presumption that basic productivities among groups cannot differ, even in average terms; cf. Kenneth Arrow, 'Models of Job Discrimination'(Ch. 1) and 'Some Mathematical Models of Race in the Labor Market' (Ch. 6), in *Racial Discrimination in Economic Life*, ed. Anthony H. Pascal (Lexington, Mass.: D. C. Heath, 1972), pp. 83–102, 187–204.

In his book *Market Signaling*, Michael Spence discusses models in which results analogous to those emerging from the models here seem to be derived. His whole analysis, however, is based on the signaling role of education and of individuals' choices of educational investment. In his discussion, Spence, like Arrow, postulates that the actual productivity distributions as between the two classes (races in his model) are identical. Differences in treatment of 'equals' in separate classes stem from the possibly differing levels of educational signals required to establish conditional probabilities for employers. Given an initial, historically determined 'prejudice', the expectations of employers and employees alike, over both classes, may prove to be self-reinforcing; cf. A. Michael Spence, *Market Signaling*, *op. cit.*, Chs. 2 and 3.

By contrast, in my model, which postulates actual differences in the mean or average productivities of the two classes, the differential treatment of 'equals' arises with no 'prejudice' or 'discrimination' present, at *any* point in time.

4.   *Regents of University of California v. Bakke*, 98 S.Ct. 2733 (1978); *United Steelworkers, etc., v. Weber*, 99 S.Ct. 2721 (1979).

14 Distributive and Redistributive Norms: A Note of Clarification[1]

In this chapter I want to clarify the distinction between distributive and redistributive norms, a distinction that has not always been kept in mind by social philosophers who analyze issues of distributive justice. By a 'distributive norm' I refer to an individual's idealized distribution in a community. To describe a situation where this norm would become directly relevant for choice, we can imagine an individual confronting the prospects of living in any one of many alternative communities, each of which embodies a different predicted distribution but all of which have the same total product. In order to avoid the particularization of the norm to a defined position, we can also imagine that the individual remains totally ignorant as to the specific position he himself will occupy in the distribution of the community that he selects (or any other community that he might select).

Despite appearances, this choice is *not* that which is confronted by an individual in a Rawlsian-type constitutional calculus. In the first choice-setting posed above, the individual is restricted to the selection of a single community from among a set of prospects, a community that is described by a specified predicted distributional pattern. By comparison and contrast, the Rawlsian-type choice problem invokes *re*distributive norms. By a 'redistributive norm' I refer to an individual's idealized distributive pattern for a specified community, *after* redistributive adjustments have been made from some initial distribution. Again, it is presumed that the individual does not know his own position before or after adjustment; he chooses behind the veil of ignorance. The individual's redistributive norm need not be, and indeed normally would not be expected to be, equivalent to that distributive norm that informs the first and quite different choice problem. Put differently, the conceptually observed distributive pattern in the community selected by the individual in the first choice-setting will not be the same as either the pre- or post-adjustment distributive pattern in the specific community in which the individual finds himself when the second choice-problem is posed.

Such possible differences in conceptually observed results may be widely acknowledged, but these tend to be attributed to production-incentive problems created by the operation of the adjustment process itself. To the extent that the implementation of any redistributive adjustments involve feedback incentive effects on the size of total product, we should not of course expect the individual's most desired post-adjustment pattern in a specific community to match his idealized distribution in a community that requires no corrective adjustments. My central point in this chapter, however, is that, *even in the total absence of all production loss*, the distributive norm and the redistributive norm differ for the individual whose 'values' remain invariant as between the two conceptualized choice settings.

Consider a highly stylized setting where persons are distributed locationally over a featureless plain in each of several communities. In every case there is a single all-purpose consumption good (manna) which is non-storable and which remains scarce regardless of quantities made available to any person. In each of these communities, the same total quantity (in pounds) is dropped from the sky each period, distributed in some fashion among the different locations on the plain. We want to look at the choice of a single person who can choose among these separate communities under the veil-of-ignorance constraint; he cannot predict which position (location) he will occupy in the community that he chooses. I shall refer to this as the first choice setting.

Under these conditions, it is plausible to suggest that the individual will select the community that will be described by equal distribution of the good among all of the locations (individuals). By presupposition, one such community will exist in the choice set, and, also by presupposition, there will be no redistribution required or allowed. My argument does not require that the individual's choice be that community characterized by full equality, but it is helpful to think of this for expository reasons.

I want to compare and contrast this first choice setting with a second and different one. Suppose now that the individual knows that he must remain a member of a given community, one that is predicted to have the same total product, or total amount of the all-purpose good, as each of the communities in the first choice setting. Again there is to be a drop of the good from the sky at the beginning of each period, but, in this second setting, this drop is known to involve a distribution among locations (individuals) in accordance with some predicted pattern, one that will involve significant inequalities. The individual is, as before, behind the Rawlsian veil of ignorance; he does not know which of the locations or economic positions he will occupy in this community. The choice that he faces is that among alternative corrective adjustment schemes, redistributive arrangements, all of which are assumed to 'work perfectly' in the sense that there is no effect on the size of total product. The same amount of the all-purpose good will be available, in total, regardless of the redistributive scheme selected.

My argument is that if we assume that the individual selected the community with an equal distribution in the first choice-setting, he will *not* select a corrective adjustment scheme that will generate full equality in the second choice-setting. Such a scheme will not represent a plausible choice for the same person who selects the equal-distribution community in the first choice.

The difference lies in the fact that, in the second setting, *re*distribution must take place in order to secure the results that may be preferred. Quite apart from predictable effects on incentives, emphasized by economists, redistribution will be predicted to involve utility losses inherent in the process of transfer itself. The transfer of units of the all-purpose good from those persons who initially receive relatively large endowments to those persons who initially receive relatively small endowments will be predicted to generate a perceived utility loss to the transferors that will, beyond some limits, exceed the perceived utility gains to the transferees.

We must of course keep in mind just what sort of utility comparisons are being made here. We are not concerned with interpersonal comparability of utilities among separate members of the community at the post-constitutional stage when the transfers are actually made. The relevant comparison for our purposes is that which takes place, within the calculus of the single person at the moment of constitutional choice among the alternative redistribution schemes. In this choice, the individual must somehow assign utilities or utility weights to himself in each one of the set of possible positions in the postconstitutional distribution, both pre- and post-adjustment. This assignment will presumably involve some predictions as to the utilities that will be perceived post-constitutionally, but that which the individual maximizes in making the selection among institutions is his own utility at the moment of choice.[2]

In the highly stylized example introduced here, there is no basis for the emergence of ethically respectable claims or rights in the initial endowments received by individuals at the separate locations in the community and hence no reason why predictions of the relevance of such rights or claims should enter into the individual's constitutional choice calculus. No arguments about 'finders-keepers', 'just desert', 'just acquisition', or the like, would seem to be worthy of consideration. Despite the acknowledged arbitrariness in the initial distribution of endowments of the good, however, 'possession' of a sort does exist (or will be predicted to exist), at least for the moment between initial receipt of endowments and the corrective adjustments. The reduction from the initial endowment received by any individual will be viewed, in some sense, as a 'taking', which will, in itself, be predicted to create a utility loss over and beyond that which would be measured by a simple difference between before and after sizes of endowments. That is to say, the person whose post-adjustment endowment is reached by a 'taking away' from his initial quantity of good will tend to be at a lower level of utility than the same person would be whose initial endowment requires no adjustment and which remains equal to the post-adjustment endowment in the other situation.

In the second choice-setting, given the assumed absence of any effect on total product, any person faced with the constitutional choice as posed, will select a transfer or adjustment scheme that will shift the distribution very substantially towards equality in the post-adjustment imputation. That is to say, the post-constitutional setting selected will embody major *re*distribution in the model postulated here. My point in this chapter is limited to the suggestion that even after 'costless' redistribution in the sense of production loss, the results will fall short of the ideal distribution that would be selected by the same person in the first choice setting.

The difference between these two conceptually observed final distributions may depend, in part, on the predicted pre-adjustment distributive pattern in the second choice-setting. The more unequal this distribution, the more transfers that will be required to generate any given post-adjustment distribution. The question of interest becomes whether the desired post-adjustment distribution is or is not modified by the predicted pre-adjustment pattern. If the utility loss predicted to occur in the process of transfer itself, that loss consequent on 'taking' and not matched by 'getting', per se, increases, and at an increasing rate, with the amount of transfer, the more unequal the predicted pre-adjustment distribution then the more unequal the post-adjustment distribution. Hence, the more different the redistributive norm from the distributive norms emergent under the first choice-setting. Differing functional relationships between the size of transfers and predicted utility loss involved in 'taking' may remove this effect of pre-adjustment distributional patterns on post-adjustment norms.[3]

In some more general sense, my argument demonstrates that the familiar and much-discussed equity-efficiency trade-off depends on the institutional structure of the society. I have quite deliberately restricted analysis to models in which no production loss takes place in order to show that the equity norm will vary with the choice setting. In the stylized example for my second choice-problem, we may convert the results into those of the first choice-problem by allowing someone to advance a proposal for a scheme that will collect all of the manna in a net above the plain, and *before* the initial individual endowments are identified. This prior collectivization of all income-wealth, if it could be done without production loss, would eliminate the predicted utility loss of the transfer process itself and would make the individual's constitutional choice one among final distributions not among redistributive institutions.

This variation on the simple example suggests that, given egalitarian objectives and totally ignoring production efficiency considerations, there may have been some vaguely plausible argument on behalf of the traditional socialist proposal for collectivization of the 'means of production'. If, through such a shift in institutional ownership arrangements, it could somehow become possible to amalgamate individual productive shares, so as to forestall 'possession', a distributive norm might be possible that would embody more equality than would be the case under market-like arrangements, with private ownership, where overt 'taking' is necessarily required to achieve any desired final distributive results. Whether or not collectivization arrangements could effectively accomplish such a divorce between productive contributions and distributive claims is, of course, highly questionable on empirical grounds.

The assumption throughout this chapter of zero production losses under redistributive schemes is of course totally unrealistic. As such losses are predicted to occur, and as they are taken into account in the individual's constitutional choice calculus, we should predict that the preferred post-adjustment distributive patterns will depart significantly from idealized distributive norms.[4] My point in this chapter has been limited to the demonstration that, even when production efficiency losses are assumed away, distributive and redistributive norms will differ, even within the calculus of a single individual.

NOTES

1. I am indebted to Geoffrey Brennan and Bruce Chapman for helpful discussion and criticism.

2. It seems inappropriate to model any Rawlsian-type choice in social welfare function terms. For example, Cooter and Helpman examine the implications of seven separate social welfare functions, one of which they label 'Rawlsian', and defined as that which maximizes the utility of the least advantaged. Presumably, the government is to be assigned the task of acting in accordance with the instructions of this function, which would in this case require some attempts to measure the utilities of persons in the post-constitutional period during which transfer schemes are implemented. But this is wholly different from the problem of the individual, behind the veil of ignorance, who chooses among separate redistributive institutions and who may be modelled as maximizing *his own utility*, at that moment; *cf.* Robert Cooter and Elhanen Helpman, 'Optimal Income Taxation for Transfer Payment', *Quarterly Journal of Economics*, LXXXVIII (nov. 1974), 656–70.

3. In an extreme and limiting case where such a utility loss is acknowledged but is assumed to be of a lump-sum nature independent of the predicted size of transfer, we get the interesting result that, if any adjustment at all is selected, the redistributive norm does become identical to the distributive norm. Only in this extreme case will the general results of my argument fail to hold, and even here the argument suggests that there may exist many pre-adjustment distributive patterns embodying some inequalities that would remain

undisturbed in that the individual would opt for no redistributive scheme while, at the same time, the distributive norm for the individual might remain that of full equality.

4.   In another work, Geoffrey Brennan and I attempt to identify the several sources of possible efficiency loss, and notably those that arise due to the necessity that any redistributive arrangement must be politically implemented; *see* Geoffrey Brennan and James M. Buchanan, *The Reason of Rules* (Cambridge: Cambridge University Press, forthcoming, 1985), Ch. 8.

15 The Ethical Limits of Taxation[1]

I. INTRODUCTION

How should tax shares be allocated among persons? Normative tax theory has been almost exclusively devoted to attempts to answer this question. The early arguments about the shape of the utility function for income were aimed at justifying this or that degree of progression in the tax rate structure. More generally, vertical equity arguments have been addressed to the design of appropriately unequal treatment for unequals, while horizontal equity arguments have involved the definition of equal treatment for equals. These discussions have been carried on in almost total neglect of the expenditure side of the fiscal process. Presumably, the same normative principles for the allocation of tax shares have been held to be applicable whether the total tax share in aggregate income is 10 per cent or 90 per cent, or anything between such limits. That is to say, traditional normative tax theory has been silent on the absolute level of taxation; it has contained no implied limits.

My purpose in this chapter is to explore this unexamined question. Quite apart from normative criteria for the allocation of tax shares, are there normative criteria that may be introduced to set *limits* on the absolute level of taxation? I shall suggest that this question may be answered affirmatively, and I shall indicate that tax limits may be derived from the application of widely shared ethical norms. 'Justice' in taxation involves the question of how much of the national income is to be extracted for collective purposes as well as how that share which is extracted is to be allocated among different persons.

It will first be necessary, in section II, to set the problem by summarizing alternative paradigms for analyzing the taxation-expenditure process. Section III introduces the normative treatment with a generalized discussion of the ethical legitimacy of taxation, a necessary way-station for any argument that seeks to establish some ultimate limits. Section IV advances the ethical precept upon which the derivation of tax limits is based, and section V uses numerical examples to suggest the specific limits that are implied. The sensitivity of the results to critical parameter values is discussed in section VI. Section VII places the whole argument in its general context.

165

II. ALTERNATIVE PARADIGMS FOR TAXATION

Taxation may be, and has been, perceived and interpreted by citizens and tax economists in several paradigms. First of all, taxation can be viewed as the cost side of an inclusive fiscal exchange process, with taxes being treated as 'prices' that persons pay for the benefits provided by collectively financed goods and services made available to them by the government. Second, taxation can be thought of, and modelled, as the embodiment of fixed charges that the community is obligated to meet, charges that are made necessary by the financing requirements for politically determined outlays that are not directly related to individually-imputable benefit flows. Third, taxation may be considered as a set of coercively imposed charges imposed on those who are politically weak by those who are politically strong (a ruling class, an establishment elite, a majority coalition, a party hierarchy) for the purpose of financing private goods and services enjoyed by the latter. Finally, taxation may be conceived by a self-contained collective enterprise, characterized by positive and negative transfers that have as their ultimate purpose the achievement of collectively chosen patterns of post-tax, post-transfer distributions.

It is clear from the definitional listing alone that the relevance of ethical limits depends on the perspective from which the taxing–spending process is examined. In the first of the paradigms, the limits to taxation are those determined by the preferences of citizens themselves for collectively provided goods. In this model the fiscal process is one of voluntary exchange, as it has been developed basically by Knut Wicksell and Erik Lindahl.[2]

In the second model, taxation is isolated from the political process, and the absolute level of revenues required to meet predetermined fiscal obligations is considered to be outside of and beyond any application of ethical norms.

In the third perspective there are no useful ethical limits, except those that might be advanced as guidelines for the ruling elites. Positive limits on the absolute level of taxation in this paradigm may be derived from the application of straightforward wealth-maximization models of sovereign behaviour.[3]

Only in the last of the fiscal paradigms defined above does the question of ethical limits apply directly. To what absolute limits of taxation should the collectivity, as a unit, be restricted when taxes, in part or in total, are levied expressly for the accomplishment of transfer or redistributive purposes? How much fiscal redistribution should take place? How much fiscal redistribution is dictated by adherence to principles of justice?

III. THE LEGITIMACY OF THE TRANSFER STATE

To what extent does the collectivity, as a unit, hold an ethically justifiable claim against the income flow generated by individual effort in an economy that is characterized by specialization and trade? Within the appropriately functioning laws and institutions that protect property and contract, a distribution of valued end-products emerges from the interactions of demanders and suppliers in input and output markets. Independently of ethical considerations, individual owners of inputs tend to secure shares in aggregate value of output commensurate with the contributions of those inputs to such value. What claim, then, can the collectivity advance to a share of value, and, if any claim at all is legitimate, how can its extent be determined?

Some state claim against valued output of the economy must be acknowledged once the productivity of the legal-governmental framework is recognized. Without an institutional regime that protects property and enforces contracts, there might be little or no total output to be claimed. The economy of Hobbesian anarchy is not efficient by any standards, and those who dream of competitive protective associations in anarchy do precisely that, they dream. In a setting where there is no enforced and protected difference between 'mine and thine', individuals will exert relatively little effort, and a large share of that which is exerted will be devoted to predation and defence.[4] The collective provision of order is productive. Hence, a claim on value of output by the institutions that provide such order, the collectivity or state, is established, even on the most extreme productivity ethic.[5]

What measures the extent of such a claim? If the orthodox imputation process is carried out, the collectivity might claim a predominant share of total value. A conceptual experiment in which the legal-governmental order is removed would surely indicate that the 'marginal product' of the state is extremely high. The payment of all input factors, including the state, in accordance with the values of internal marginal products, would more than exhaust the total product of the economy. The inclusive production functions exhibit increasing returns, due to the scale economies in the provision of protective-enforcement services. We seem to be plunged into the analogue to the classical joint cost problem, with a comparable indeterminancy in solution.

One possible response is offered by the purely procedural contractarian. The patterns of distribution that emerge from whatever institutions that are agreed on in the conceptualized contractarian setting are defined to be 'just' or 'fair' because of the procedures through which they are produced. No further normative criteria are required or needed. In this setting, individuals are placed behind some veil of ignorance and/or uncertainty where they cannot identify their own positions under the operation of the institutions to be selected. The institutions so selected may include a transfer sector, and, with it, taxation that is outside any meaningfully defined exchange process. The absolute level of taxation is not, however, determinate. The limits on taxation are those that emerge from the idealized procedure, which itself becomes the object of the normative or ethical evaluative exercise.

The procedural criteria for justice or fairness may be retained as the ultimate test for any proposed set of institutional arrangements. The normative analyst may, however, seek to go beyond purely procedural restrictions and examine institutional alternatives that may be put to the procedural test. What ethical-moral precepts guide the choice among alternatives in the idealized contractual setting?

IV. THE FIRST RAWLSIAN PRINCIPLE: MAXIMAL EQUAL LIBERTY

This was precisely the task that John Rawls set in his highly acclaimed book *A Theory of Justice* (1971).[6] He derived two basic principles of justice and suggested that these would guide agreement among parties in the idealized contractual setting. The two principles were those, first, *maximal equal liberty*, and, second, the *difference* principle for the distribution of primary goods. The Rawlsian argument generated lively discussion, among economists as well as philosophers and other social scientists. Almost all of the economists' treatment was concentrated, however, on the second of the two suggested principles, the maximin or difference principle of distribution. Attempts were made to derive the taxing implications of satisfying this second principle. And, for the most part, Rawls was interpreted as having offered persuasive ethical argument in support of institutions that embody considerable redistribution of incomes and wealth among persons.

What these interpreters of Rawls' work overlooked, however, was the assignment of *lexical* priority to the first principle of maximal equal liberty. Rawls was careful to state that this first principle was to be met before the application of the second principle is attempted. Institutions that fail the test for satisfying the first principle are necessarily ruled out of consideration, regardless of their possible efficacy in seeming to further the objectives defined in the second principle.

I shall argue that limits on the absolute level of taxation are implied by the first of the two Rawlsian principles of justice, that of maximal equal liberty, and, hence, that the difference principle can only become relevant within these limits. Further, my argument suggests that the ethical support for the first Rawlsian principle, based exclusively on liberty, may be accepted even by those critics who may not go along with the second principle.

Equal Liberty There are two elements in the first principle of liberty. Institutions that are to be put to the procedural test must meet dual requirements. Liberties among persons must be *equal*, and these equal liberties must be *maximal*. Each one of these two conceptually separate requirements becomes important in any analysis of tax structure and tax limits. I shall not, in this chapter, concentrate my attention on the equal liberty requirement. This neglect is prompted exclusively by considerations of space and not by any absence of challenging issues waiting to be analyzed. These issues are those raised in orthodox normative tax theory, noted at the outset, and the Rawlsian approach may yield helpful insights into familiar territory. In its broad sweep, however, the equal liberty proviso lends support for the standard precepts of generality in taxation and rules out overtly discriminatory tax treatment. But in all this discussion, the concern is with justice or fairness in the allocation of tax shares among persons and not with the absolute level of taxation, within the confines of the equal liberty criterion. For example, a set of fiscal institutions might meet the equal liberty requirement and yet extract 90 per cent of valued output from the economy for collective purposes.

In the discussion that follows, I shall assume that all institutions to be considered meet the equal liberty criterion and that agreement has been reached on precisely how this requirement is to be defined. I shall be more precise and assume, without argument in defence, that taxes must be proportional to meet the equal liberty proviso, and that all transfer payments take the form of equal per-head demogrants.

Maximal Liberty I shall demonstrate that the satisfaction of the maximal liberty criterion does imply a limit on the absolute level of taxation.[7] In order to do this, I must first advance at least a working definition of liberty itself, and without getting bogged down into long-winded philosophical debate. I shall define liberty only in its negative sense: an individual is at liberty or free to carry on an activity if he or she is not coerced from so doing by someone else, be this an individual or group. Whether or not the individual has the ability or power to undertake the activity that he is at liberty to undertake is a separate matter, and it can only confuse discussion to equate liberty with ability or power or to extend its meaning to include these qualities.

My working definition can be illustrated in an example used by Amartya Sen. A person is at liberty to sleep on his back or his belly if no other person or group interferes with the exercise of such choice. A physical disability that may prevent one of the two options being chosen is not a constraint on the person's liberty, as such.

We may think in terms of a listing of all the activities that persons may be at liberty to undertake, subject only to the requirement that all persons in the relevant community be allowed the same or equal liberties. The familiar set of civil liberties come to mind: liberty of speech, press, religion, voting, association. To these may be added the 'economic liberties': consumption patterns, location, occupation, trade, property holdings.

Consider, now, two possible regimes, A and B. In Regime A, the collectivity, as an organized political unit, levies a tax of 90 per cent on valued output. From the revenues so collected, the collectivity supplies the legal-protective-enforcement environment, which requires an outlay of 10 per cent of total product. The remaining revenues are distributed to all members of the political community in a set of equal-per-head demogrants. (I assume away incentive effects feedbacks on output. Persons work equally hard at all levels of taxation and demogrants.)

In Regime B, by contrast with Regime A, the collectivity collects only 10 per cent of valued output, again through a proportional tax. Such tax generates revenues in the minimal amount required to finance the supply of the legal-political order. There are no demogrants.

In both regimes, individuals possess equal liberties to speak, write, vote, exercise religion, associate, and to choose their own consumption pattern, location, occupation, trading partners, and private assets. Is it then possible to state that individuals possess more liberty in B than in A? Clearly, persons have different abilities to satisfy their own desires in the two regimes, but it is not clear that individual liberties are different, under the definition posed earlier.

I suggest, however, that an inclusive list or array of activities might also include the liberty of individuals to *form new polities* from within the existing one—the liberty to secede. Singly, or in coalitions of any size, persons would be allowed to withdraw simultaneously from both the tax and benefit sides of the fiscal account, which would require that they provide *all* public services, including legal order, on their own. Such an internal exit option is a meaningful addition to the set of liberties normally considered, and a society in which this equal liberty of secession exists clearly is superior, on grounds of the first Rawlsian principle, to a society where this liberty does not exist.

The relationship of this particular liberty to the limits of taxation should be clear. The collectivity cannot ethically justify a claim on the economy's valued product that is over and beyond that level of taxation that would encourage any subset of the community membership to form their own separate polities. The idealized internal exist option places ethical limits on the absolute level of taxation, and it is only within these limits that the second Rawlsian principle, or indeed any other distributional principle, can be legitimately applied.

V. NUMERICAL EXAMPLES

The limits of taxation imposed by the equal liberty of secession may be illustrated numerically. Assume that there are seventy-five persons in the political community, made up of the two separate groups, each one of which contains internally homogeneous members. There are twenty-five X workers, and fifty Y workers, and an X worker is twice as productive as a Y worker. Aside from these two qualities of labour, the only other productive input is the legal-governmental order. Workers are equally productive in any combination.

Since we have assumed away any incentive effects, suppose that the economy generates a total product of a hundred units under any fiscal regime. These units are in the dimension of a single all-purpose consumable good. There is no saving or capital.

Withdrawal of a single X worker reduces total product by 2 units; withdrawal of a Y worker reduces total product by 1 unit. For simplicity, suppose that abandonment of the legal-protective framework reduces total product to zero.

Consider, now, the situation in Regime A, described above, where the collectivity levies a proportional tax of 90 per cent on all valued output. From the 90 units in revenues that it collects, the state then uses 10 units to provide the legal-protective umbrella for the economy. The remaining 80 units are returned to all members of the community in equal-per-head demogrants, with each of the 75 members getting 1.067 units.

Positions of individuals in the two groups will be as follows:

Individual	Pre-tax Wage	Tax	Demogrant	Net
A_1	2	1.8	1.067	1.267
B_1	1	.9	1.067	1.167

The 90 per cent level of taxation is *not* ethically justifiable on the principle of maximal liberty. To show this, consider the prospects for members of the X group. Assume that the legal-protection 'good' is completely lumpy; it takes 10 units to provide this good for any level of community membership. Assume that there are no scale advantages to the size of the market as such.

By seceding and forming their own political unit, the X workers can generate a total product of 50 units, of which 10 units, or 20 per cent, will be required to provide the legal-protective umbrella. The 40 units that remain can be retained by the persons in the group, for a net value of 1.6 units per person, which is higher than that secured under the operation of Regime A. Any level of taxation that leaves a member of the X group with a net consumption capacity below 1.6 is not sustainable under the liberty of secession option.

Note, however, that the application of the principle of maximal liberty does *not* remove all indeterminancy in the level of taxation chosen and does *not* prevent the state from undertaking transfer activity through its fiscal structure. There is nothing in the argument that supports taxation at the minimal level required to finance the legal-protective order, or 10 per cent in the example. The range of indeterminancy extends from 10 per cent, at its lowest, to 40 per cent, at its highest.[8] Any level of absolute taxation within this range satisfies the precept of maximal liberty in the conditions specified in the examples. Choice of level of taxation within this range must be made on grounds other than the application of the first Rawlsian principle. It is at this stage, and only at this stage, that the second Rawlsian principle, or some other principle of distribution, might be legitimately introduced. Application of the difference principle, within the range of values allowed by the principle of maximal equal liberty, would of course restore determinancy in the definition of the 'just' tax-transfer structure.

VI. CRITICAL PARAMETERS

The numerical examples are helpful in calling attention to the several critical parameters that become relevant in setting the limits on taxation that may be dictated by adherence to the principle of allowing equal liberty of secession to all persons in the economy, a liberty that I have suggested must be included in the array of activities along any Rawlsian dimension. Changes in the values for these parameters will clearly modify results.

Perhaps the most obvious parameter of critical importance that is suggested by the numbers is that which describes the relative sizes of the two groups in the economy. If, on the example, there should be only 10 X workers, along with 65 Y workers, with all other conditions remaining as postulated, total product would of course be only 85 units. The minimal proportional tax rate required to finance the legal-protective services would be 11.8 per cent. The maximal rate consistent with adherence to the maximal equal liberty precept increases to 100 per cent. The number of X workers in this case is simply too small to make the secession option economically viable. On the other hand, if the number of X workers in the total population of 75 persons should be 35 rather than 25, then, given the other parameters, the maximum tax rate with the liberty of secession option falls from 40 to 29.4 per cent. The arithmetic suggests that the ethical limit on taxation, dictated by the principle of maximal equal liberty, falls as the size of the group that is relatively more productive increases, and quite apart from any direct exercise of potential political power. So long, however, as there exist any economies of scale in the provision of the services of the legal order, there must remain some room for net fiscal transfers over and beyond the minimal tax limits.

As a second parameter, consider the public-goods characteristic of the provision of the legal-protective services. In the numerical examples, I have assumed extreme jointness, in that the same outlay is required for provision of such services independently of the size of the collective group. At the other extreme, of course, where there is no jointness, no scale economies, in provision of these services, we are back in the private or partitionable goods model. But, as previously noted, this anarchist Utopia is not intellectually recognizable. However, the scale economies may lie somewhere between the two extremes; equal outlays need not be required to provide legal-protective services for differing-sized communities. In the central example, the group of the 25 X workers might, say, be able to finance the required services here for a total outlay of 8 units, by comparison with the 10 units required for the inclusive community of 75 persons. In this case, the absolute limit to taxation that the inclusive community could impose, while honouring the liberty of secession requirement, would fall to a maximum of 28 per cent, by comparison to the 40 per cent indicated under the other model.

A third critical parameter describes the relative productivity of workers in differing combinations. In the example of section V, I assumed that workers were equally productive in any input arrangement. If, by contrast, an X worker would only be productive if his efforts were combined with Y workers, the standard imputation process would not apply. Secession on the part of the X workers would be precluded technologically, and there would be no limits imposed by the liberty of secession criterion. Again, however, something in between the extreme models might be plausibly considered. Suppose that in the central example X workers might, indeed, produce independently, but that, outside the nexus that includes some Y workers, each worker might generate a 'marginal product' of only 1.8 units rather than 2 units. In such case, the liberty of secession requirement would be less restrictive on the absolute level of taxation, with the upper limit being raised to more than 65 per cent.

A fourth critical parameter is that which describes the economies of scale for the economic nexus in the large. If the specialization and division of labour are such as to make a large economy necessarily more productive than a small economy, and if trade among persons in separate political units is prohibited, this parameter will become relevant. In the example, I assumed that such scale economies did not exist. If, however, we assume that the smaller economy of twenty-five persons is less productive, because of its size alone, we get results comparable to those introduced above by technological advantages of particular input combinations. It seems questionable, however, whether this particular parameter should be treated as potentially relevant. If a new polity forms within an existing unit, there need be no presumption that trade among members of the now-separated political units should cease. That is to say, the scale economies of the inclusive market area, if these exist, need not be lost through potential political separation.

A fifth critical parameter has been neglected because of simplicity in exposition. In the examples presented in section V, I assumed that incentive-effect feedbacks on work effort, either due to the imposition of taxes or to the payments of demogrant transfers, did not exist. Clearly, the reaction of taxpayers-transferees to varying levels of fiscal activity would be relevant in any determination of the critical upper limit to levels of absolute taxation. To the extent that higher levels of taxation and/or higher levels of transfers affect work effort negatively, the upper limit on taxation imposed by the liberty of secession criterion is reduced.

Finally, I have not mentioned the potential barriers to political secession that would be imposed by the costs of organizing coalitions. There may exist groups of persons who would secure net gains from securing political independence in a separated unit, but these groups may never be formed because of organizational costs. Free-rider incentives may prevent the emergence of the entrepreneurs that would be necessary to get such coalitions effectively organized. As with the economy-wide issue of scale advantages, however, it seems questionable whether this parameter should be treated as relevant for my purposes. In any actual assessment of potential secession, these costs must clearly be reckoned. But for my purposes of discussing the secession option as an ethical principle for assessing levels of taxation, the organizational costs barrier is not necessarily relevant.

My intention in this section has not been to discuss the critical parameters exhaustively and in detail but rather to indicate how the results are sensitive to changes in these underlying behavioural, technological, and economic characteristics of the political-legal-economic interaction. Any attempt to determine empirically the precise upper bounds that would be imposed by the operation of the liberty of secession principle would require an estimation of the values for each of the parameters noted, and many more in addition. My aim has been, instead, to indicate that, in any given setting, such an upper limit exists and could, at least conceptually, be empirically estimated.

VII. ECONOMICS AND ETHICS

The last two sections suggest that the limits to taxation, which I advanced as being those dictated by adherence to an ethical norm depend critically on *economic* characteristics, and the analysis seems to have shifted to areas familiar within economics: the theory of public goods, the theory of clubs, the theory of the core of an economy, and related subject matters. The demonstration of just such an integration between ethical precepts and the realities of economic process is itself a useful by-product of the exercise. The constitutional organization of a tax-transfer system based on adherence to the principle of maximal equal liberty will *not* in itself offer determinate guarantees for particular upper limits to taxes. It will do so only within the context of the parameters that describe the economy. Given any such values, however, or given any pre-constitutional estimates for the ranges of such values, upper bounds to taxation emerge. These limits provide ethical-normative criteria for fiscal structure that have been absent, to my knowledge, in normative fiscal theory.

The ethical justification for the upper limit to taxation emerges from the idealized application of the principle of maximal equal liberty. It does not require models of political reality that are themselves embodiments of the ethical idealization. In other writings, noted earlier, I have analyzed tax limits largely on the basis of predictions about how politics might work in practice. The results in this chapter require no such political imperfection. Even if the fiscal structure chosen and put in place at the constitutional level should operate perfectly, the limits discussed here would remain fully applicable.

Further, the derivation of the ethical limits to taxation does not depend on any presumption that persons respond only to economic self-interest, as the numerical examples might have seemed to suggest. Given liberty of secession, members of particular groups may select the internal exit option, even if such action was counter to measured economic interest. Or, given a sufficient sense of inclusive community solidarity, individuals may remain within an organized collectivity even if economic self-interest should dictate secession. My concern is with a normative derivation of the absolute limits to taxation and not with any positive prediction as to when such limits may be reached. The argument carries through whether or not persons respond to measured self-interest.

The central argument is Rawlsian in that I have used his first principle to generate the results. But the argument does not require extension to or acceptance of the second Rawlsian principle of justice, the difference principle of distribution. The argument does depend on acceptance of the principle of maximal equal liberty behind the eil of ignorance and/or uncertainty as a basic precept of justice that might be used as a guide in the organization of a fiscal structure. And, as noted earlier, the results are presented in the form of hypotheses to be put to the conceptual contractarian test.

It is important to emphasize that my concern is with the organization of the tax-transfer system rather than with the larger and more extensive political organization of society. I have suggested that the equal liberty of secession is a measurable activity along the Rawlsian dimension. And this liberty, if it exists, imposes predicted limits on levels of taxation. But even if this liberty of secession does not in fact exist, the organization of the fiscal structure may be guided *as if it did*. In other words, there is *no* ethical-normative justification for extending taxation beyond the indicated upper limits, because political reality does not itself allow an equal liberty of secession. My argument is precisely the reverse: because the equal liberty of secession may not in fact exist, its conceptualization as a norm offers guidelines for the organization of a fiscal structure that may lay claim to ethical-moral legitimacy.

The emphasis has been on the internal exit option, the equal liberty of secession. The economic analysis is of course analogous to the treatment of the external exit option, summarized under the rubric 'Tiebout models'.[9] To the extent that persons are free to migrate across boundaries of separate political jurisdictions, effective positive limits are placed on tax-transfer activities within any given political unit. In many particular cases, these limits may suggest lower boundaries on taxation than those emergent from application of the internal exit option. The ethical-normative issues involved in the equal liberty of persons to migrate among separate polities are more complex and more extensive than those that are required to generate the results of this chapter.

NOTES

1. This chapter was initially published in *Scandinavian Journal of Economics*, Vol. 86, No. 2 (1984), 102–14. I acknowledge permission to reprint the material here, with only minor changes. I am indebted to Geoffrey Brennan, Daivd Levy and Loren Lomasky for helpful comments on earlier drafts of this paper.

    In several earlier papers, written separately and jointly, I have analyzed limits on taxation from a constitutional perspective. *See*: James M. Buchanan, 'Constitutional Constraints on Governmental Taxing Power', *ORDO*, Bd. 30 (Stuttgart: Fischer, 1979), pp. 334–59; 'Procedural and Constitutional Constraints on Fiscal Authority', in *The Constitution and the Budget*, ed. W. S. Moore and R. G. Penner (Washington: American Enterprise Institute, 1980), pp. 80–4; 'The Limits of Taxation', in *The Constitutional Challenge*, ed. M. James (St. Leonard's, N.S.W.: Centre for Independent Studies, 1982), pp. 113–30; and James M. Buchanan and Geoffrey Brennan, 'The Logic of Tax Limits', *National Tax Journal*, 321 (June 1979), 11–22. The justification of tax limits in this perspective was largely, if not exclusively, based on the predicted working properties of post-constitutional political processes.

2. Knut Wicksell, *Finanztheorietische Untersuchungen* (Jena: Gustav Fischer, 1896); Erik Lindahl, *Die Gerechtigkeit der Besteuerung* (Lund, 1919); *see also*

my paper, 'Taxation in Fiscal Exchange', *Journal of Public Economics*, 6 (1976), 17–29.

3. For such models, *see* Geoffrey Brennan and James Buchanan, *The Power to Tax* (Cambridge: Cambridge University Press, 1980).

4. For analysis, *see Explorations in the Theory of Anarchy*, ed. Gordon Tullock (Blacksburg: Public Choice Center, 1972); *see also*, James M. Buchanan, *The Limits of Liberty* (Chicago: University of Chicago Press, 1975).

5. J. R. Kearl has supported the collective claim to a share of valued output along essentially the lines sketched here. Kearl, however, explicitly states that the question as to the extent of this claim 'has no quantifiable answer' (p. 80); *see* J. R. Kearl, 'Do Entitlements Imply that Taxation Is Theft?', *Philosophy and Public Affairs*, 7 (Fall 1977), 74–81.

6. John Rawls, *A Theory of Justice*, (Cambridge, Mass.: Harvard University Press, 1971).

7. I am particularly indebted to Loren Lomasky for pointing out to me the Rawlsian emphasis on maximal liberty. I had earlier, like many others, interpreted the first Rawlsian principle largely in terms of the equal liberty element. For a paper in which both these elements of the Rawlsian principle are used, *see* James M. Buchanan and Loren Lomasky, 'The Matrix of Contractarian Justice', *Social Philosophy and Policy*, 2 (Autumn 1984), 12–32.

8. In the examples here, I have left out of account any explicit strategic threat behaviour on the part of the members of the potential secession coalition. By choosing the internal exit option, members of this group do of course impose costs on all persons who remain as members of the original polity. And recognizing this set of tax externalities, threat potentials do exist which would need to be taken into account in any positive, predictive theory. My concern, however, is not with what a potential coalition might be able to enforce but is, instead, with what level of taxation can be ethically justified.

9. *Cf.* Charles Tiebout, 'A Pure Theory of Local Expenditures', *Journal of Political Economy*, 64 (Oct. 1956), 416–24.

16 Dismantling the Welfare State[1]

I. INTRODUCTION

During the middle years of this century the welfare state has emerged full grown in all Western nations. There is widespread agreement that many of the consequences were unintended and undesired. When viewed from the perspective of the 1980s, we can agree that things 'might have been' better had the course of history been different from what it was. To agree on this proposition is *not*, however, equivalent with agreement on an apparent corollary proposition that steps should *now* be taken to dismantle the set of social institutions that describe the modern welfare state. This corollary proposition is much more controversial than the mere assessment of history, and not only at a level of actual implementation. To defend the corollary proposition it is necessary to bring to bear wholly different intellectual arguments.

Let me offer a simple example. A man (or woman) may arrive at the conclusion that a marriage was a mistake; it 'would have been better' if the marriage had never happened. Nonetheless, the man (or woman) may, at the same time, decide that, given the fact of the marriage, divorce is *not* a rationally desired step to take. Failure to distinguish between the identification of a past mistake and the inference from this identification that the institution once established should be replaced has marred constructive discourse by both scholars and practical men of affairs. My concern in this chapter is exclusively with the apparent corollary proposition related to the modern welfare state. I address the question that given the welfare state *as it exists*, should it be dismantled and, if so, how should the process be implemented?

II. SOME PRELIMINARIES

A first step is to define terms. I shall distinguish between the *socialist state* and the *welfare state*. The *socialist state* embodies collective ownership and operation of productive enterprise. The welfare state, in its pure form, involves no such ownership and operation. Instead, it imposes a set of collectively determined coercive income and wealth transfers upon the operation of a private-ownership, market directed economy. Until the middle of the 1970s, Sweden offered the closest real-world approximation of the pure welfare state. By the 1980s, Sweden, along with most other Western nations, was best described as some mixture of a welfare state and a socialist state.

In this chapter, I shall discuss only the welfare state, as if it exists in its pure form, and independently of its socialist-state counterpart. (It is much easier to make out an argument for dismantling the socialist state than for dismantling the welfare state. The efficiency gains promised by the shift from public to private enterprise are sufficient to dominate other elements in any relevant decision.)

Within the welfare state rubric, as I have defined it, there are many varied kinds and types of income and wealth transfers to be observed. It is impossible to treat all of these as if they were identical in effect and as if they present the same difficulties in making constructive reforms. I propose, therefore, to limit my inquiry further. I shall confine direct discussion to the single most important set of transfers in the modern welfare state; namely, the set of transfers from the currently productive members of the economy to the currently unproductive members, primarily to pension recipients. For purposes of exposition and understanding here, we may think of the analysis as applying to a large, growing, unfunded scheme of retirement pensions (what we call in the United States the Social Security System).

III. CRITERIA FOR REFORM

I promised to address the questions of whether the welfare state should be dismantled and, if so, how the process should be implemented. It is evident that I cannot answer such questions without some normative criteria. I might, of course, state simply that the welfare state should be dismantled because I do not like it, either for reasons of private interest (I am a net loser), or of ideological commitment (I do not like collectivized pension schemes). I might go further and suggest that government should simply follow my advice and abolish the transfer system, and that is that. Arguments of this sort would deserve what they get, little or no attention from anyone.

I propose to rely on the advice and counsel of the greatest of all Swedish economists, Knut Wicksell (and I am tempted to leave out the modifying word 'Swedish'). If an existing institutional structure is genuinely inefficient, there must exist some means of changing or reforming elements of this structure so as to benefit *all* persons and groups in society. And if the observing economist tries and fails to locate some such means (there may, of course, be several), he is not allowed to say that the existing structure 'should' be changed. The Wicksellian test of conceptual unanimity offers the only defensible normative criterion for evaluating reform proposals. (Professional economists will recognize the similarity between Wicksellian and the more familiar Paretian criterion. I prefer to use the Wicksellian criterion because it concentrates attention on potential agreement as well as upon institutional-constitutional change rather than upon more formal allocative requirements.) The conceptual unanimity test allows me to seek answers to both of the questions simultaneously. If I can locate a means of changing the existing structure so that *everyone* benefits (or at the least no one loses), and hence should agree to the change, I have both validated the argument that change should be made and indicated one way it might be implemented. If I cannot come up with some such proposal for change, I should be forced to acknowledge that the existing state of affairs is 'Wicksell-efficient' (Pareto optimal) no matter how much my own dislike for this state of affairs may be.

IV. ENTITLEMENTS AND CLAIMS

The first step in any search for possible reform involves a careful description of the existing structure of entitlements and claims against the welfare state held by separate persons in the society. Under tax-transfer structures, the 'contract' made between government and claimants (those already retired or those who have accumulated credits towards retirement pensions) is implicit rather than explicit. The contractual basis is, nonetheless, widely acknowledged, and current and potential recipients make life-cycle plans on the expectation that the implicit commitments will be honoured by governments which hold ultimate taxing and spending powers.

Any proposal for reform or change that aims to meet the Wicksellian test must embody the meeting of all legitimate claims. Governments cannot, and should not, simply violate their implicit contracts with citizens. If this basic principle for reform is accepted, it then becomes necessary to identify and compute the net entitlement or claim of each person at some specified point in time, say, 1 January 1986. A person's claim against the system may be positive or negative, with the precise amount depending on the structure of taxes and benefits, on the age and status of the potential recipient, and on many other variables. Once a claim is specified for a particular person, we then have a benchmark against which the effects of all proposals for change may be measured. If a person's properly computed net claim (present value of anticipated benefits minus present value of anticipated tax payments) is, say, $10,000, any modified or changed structure must yield this person a net present value of at least this amount. If the properly computed net claim is negative, say (-) $10,000, then any proposed structure must represent a net obligation of less than $10,000 for this person.

V. THE AGGREGATE LIABILITY OF TAX-TRANSFER SYSTEMS

The tax-transfer systems of modern welfare states are not in what we might call 'actuarial balance'. As they exist today, these systems are characterized by massive net liabilities, defined in the aggregative sense. That is to say, if we compute the net claims of all persons in the manner indicated in section IV above, the aggregate value of currently anticipated benefits would far exceed the aggregate value of anticipated tax payments under the systems. In the United States social security system, for example, the aggregate net liability amounts to several *trillions* of dollars.

This aggregate net liability of any tax-transfer system represents implicit national debt that cannot be forfeited or cancelled, even by inflation. It should be explicitly recognized to be such, and this debt should be entered into any national balance sheet accounting. Each holder of a net positive claim should be treated equivalently with the holder of an indexed governmental security.

The aggregate net liability of modern tax-transfer systems increases over time because none of these systems has ever attained, and can never expect to attain, a steady-state equilibrium. A major principle for constructive reform must be that the aggregate net liability should be stabilized at current levels, say as of 1 January 1986. *Additional 'issues of implicit national debt' must somehow be avoided.*

VI. PAYING OFF INDIVIDUALIZED CLAIMS AND THE ISSUE OF EXPLICIT NATIONAL DEBT

If government is to honour all implicit claims of current and potential benefit-payment recipients, and if the aggregate net liability of the system is to be stabilized at levels of some specified date and not allowed further to increase, there must be an abrupt halt to taxes and benefit flows within the system as of the chosen effective date. As of this date, say 1 January 1986, the government must pay off all individual claims; the implicit national debt must be retired. Persons with positive net claims should be compensated in terms of cash capital values. Persons with negative net claims should be billed for the capital value of their net obligations. From the specified point in time, the system, as previously organized, would simply cease to exist. No taxes would be collected within the system; no benefit payments would be made.

As noted above, however, the aggregate net liabilities of modern pension schemes are of tremendous magnitude. How can governments finance the horrendously large claims? How can governments retire the implicit national debts that the pension schemes represent?

I propose that those who hold claims be 'paid off' individually in capital sums. I do *not* propose that the burden of payment be saddled onto the current generation of taxpayers. I propose that funds for meeting the individual claims within the system be raised by the explicit issue of general-purpose national debt, with the perpetual interest charges on this debt to be levied equally against current and *all* future generations.

The modern welfare state represents the mistakes of almost a century. It is fully analogous to the failure of a nation to accumulate a capital stock over a comparable period of time. Having made such mistakes, however, we must live with them, and the nation must carry forward, *forever*, the annual costs of these mistakes it has made. *Reform involves stopping the net increase in aggregate liability; it does not involve the imposition of differentially onerous burdens of taxation and/or inflation on the particular generation of persons who are producing income at the time of the structural change.* Clearly, any attempt to impose such differential burdens would violate the Wicksellian unanimity test. Current-period taxpayers can, of course, meet the annual interest charges on the aggregate net liability since this group, even before any structural change, is bearing at least this cost of the system.[2]

After the tax-transfer pension system is abruptly closed down, and all compensations are paid, there will be demonstrable increases in the productivity of the economy due to the reductions in excess burdens generated by both taxes and benefit payments. This productivity gain will allow the economy to carry forward the annual interest charges on the accumulated welfare state overload (which would then be represented by explicit national debt) with a gradually decreasing weight relative to annual gross product in the economy.

VII. PROVISION FOR PENSIONS AFTER THE WELFARE STATE TAX-TRANSFER SYSTEM IS ABOLISHED

To this point, I have said nothing at all about provision for retirement pensions *after* the existing structure ceases to operate. The reform measures sketched out above offer a means of closing down the old system without harm to anyone in the society. The reform proposals do not address themselves to the establishment of some new, replacement structure of retirement pensions.

Nonetheless, after the old system is closed down, the way is cleared for the construction of a fully funded, actuarially sound pension scheme with separated and identified individual accounts. Persons can be offered the option of making their own private provision for retirement through market-organized insurance schemes or joining a government insurance enterprise. In either case, their payments would be directed into a fund from which *their own* retirement pensions would eventually be financed. These genuine 'retirement contributions' should be categorically separated from any coercive taxes imposed to service the national debt made explicitly necessary by the closing down of the old system.

VIII. REDISTRIBUTION

An actuarially based, individualized system cannot of course embody within it redistribution among separate persons and groups. The abolition of the old welfare state system carries the major advantage of providing the opportunity of separating, once and for all, genuine retirement pension schemes from redistributive schemes. There is, of course, no reason why redistribution schemes may not be set up along with the efficient pension schemes if these are deemed desirable by the citizenry.

The closing down of the mixed-up, unsound, and confused system of retirement pensions and redistribution arrangements will offer societies the opportunity to modify, perhaps dramatically, the whole redistributive apparatus of the welfare state. Under the approach suggested here, all potential recipients of net transfers will have their accumulated claims (entitlements) fully satisfied. Their expectations of possible 'cradle to grave' support from government will be validated. But there is *no* implication in the set of proposals for reform that any *future* members of society, those who have not entered adulthood or even have not been born, should be able to accumulate *new* claims against the productive members of the economy. The critically important feature of the reform proposals advanced lies in the stabilization of the aggregate net liability. Implementation of the reforms suggests that persons born at different points in time must be treated differently. A person born in the first half of this century may have been allowed to accumulate net positive claims against the society. These claims must be paid off. But a person, in a similar relative economic status, who is born *after* the existing welfare state structure is abolished, need not be allowed to accumulate comparable claims. Whether or not such a person might or might not qualify as a net transfer recipient under a newly chosen redistributive scheme would be determined in the post-reform stage of revaluating all redistributive objectives as well as the costs of attaining them.

IX. COMPENSATION AND AGREEMENT AS BASES FOR POLITICALLY ATTAINABLE REFORMS

I have sketched out an approach to reform of the modern welfare state by concentrating on the retirement-pension example. The approach utilizes the Wicksellian test of conceptual unanimity to determine the possibility of genuinely efficient or desirable changes in the existing institutional structure. To secure unanimity, even in some proximate sense of consensus among most persons and groups in society, those who are positive claimants under the existing structure must be 'paid off'. Compensation is necessary for agreement. This compensation approach to reform admittedly involves major costs that might seem to be avoidable if the ruling political coalitions could be induced to renege on the implicit contractual obligations that governments have made over the decades of the welfare state. Such a policy of open default would, however, involve major costs of quite a different sort. The sense of unfairness generated might be such as to undermine severely the sense of legitimacy without which modern governments could not survive.[3]

It seems highly unlikely, however, that ruling political coalitions would ever choose to default in any important measure on the implicit contracts made under the guise of the modern welfare state. Faced with the stark choice between continuing to allow the net liability of the ongoing welfare state to increase, even with its admitted consequences, and closing down the system by default, democratically influenced governors will almost surely opt for continuation. Those economists who advise governments to proceed with action contrary to the political interests of the actors in the process are likely to experience repeated frustration.

Political leaders need not be faced with the dichotomous choice between continuation of an admittedly misconceived and worsening structure on the one hand and massive default on the set of implicit contracts that the structure embodies on the other. Political economists fulfil their proper role when they can show politicians that there do exist ways to close down the excesses of the welfare state *without* involving default on the contracts that this State has obligated itself to.[4] This approach to reform not only meets ordinary precepts of fairness; it also facilitates the political leader's task of organizing the consensus necessary to allow any institutional changes to be made at all.

X. CONCLUSIONS

Should the welfare state be dismantled? If so, how should the process be implemented?

My response to these questions posed at the outset may be simply summarized. The welfare state should be dismantled if those who gain from the change can pay off those who have positive claims and still have some surplus left over. The process can be implemented politically if the pay-offs are actually made, but not otherwise. I do not suggest that reforms based on this Wicksellian approach will be easy to accomplish. The detailed working out of the set of compensations required will indeed be complex and tedious. And as I have already noted, there should be no illusion about the apparent cost that the reforms would make explicit. The political and ideological errors of more than a half-century cannot be erased as if they had not happened. In the larger sense, however, the cost of continuing the existing welfare state structure without substantial change looms much larger than that of taking the decisive action that I have suggested. The fundamental question is whether or not the political decision structures of modern Western nations are capable of taking the decisive reforms that are clearly within the realm of the politically attainable.

NOTES

1. Material discussed in this chapter was first presented at a Regional Meeting of the Mt Pelerin Society in Stockholm, Sweden, in August 1981.
2. For a more detailed analysis, with numerical examples, *see* James M. Buchanan, 'Comments on Browning's Paper', in *Financing Social Security*, ed. Colin Campbell (Washington: American Enterprise Institute, 1979), pp. 208–12.
3. As Gordon Tullock has noted, politicians may shift the boundary between the set of positive net claimants and negative net claimants. Persons in the second set will, of course, support an open policy of default on all claims. To the extent that this group of potential net gainers from default increases in size so as to approach that of the group of potential net losers from default, the whole structure is likely to develop into essentially a zero-sum political struggle; *see* Gordon Tullock, *Economics of Income Redistribution* (Boston and The Hague: Kluwer-Nijhoff, 1983). My approach in this chapter is based on the presupposition that such a struggle is not desirable, that even for those persons who now are legally net debtors to the system might prefer the sort of changes suggested to open default of claims of legal creditors.
4. For an early discussion of this role for the political economist, *see* James M. Buchanan, 'Positive Economics, Welfare Economics, and Political Economy', *Journal of Law and Economics*, II (1959), 124–38; reprinted in Buchanan, *Fiscal Theory and Political Economy* (Chapel Hill: University of North Carolina Press, 1960), pp. 105–24.

Part Four
The Political Economy of Debt and Deficits

17 The Moral Dimension of Debt Financing[1]

I. INTRODUCTION

Economists have almost totally neglected moral or ethical elements of the behaviour that has generated the observed modern regime of continuing and accelerating government budget deficits. To the extent that moral principles affect choice constraints, such neglect is inexcusable. It is incumbent on us, as economic analysts, to understand how morals impact on choice, and especially how an erosion of moral precepts can modify the established functioning of economic and political institutions. A positive and empirical theory of the operation of moral rules is in order even if we want to leave the preaching to the moralists.

An understanding of how moral constraints affect patterns of political outcomes need not require comparable understanding of the origins of moral rules themselves. Indeed, one of the arguments I want to develop depends critically on the 'non-rational' attributes of such moral rules. The effects of moral constraints are, of course, fully symmetrical. If moral rules constrain choices, if there exists what we may call a moral feasibility frontier, then it is also the case that an erosion or destruction of moral norms relaxes the constraints and thereby shifts the frontier locus 'outwards', and with consequences that we, as economists, can analyze.

I shall argue that the explosive increase in debt or deficit financing of public consumption outlays can be explained, at least in part, by an erosion of previously existing moral constraints. The political decision-makers did not 'discover' a new technology of debt financing midway through this century. Their rational self-interest has always dictated resort to non-tax sources of public revenues. What happened in this century was that debt financing ceased to be immoral. We have here an almost perfect example of the harm that 'rationalist constructivism' (to use this term pejoratively in the Hayekian sense) can produce. The attempt to impose 'rational choice' behaviour on those who were constrained by previously existing and culturally evolved moral rules has in fact allowed a reversion to the more primitive instincts that were previously held in check.

This moral dimension of the modern fiscal dilemma must be appreciated if there is to be any hope for escape. Abstract rules that have evolved unconsciously cannot themselves be rationally restored. However, rationally chosen constraints can be introduced that will serve, in part, as substitutes for the eroded moral rules. Balanced budgets that were dictated once by moral standards were never explicitly mentioned in formal constitutional documents. Without such standards, however, balanced budget constraints must be explicitly chosen, imposed, and enforced.

II. THE TRIBAL HERITAGE

I am neither ethnologist nor anthropologist, and I make no claim to more than minimal lay knowledge of such areas of inquiry. Hence, my remarks should be treated as conjectural rather than as recorded history. With this disclaimer made, let me suggest that there is nothing in our genetic or biological 'nature' that dictates an abiding interest in the abstract future of the human species, or even in the future of the arbitrary collectives that include large populations and that claim dominion over large territories. Biologically, we remain tribal animals, and our natural instincts have not evolved beyond those that emerged in very small human communities. Those precepts for behaviour that we often call moral often reflect merely our communitarian sense of loyalty to fellow members of the tribe.

The post-Englightenment attitudes towards the formation, accumulation, and maintenance of capital (stored up capacity to satisfy wants) evolved in application to the extended family in its role as the relevant tribal unit. Through the process of group selection, those families whose members exhibited financial prudence survived and prospered. Generalized norms for our behaviour in respect to the build-up and maintenance of wealth and property were unconsciously directed towards family interests, not primarily those of individuals and not at all to the interests of political entities akin to modern nation-states.

III. FROM MORAL COMMUNITY TO MORAL ORDER

I have found it useful to use the terms 'moral community' and 'moral order' to distinguish between the two sets of human interaction relevant for the discussion here (see Ch. 11). Persons belong to a moral community if they share loyalties to the group. They participate in a 'moral order' if they share commonly accepted codes of conduct that enable productive interaction to take place between persons of differing moral communities. Norms for fiscal prudence on the part of persons who act on behalf of political entities are norms for a 'moral order' rather than norms for a 'moral community'.

These norms for collective fiscal prudence run counter to basic genetic drives. As Hayek in particular has emphasized, the norms for 'moral order' have emerged in a long process of cultural rather than biological evolution.[2]

Modern man gradually came to adopt modes of behaviour that enabled him to leap beyond the limits imposed by his tribal heritage; he learned to behave in accordance with moral norms that are not of genetic origin but which, nonetheless, are not consciously or rationally learned. As he did so, he was able to leap into what Hayek has called 'the great society', which is equivalent to what I have called 'moral order'. Man came to behave vis-à-vis persons who were not recognized members of his own tribe in such fashion that reciprocal dealings become possible. In this way, ownership rights came to be mutually respected, even between members of wholly separate tribes. Trade and exchange as we know it in all its forms, from simple to the most complex, emerged; the specialization of labour was extended, and we achieved the miracle of coordination that modern markets describe.

My purpose here is neither to criticize nor to elaborate the Hayekian story. My purpose is the more limited one of suggesting that we can apply this move from moral community to moral order directly to the shift in the norms for fiscal prudence on the part of those who make decisions for the relevant polities. There is nothing in our tribal heritage that tells us to respect our 'national capital stock', any more than there is that which tells us to respect the lives and property of persons whom we do not and have never included as being members of our moral community. The behaviour that exhibits respect for the capital stock of the nation, as a unit, is (or was) a product of *cultural* evolution, not an outgrowth of any genetic heritage. The fiscal norms of the Victorians, which we may now view as praiseworthy, were culturally evolved norms. The shift from those attitudes towards family capital, which may be biologically derived, at least in part, to comparable attitudes toward national capital, was a shift that involved cultural evoltuion. We note with considerable interest in passing that this shift was well under way when Adam Smith decided upon the very title of his book.

IV. KEYNES AS A MORAL REVOLUTIONARY

The Victorian fiscal morality, that set of behavioural precepts that dictated adherence to strict budget balance, to a limited absolute level of taxation, and to a self-enforcing monetary regime, was neither rationally nor biologically derived. It was an outgrowth of a cultural evolutionary process that those who shared the morality did not understand. It existed in continual tension with the tribal morality that remained essentially indifferent to the rules for fiscal behaviour and with the occasional attempts to introduce allegedly rational arguments for fiscal-monetary debauchery.

On the moral dimension that is my emphasis here, Keynes may be viewed as a successful revolutionary who destroyed the Victorian precepts. He did so for rationally based reasons, and he sought to replace the strong but essentially unconscious adherence to long-standing rules by what seemed at the time to be a well-reasoned 'logic of policy'. Where Keynes totally failed was in his recognition that the long-standing rules for fiscal-monetary prudence were required to hold the tribal instincts in check, and that once the Victorian precepts were eroded, the latter instincts would emerge with force sufficient to overwhelm all rationally derived argument.

That which we observe is what we might have predicted from the simple public-choice analysis of political behaviour. Constituents enjoy receiving the benefits from public outlays, and they deplore the payment of taxes. Elected politicians attempt to satisfy constituents. There is little need here to elaborate on this simple model of public choice, which now seems so straightforward. I have discussed this model in my book, *Democracy in Deficit*, written with Richard Wagner.[3] This chapter goes beyond the model in that book by offering an explanation as to why the natural proclivities of citizens and politicians alike emerged only in the post-Keynesian era. I have previously referred to the fact that the Keynesian theory of economic policy essentially repealed the implicit fiscal and monetary constitution.

V. THE VULNERABILITY OF CULTURALLY EVOLVED NORMS

Why did the implicit rules exist and why were these rules made so vulnerable? I have introduced the Hayekian differentiation between culturally evolved codes of conduct and biologically driven instincts to assist me here. The human animal, as he behaves in modern political structures, has chosen to 'eat up' the capital stock of his nation. (For let us make no mistake about it, this is precisely what the debt financing of public consumption is, an 'eating up' of national capital.) This choice has been taken because of the shift in moral standards that the Keynesian revolution embodied. It is no longer immoral to mortgage the future flow of the national income, at best an abstraction that commands little moral assent.

The erosion of the standards of fiscal morality applied to political units has exerted predictable spill-over influences on the standards of morality applied to family and personal portfolios. There remains, nonetheless, the major difference in the vulnerability of the two sets of standards. To some extent at least, the immorality of destroying family or personal capital stems from biological origins. Public profligacy now seems almost unlimited because of the breakdown in moral standards that were clearly produced in a cultural evolutionary process. Private profligacy continues to be held in check by moral standards that are only in part culturally determined.

In the perspective taken here, it is interesting to observe that attempts by modern economists to de-emphasize the effects of the shifts that have occurred in our behaviour with respect to public debt issue have included the revival of the Ricardian equivalence theorem, which involves the conversion of public debt into its private debt equivalents. To the extent that such conversion does in fact take place, individual standards of morality with reference to the consumption of family or private capital stocks are implicitly extended to the aggregative national capital stock. These models are deficient, however, in precisely the same sense as the simple public choice models. They provide no explanation at all for the explosion in public-debt financing of ordinary public outlays in the middle decades of this century. If, indeed, individuals act as if modelled in supra-rational Ricardo-Barro terms, why did the financing mix between taxation and debt shift so dramatically in the post-Keynesian era?

VI. CULTURALLY EVOLVED NORMS AS PUBLIC CAPITAL

If my basic diagnosis is correct, if we have lived through a period in which culturally evolved rules of fiscal prudence, as applied to the behaviour of public choosers (in all capacities) have lost their previously existing moral force, it is first necessary to acknowledge that we have destroyed a valuable portion of our public capital stock. The metaphor is useful in that it suggests that there is a quasi-permanency involved here, even if it were possible to 'reconstruct' that which has been destroyed. If moral rules must evolve slowly and without deliberate construction, then there is little to hope for by way of any attempt at restoration. We can take a somewhat more optimistic view, however, if we recognize that there is always some degree of a substitutability between rules for behaviour that reflect moral norms and those that are explicitly chosen as constraints.

If this substitutability is accepted, then an observed erosion in constraining moral norms can be offset, at least in part, by deliberate adoption and enforcement of behavioural constraints. If, in our varying capacities as public choosers (as voters, as members of special interest groups of benefit recipients, as taxpayers, as members of political parties, as elected politicians, as bureaucrats), we are constrained by no moral sanctions against the accelerating destruction of our national capital stock through the deficit financing of public consumption, we must look to the more formal rules of the political institutions within which we make public decisions. It is not at all contradictory or inconsistent to recognize that the rules under which we choose may be non-optimal while at the same time behaving within those existing rules in accordance with rational utility-maximizing norms. Given the absence of moral constraints, and given the observed open-ended rules for fiscal decisions, rational behaviour on the part of public choosers ensures the regime of continuing and accelerating budget deficits.[4] Given the difficulties if not the impossibilities of any deliberative restoration of moral precepts, we must indeed look to the explicit rules if reform in the pattern of results is to be expected.

I think that the discussion on the constitutional amendment to require governmental budget balance offers the most constructive advance in policy reform in several decades. Having lived through the destruction of the fiscal morality by the Keynesian mind-set, we must make every effort to replace this morality with deliberatively chosen constraints that will produce substantially the pre-Keynesian patterns of results. Economists, in particular, need to be brought up to date in their own thinking on all such matters and to rid themselves once and for all of the notions that they need only proffer advice to the benevolent government that waits ever on their call.

NOTES

1. Presidential Address presented at Western Economic Association meeting, Las Vegas, 28 June 1984. The address was initially published in *Economic Inquiry*, XXIII (January 1985), 1–6. I acknowledge permission to republish the material without substantial change.
2. See, F. A. Hayek, *Law, Legislation, and Liberty*, Volume III, *The Political Order of a Free People* (Chicago: University of Chicago Press, 1979), especially 'Epilogue', pp. 153–176.
3. James M. Buchanan and Richard Wagner, *Democracy in Deficit* (New York: Academic Press, 1978).
4. There are, of course, limits to deficit financing. Continued increase in debt-service charges cannot be characteristic of economic or political equilibrium. Explicit default, or default through inflation, will of course impose such limits. Even fear of such default may, however, be sufficient to generate the requisite political support for *temporary* reductions in deficit size. But there is nothing in modern democracies to generate permanent changes in the pattern of results.

18 Public Debt and Capital Formation[1]

I. A SUMMARY HISTORY OF SOME IDEAS AND THEIR CONSEQUENCES

To the Victorians, the consumption of capital was venality itself, and even full consumption of income was prodigal in the extreme. Ordinary prudence demanded that some share of income be put aside for adding to the capital stock. In their world, capital, once created, was indeed permanent, whether it was measured separately in each family's portfolio or jointly in the national aggregates. Further, there were no essential differences in the precepts for fiscal prudence applicable to the family and to the nation. Basically, these same attitudes carried over into the Victorians' approach to the institutions of law, politics, and the economy. The Gladstonians did not really expect to live forever, but they acted as if they did, and their moral precepts matched their behaviour. (The Ricardian theorem on the equivalence of public debt and taxation may, indeed, have been descriptive of the behaviour of at least some of the Victorians.)

We are a century away from 'capitalism's finest hour', if we restrict our definition of 'capitalism' to refer to prevailing public attitudes on the accumulation and maintenance of 'the capacity to satisfy wants stored up in things'.

How distant these Victorians seem to us now! We have passed through several shifts in ideas and attitudes. Even before Keynes, economists had challenged the classical (and Victorian) equivalence of public and private debt. Fallacies of aggregation antedate the Keynesians, and the argument that 'we owe it to ourselves' was not totally new to this century. This aggregation fallacy, to the extent that it gained acceptance, served to loosen somewhat the precepts of fiscal prudence for governments, although the principle of budget balance kept public debt creation within bounds of reason. Norms for private capital accumulation and preservation remained pervasive, however, until Keynes and the Keynesians promulgated the 'paradox of thrift'. With this step, even the norms for private, personal prudence came to be undermined. Spending not saving spilled over to benefit society. Alongside this inversion of private norms, the Keynesian theory of public policy directly undermined any intellectual basis for the maintenance of balance in governmental budgets. The modern era of profligacy, public and private, was born.[2]

Ideas do have consequences through their effects on public and political attitudes. But these consequences emerge slowly and with significant time lags. After Keynes, the anti-classical, anti-Victorian ideas were firmly in place in the academies and in the dialogues of the intellectuals. But politics reflects the behaviour of politicians, whose ideas change but slowly. Hence, during the years immediately after the Second World War, many politicians adhered to the old-fashioned precepts for fiscal prudence, only to be treated condescendingly and with scorn by their academic-intellectual peers. Some of us recall amusingly, if sadly, the derision that greeted President Eisenhower's reference to public debt as a burden on our grandchildren.

By the late 1950s, the partial derivative of the mind-set of economists shifted in direction. There was a revival of essentially classical ideas on the incidence and effects of public debt. These then-novel notions were by no means universally accepted by academic economists, but the challenge to the aggregation fallacies was not refuted. Among academic economists, the discussion of public debt changed, slowly but surely, towards the earlier verities, change that took place over the 1960s and 1970s.

As with the onset of the Keynesian ideas three decades earlier, however, public and political attitudes lagged behind those emergent in academia. The politicians who made the policy decisions of the 1960s and 1970s had fully absorbed the Keynesian lessons on both macroeconomic policy and on public debt. They were ready and quite willing to apply the policy messages appropriate for the 1930s to the policy environment of the 1960s and 1970s because these messages offered apparent intellectual support for their natural proclivities to spend and not to tax. The era of seemingly permanent and increasing governmental deficits was upon us, an era from which we have not yet escaped.

In the mid-1980s we can only hope that the political decision-makers of the late 1980s and 1990s will have become familiar with the post-Keynesian challenges to the aggregation fallacies and that something akin to the classical Victorian precepts for private and public prudence will come to inform the observed politics of these decades. The restoration of old ideas that have been for a long time displaced by fallacies is at best more difficult than acceptance of ideas that have been carried forward in an unblemished tradition. We can hope that such restoration goes forward. As of 1985, there are both encouraging and discouraging signals to be observed. The financial politics for the remaining years of this century remain unpredictable.

II. THE ELEMENTARY LOGIC

A debt instrument (bill, note, or bond) is a contractual obligation on the part of a person or entity that promises payment of stipulated amounts of things (or claims on things) over a sequence of designated periods subsequent to the period in which the contract is signed. That is to say, debt is an obligation to pay *later*. Taken separately, therefore, the contracting of debt by an owner of a portfolio of assets amounts to a claim against the anticipated stream of net returns from those owned assets. This claim must reduce the present value of the assets, which is determined by discounting the anticipated stream of net returns. At this level of very elementary logic, the issue of debt is identical to the destruction of capital value.

This basic relationship between debt issue and the destruction of capital value tends to be obscured or overlooked because of the mind-set imposed upon us by double-entry bookkeeping or balance-sheet accounting. The issue of debt, the incurrence of the obligation to make payments in future periods, is more or less automatically treated as only one side of a two-sided transaction. The issuer of debt is a borrower, who receives a transfer of payment during the period of the contract itself. This payment *now* is that which is received in exchange for the promise to make payments *later*. In this two-sided treatment, the balance sheet of the borrower is adjusted by adding the present value of the debt instrument to the liability side of the account and the present value of the current payment received to the asset side. There is no change in net worth. There seems to be no destruction of the capital value of the whole portfolio or enterprise.

The legitimacy of this double-entry procedure is based on the implicit presumption that the funds secured currently in exchange for the debt instrument will be used productively, at least in some prospective or anticipated sense. Such a presumption is invalid when the borrower simply uses up or consumes the funds that are currently received in exchange for the promise of future period payments. In this case, the separated or one-sided model of debt issue is more helpful than the double-sided model. Debt issue becomes equivalent to the 'eating up' of capital value, pure and simple.

This elementary logic of debt applies, of course, to any intertemporal contract. There is no difference between individual, firm, agency, or public borrowing. In all cases, the issue of debt for the purpose of financing current-period use or consumption is equivalent to the destruction of the capital value of the asset stream that is anticipated. This basic proposition holds independently of the value of the portfolio. If there is no capital value, the creation of debt will, in this case, produce negative capital. If the capital value is initially negative, debt will merely increase the negative total.

III. PUBLIC DEBT AND PUBLIC CONSUMPTION

What has the elementary logic of section II to do with the summary history of ideas sketched out in section I? Indeed, what has it to do with the title and purpose of this chapter? The connection and relevance should be clear enough. The public debt incurred by the United States government over the regime of ever-increasing and apparently permanent budgetary deficits has financed public or government *consumption* rather than public or government investment. The classical rules for fiscal prudence have been doubly violated. Not only has government failed to 'pay as it goes', government has also failed to utilize productively the funds that have been borrowed. There has been no offsetting item on the asset side to match the increase in net liability that the debt represents. The capital value of the income stream of the national economy has been reduced, dollar-for-dollar, with each increase in present value of liabilities represented by the debt instruments issued.[3]

Proper accounting would therefore require that any estimate of 'national capital stock' derived by discounting the net national income be written down or reduced by the present value of the outstanding national debt instruments. A somewhat different way of putting this point is to say that a share of the anticipated national income over future periods has already been precommitted for the payments of amortization and interest charges on the debt. This share is simply not available for free disposition, either privately or publicly, in accordance with the preferences of persons who nominally 'earn' the income in the periods to come. The national debt obligation is an overload, a burden, that carries forward with it no compensating asset or claim. For citizens, the national debt is fully analogous to a private debt that has been incurred to finance a consumption spree in some past period.

Objections may be raised to my simplistic approach to such weighty issues of national fiscal policy. An initial, if unsophisticated, argument might suggest that federal government outlays (that have, admittedly, been partially financed by debt) have not been 'wasteful' and that any analogy to a private consumption spree is misleading. After all, or so such an argument might run, these outlays financed spending on the provision of goods and services that were deemed to be collectively beneficial, including transfers to the needy and to those who hold legitimate entitlement claims.

My analysis does not, however, imply that the outlays made by the government were 'wasteful' in any such sense of the term. The spending that was debt or deficit-financed during the 1970s and 1980s may well have provided benefits that were valued in excess of the then-present value of the debt instruments that were required to finance such spending. But precisely the same point may be made about the spending made by an individual during a private consumption spree. The to-be-pitied slob who, after having blown his whole week's wages, borrowed still more funds to finance last Saturday's spending at the local pub, may well have enjoyed Saturday-night benefits that he estimated, *then*, to be higher than the opportunity costs of the debt obligation that he assumed. The rationality or irrationality of the choices made last Saturday night cannot, however, affect the burden of the debt obligation at next week's payday. The slob may, of course, have warm memories regarding last Saturday's pleasures, and he may sigh that 'it was worth it all', but, come Friday, he will have fewer dollars of net income available for current spending than he would have had if last Saturday's binge had not taken place at all. The fact that the benefits or pleasures then enjoyed may have been more than, equal to, or less than the properly estimated choice-influencing opportunity cost becomes irrelevant to the temporal location of the post-choice costs. The benefits, no matter how great or small they might have been, *have been enjoyed*. The post-choice consequences must be suffered *now*.[4]

IV. PUBLIC DEBT AND PUBLIC INVESTMENT

A more sophisticated argument may commence with an explicit denial that federal outlays financed by debt have in fact been exclusively devoted to current public consumption. It may be suggested that some share in federal government outlays represents investment spending on long-lived capital assets. To the extent that federal outlays are investment-like, it is appropriate that these be financed with debt issue. Government practice in this respect is not different from ordinary business procedures, and responsible financial planning must allow for borrowing to finance the purchase of genuine asset items. A practical suggestion that often emerges from this argument is that the government's fiscal account should be improved by the introduction of categorical separation between consumption and investment items, between the current consumption and the capital budget, sometimes referred to as above-the-line and below-the-line items. This distinction does characterize public accounting procedures in several countries.

Cursory examination suggests that this argument warrants close consideration. If in fact the share of federal government outlay financed by debt should be roughly similar to the share that might appropriately be classified to be investment in public capital, there would be an offsetting item on the asset side of the nation's balance sheet that would match the liability that the present value of debt represents. In this setting, when *both* sides of the transaction are recorded, both the issue of debt and the purchase of the assets, there need be no net change in the present value of the national capital stock. Indeed, if the investment outlay should prove productive in some net sense, a properly measured present value should record some increase.

The question would seem to be empirical. How much federal spending during the observed era of deficits can properly be classified as public capital investment? Does this estimated share in total outlay come close to the share that has in fact been financed by debt?

Care must be taken, however, to specify precisely what is required for an item of budgetary outlay to be classified as a public capital investment. The durability of an asset alone is not sufficient to make the purchase of such asset qualify as capital investment for purposes of the exercise here. In order that an item of governmental outlay be labelled a net asset, with a positive present value to be entered on the balance sheet as offsetting the debt liability, there must be an increment to the net income stream directly attributable to that asset.

As an example of a long-lived asset that cannot qualify as public capital for our purposes, consider a monument that is designed to last forever. There is no measured income flow associated with the monument. While there may be benefits anticipated from the monument over the whole sequence of future time periods, these anticipated benefits cannot be appropriated as a source for the tax payments that may be required to service the debt if the initial outlay is debt financed.

In terms of criteria for tax equity, the anticipated flow of benefits over time may seem to suggest the appropriateness of debt rather than direct tax financing. In this sense, the outlay on public 'capital' like monuments is quite different from that on current public consumption, the benefits from which accrue during the period when the public goods are actually consumed. The anticipated benefits from the monument add to the stream of psychic income or utility. And a measure of utility levels in any future period should ideally include some imputed value for these particularized benefits. Note, however, that persons receiving these benefits have no choice as to the form that these take, and there is no prospect of converting income benefit flows into other channels that might be helpful in covering amortization and interest charges on the debt.

Public 'capital' like monuments, which does seem to include much durable investment of government (public buildings, defence hardware) may be likened to personal, private investment in specific human capital designed to yield consumption benefits over time. Consider, as an example, outlays for a course in music or art appreciation. The anticipated benefits extend over a lengthy sequence of periods, and utility streams over these periods is higher than they would otherwise be without the initial investment outlay. But, once the initial outlay is made, these benefits are 'locked in', so to speak; they are inalienable in the sense that there is no prospect of converting them into realizable monetary equivalents. The person who has incurred a debt obligation to take the course on art appreciation may enjoy knowing all about art, but the enhancement in his utility in this respect will not reduce the burden of the debt overload during the relevant payout or debt retirement periods. If double-entry books were kept in utility dimensions, the inclusion of an offsetting asset value to the debt liability might seem appropriate. Double entries in accounts normally, however, refer only to realizable values and enforceable obligations. Unless this elementary precautionary precept for prudence is followed, persons who might indeed be wealthy in the utility dimension will find themselves in the bankruptcy courts.

For governments, this precept for fiscal prudence would suggest that assets be classified as 'public capital', and hence introduced as offsetting items on the balance sheet, only if measurable and realizable money income flows are anticipated. For example, if government constructs a toll highway or an urban transport network, it is appropriate to discount the expected stream of anticipated facility revenues or fees to produce a capital value of asset that the facility represents. This asset value should, however, be limited to the discounted value of the fees that are actually expected to be collected. It should not include the full cost outlay on the facility if fees are not expected to cover these costs. Government's announced or expressed unwillingness to collect fees from a debt-financed facility's users sufficient to cover full costs becomes equivalent to precommitment of a share of non-facility income. The result is precisely the same as if the funds secured in exchange for the debt instruments are used for current public consumption.

Since we know that a relatively small share of governmental outlays reflect 'public capital investment', even in the broadest definition, and since even within this share there are precious few facilities or projects that carry an associated direct income stream, the analytical treatment of all public outlays as current public consumption does not seem far off the mark, and surely not far enough off to yield wildly misleading conclusions. This result should not be surprising in itself, since federal fiscal accounts are not arranged or discussed in terms of the distinction between current and capital outlays, and decisions on the sizes of the deficit are never related to the composition of the budget.

V. BUT, AFTER ALL, WE DO OWE IT TO OURSELVES

The elementary logic carries through. The issue of public debt to finance the great and continuing fiscal spree of the 1960s, 1970s, and 1980s has been equivalent, in all relevant respects, to the destruction of capital value. A substantial and ever-increasing share of our future income has been precommitted. There are no offsetting asset items in the national balance sheet.

As I suggested in section I, this spree is at least partially the result of the widespread acceptance of aggregation fallacies, a set of ideas that were in the air long before Keynes but which were putatively legitimized intellectually by the Keynesian macroeconomic methodology. It seems useful at this point to see precisely how this methodology served to undermine the classical Victorian theory of public debt.

To do this, let us return to the elementary logic of the personal consumption loan. An individual, let us call him B for *borrower*, desires funds in excess of those available to him during time period, t_0. To secure these required funds, he contracts a loan; he issues debt, and proceeds to finance current spending for consumption in t_0. Having consumed the funds, but with the contractual promise to pay later still before him, B has suffered a reduction in his net wealth position. He has, in effect, eaten into his capital, he has precommitted some share of his anticipated future income.

The funds that B used in t_0 were obtained from the lender, whom we shall call L. She gives up funds in t_0 in exchange for B's debt instrument, B's promise to pay later. Let us now look at the balance sheet adjustment for L. At the time of the contract, in t_0, she writes down the *Cash* item and writes up the *Notes Receivable* item, both on the asset side of the ledger. There is *no* change in L's net worth in the transaction.

Let us now marry B and L and combine their two separate balance sheets to create a single family account. The combined balance sheet will record the debt liability item of B and the notes receivable item for L, which seem to offset each other. But the balance sheet, struck as of t_1 after the marriage, will not directly reflect the history of the transaction. By comparison with the family balance sheet that might have been had B not engaged in the consumption spending spree, the net wealth of the family is lower by the size of the debt liability.

Straightforward, simplistic, elementary. Indeed so. But it is the failure to go through these very simple steps that led many fine intellects to go wildly wrong in their analyses of public debt. The central failure was that of comparing irrelevant rather than relevant alternatives. In our highly simplified two-person example, the macroeconomic methodology would have involved taking a balance sheet snapshot of the combined account of B and L, whether or not the conjectural marriage has taken place. Such a snap would have revealed the debt liability of B and the offsetting claim of L. From this simple offsetting balance, the conclusion emerges that there is no net debt for the community as a unit. To be sure, or so the argument would have proceeded, B holds a present-value liability and L a present-value claim. But these are precisely cancelling in the net. There can, then, be no community 'burden' of debt. The conclusion appears totally absurd in this two-person model. It is not the two-person 'community' that has incurred the debt; B has, and B must pay L. And it is not the 'community' that has enjoyed the consumption spree; B has done so. Indeed, L has financed the spree by voluntarily giving up command over resources in t_0, but only in explicit exchange for the debt commitment.

The aggregation fallacy surfaces when the 'community' in the form of a government that acts for all citizens assumes the role here of B, the borrower in the two-person example. Here it is the government, acting on behalf of the whole 'community', that spends beyond its means in t_0, and, in so doing, incurs the debt obligation. The fact that the lenders, the L's, may also be members of the community is totally irrelevant to the calculus. These persons, the lenders, sacrifice or give up purchasing power over goods or other assets in exchange for the promises of future payment written into the debt contract. In this latter capacity, these L's act privately and not at all for the 'community'. A proper combination of private and public accounts can only record a net decrement of the community's net wealth as a result of the consumption spending-debt issue transaction. Analytical clarity requires that the macroeconomic aggregates be broken down into relevant components attributable to private and to public or governmental accounting records.

VI. IS PUBLIC DEBT EQUIVALENT TO A TAX ON CAPITAL?

The elementary logic of section II cannot be challenged. The financing of public consumption outlay by government borrowing is equivalent to reducing the income stream available for private/and/or public disposition in all periods of time subsequent to that period in which the funds are initially transferred from lenders and the revenues utilized. If the national capital stock is measured as the present discounted value of the anticipated future income stream, debt-financed spending of this sort amounts to a destruction of this stock.

This simple result must stand. But this result is not identical to the related but different proposition to the effect that public debt financing and capital taxation are equivalent. These two revenue-raising instruments become equivalent in all respects only under a particular set of circumstances. And these circumstances are not those that are usually associated with the two alternatives in practical fiscal operation.

In the first place, capital taxation, as this fiscal instrument is normally discussed, does not often include the present value of anticipated income from labour in the tax base. In other words, human capital, or the value thereof, is often not subject to the capital levy. Unless its is so subjected, however, the so-called capital tax is, however, only partial. Such a tax is in no sense identical in effect to the issue of debt if the interest and amortization charges on the latter are to be financed by general taxes on income flows. The important difference is suggested in the above statement. This difference lies in the fixing of the pattern of incidence in the one case and the effective postponement in the other. With a tax on capital, whether this be entirely general or limited to particular forms of capital, the imposition of the tax defines once and for all the distribution of the burden. With public debt issue, by contrast, there is no immediate or first-period definition of the ultimate pattern of incidence. To make the debt equivalent to the tax it would be necessary to assign to each current asset holder a specific share in the liability that the public debt represents. Through such a procedure, any public debt could be converted into an instrument that is fully equivalent to any tax on capital, whether this be general or specific. Unless such first-period assignment of liability is made, however, the actual incidence of debt would seem to be highly unlikely to be equivalent to that resulting from the levy of the equal-revenue capital tax that might have been imposed in lieu of debt issue.

VII. DEBT RETIREMENT AND CAPITAL CREATION

The elementary logic is fully symmetrical. If an issue of debt to finance current consumption is equivalent to a destruction of capital value, then the retirement of existing debt that is financed by the drawing down of current consumption must be equivalent to the creation or restoration of capital value. This simple result holds for either private or public debt. To retire outstanding debt from current consumption is identical to the financing of new income-yielding investment. In balance-sheet terms, the value of the liability item measured by the debt is reduced; there is no explicit change on the asset side of the account. Net worth, or capital value of the enterprise, be this of a person, firm, or nation, is increased, dollar for dollar, by the net pay-off of debt.

The symmetry carries through, however, only if both sides of the account are analogous. Debt creation to finance current consumption destroys capital value; debt retirement financed from current consumption creates capital value. But debt retirement out of current investment does no such thing. If a debt amortization programme is financed from funds that would otherwise be destined for investment, the effect is neutral with reference to the value of capital. From this result it follows that the explicit retirement of outstanding national debt by the imposition of a once-and-for-all capital levy will not affect the properly measured value of the national capital stock.

The analogy with capital taxation to finance outlay in lieu of debt applies in reserve here. There will normally be significant differences in the effective distributional incidence of any capital levy aimed at debt retirement and the distributional incidence of the continuing liability that an existing debt embodies. The explicit imposition of a capital tax will fix once and for all the final incidence of the aggregate charges for the outlays that were initially debt financed. On the other hand, and by contrast, the carry-forward of the debt allows such final incidence to be in part postponed. *Someone* in the polity, now or in some future period, owes the full liability value of the debt that is on the books. But *no one* has an assigned share in this liability. A person may behave under the expectation that successful political strategy can remove, from himself, all or most of the debt-measured liability. The debt liability is a continuing zero-sum game.

There is a direct public choice implication of this comparative incidence of the two institutions. Precisely because any tax levy, whether on consumption or investment, fixes the distribution of the ultimate charges, there will be directed political opposition by those persons and groups on whom the tax incidence falls. Politically, therefore, the choice is far from neutral. There will be a natural bias against any proposal to retire debt from tax-financed revenues. Those who are to be taxed will oppose; those who may be the net beneficiaries may not exist (future generations) or, if they do, may not treat the aggregate reduction in liability as personally experienced increases in their own net wealth. For the same reasons that politicians find it much easier to finance outlays with debt rather than with taxes, they also find it much easier to carry forward debt, once issued, than to retire debt from tax sources. In a very real sense, the Victorian model has been reversed. National capital, once destroyed by debt creation, will not be restored; or, to put this point differently, public debt, once created, is *permanent*, regardless of the initial usage to which the funds might have been devoted.

VIII. DEFAULT, INFLATION AND CAPITAL VALUE

The only means through which public or national debt is likely to be 'retired' is via default, whether this be explicitly or implicitly carried out. But default does absolutely nothing towards restoring the capital value destroyed when the debt was created and the resources used up. Default is equivalent to the levy of a discriminatory tax on those persons and entities, internal and external, who hold debt instruments in their investment portfolios. Consider first a model in which all holders of debt are citizens of the issuing jurisdiction. Repudiation of the government's debt obligation will reduce to zero the liability item in the imagined balance sheets of all future taxpayers. It will also reduce to zero the sum the capital value of the debt instruments carried in the balance sheets of all holders of the relevant securities. Since these two items, aggregated over the whole community, are precisely offsetting, there is no net effect on capital value. Some persons are made better off; others are harmed. There is no increase in the expected value of the national income stream over future periods and, hence, no increase in the value of the national capital stock.

The crudest of aggregation fallacies must be avoided here. Because default does not in itself affect capital value in the aggregate, it should not be concluded that the debt itself had no effect. Again, the relevant alternatives must be examined. If the debt had not been issued and the funds used up, those who invested in government debt instruments could have invested in income-yielding assets. The net income stream, and therefore the capital value, would have been greater in the absence of the debt. The fact that explicit default neither increases nor decreases the value of the national capital stock, in the aggregate, suggests only that there is no miracle of fiscal process that will remove the burden of error once made. Indirectly, of course, explicit default may reduce the effective value of the government's exploitable capital value. If, because of a past default on debt, government cannot borrow at or near market rates, government's own net worth is reduced. But in such case, government, as an entity, becomes distinguishable from the community.

If some holders of government debt instruments are foreigners, default can, by repudiating the capital values of these external holders of claims, increase somewhat the net wealth of the members of the internal community. This international redistribution of burden is fully analogous to the internal redistribution of burden in the previous model. It becomes somewhat arbitrary to aggregate only within national boundaries. In this model of externally held debt, the indirect effects of repudiation are likely to be more severe than with internally held debt. Default is likely to make it difficult for governments to borrow in international markets except on unfavourable terms. If the potential for foreign borrowing is included as an asset item in a national balance sheet, default on debt will reduce the capital stock.

Implicit rather than explicit default is the much more likely consequence of government debt. History provides more than sufficient evidence to suggest that governments find it relatively easy to default on their real-valued debt obligations through inflation. With access to money-creation powers, governments find it almost irresistible to destroy capital values of debt holders. Nominal obligations are honoured; real-valued obligations are ignored and capital values confiscated. The basic analysis is almost identical to that for explicit default sketched out above.

But there are important differences. As public debt continues to increase in a deficit-financing regime, interest charges on this debt increase. The share of total budgetary outlay devoted to the service of previously issued debt increases. At some point political pressures will ensure resort to inflationary financing, if this avenue of revenue creation is possible. Through inflation, the real value of current government outlays may be maintained, and possibly even expanded, in the face of ever-mounting interest charges on the debt, charges that are denominated in nominal monetary units rather than in real values.[5] This result would be impossible in a regime that honoured the real value of the debt claims.

So long as the inflation is unanticipated, in whole or in part, government can continue to be responsive to demand pressures for expanded outlay on goods, services, and transfers, and to counter pressures against tax increases, while appearing to remain 'responsible' in meeting its interest charges on the debt that is outstanding. Through the inflationary process, the government may, over a considerable period of time, succeed in confiscating the real values of previously issued debt claims, while at the same time it may continue to issue new debt to finance flows of current outlays. Open and explicit repudiation of public debt would confiscate values at one moment, but because of the explicit signal such repudiation would provide, the potential for exploitation would be much more limited than with the implicit repudiation through inflationary financing. As the inflationary process continues, default risk will of course come to be incorporated in borrowing rates. As such rates increase, the weight of interest charges in the budget grows, which in turn generates political pressure for still further inflationary financing of outlay, including debt service. An equilibrium of sorts is attained only when government becomes unable to borrow at any rate, a position that is then identical to that reached immediately with open and explicit default.

As the basic analysis suggests, default on public debt as such neither destroys nor creates capital value in the aggregate, except through the indirect effect on government's potential borrowing capacity. Other indirect effects may emerge, however, through incentives on private decisions to create capital. If the government defaults, explicitly or implicitly, if it levies what amounts to a discriminatory tax on the holders of its own debt instruments, individuals who might be potential investors may become concerned about potential government seizure of other forms of capital, through the fiscal structure or otherwise. The direction of effect on capital creation seems clear; individuals will tend to put aside relatively fewer resources for investment than they would in a regime characterized by government dedication to honour its own debt obligations.

Default through inflationary financing has, in this respect, even more severe incentive effects than open default. With inflation, the discriminatory tax cannot be levied exclusively on holders of public debt claims. Inflation tends to destroy the value of all assets and claims that are denominated in monetary units, including the holders and users of cash balances. In this setting, therefore, individuals who might be potential creators of capital will predict that government will indeed destroy such values once they are created. That which remains only a fear with open default becomes a predictable consequence of continued inflationary financing. In terms of criteria for capital accumulation and preservation, therefore, explicit repudiation of public debt seems clearly preferable to default by means of inflation.

IX. CONSTITUTIONAL CONCLUSIONS

In the mid-1980s in the United States we live with a large and ever-increasing national debt. Many developed and developing countries are in roughly the same situation. Funds secured in exchange for the government securities that make up this debt have been used, largely if not exclusively, to finance public consumption. The resources so commanded by government have been already used up. Whether or not these resources may or may not have been 'worth' the value that the debt liability now embodies is an irrelevant question. Capital value has been destroyed that cannot be restored. We live with a capital stock that is permanently lower than that stock might have been had the government not embarked on the great fiscal spree of the 1960s, 1970s, and 1980s.

If we look at political reality, it seems unlikely that we shall act to restore the national capital stock by retiring debt out of funds drawn from current consumption. We shall not deliberately reduce the flows of goods and services, public or private, that we enjoy. We may, and presumably will, continue to default on real debt obligations through inflation, but this behaviour will in no way restore capital value already lost.

Realistically, we can at least hope to 'stop the bleeding'. We can stop the continuing destruction of capital value through deficit-debt financing. As our institutions are now organized, however, we cannot hope to accomplish even this minimally desired result. The temptations of ordinary pressure or interest group politics are simply too overwhelming for those who hold elective office, whether in the executive or legislative branch of government, to resist. The response behaviour exemplified in ordinary politics cannot be that which would satisfy the demands of reasonable fiscal prudence.

What to do? Our politicians will not be reconverted easily to the Victorian fiscal religion, especially since the Keynesian alternative fits so closely with their natural proclivities to spend without taxing. But we can, as politicians, as academicians, and as laymen, recognize what is happening. And diagnosis is the first step towards cure. Once sufficiently recognized, fiscal profligacy can be contained by appropriate *constitutional* remedies.

Ordinary politics will simply not allow fiscally responsible outcomes to emerge from modern democratic institutions. But ordinary politics operates within a set of *constitutional rules*, and these rules have been and may be changed so that more desired patterns of outcomes will emerge.

In this respect, the proposed constitutional amendment that would require budget balance on the part of the national government becomes the most important fiscal reform that has been discussed in the century. Such an amendment, considered as a *general rule* of fiscal prudence, can be discussed, evaluated, and possibly approved largely in independence from the demand-side pressures of day-to-day politics. The fiscal outcomes of ordinary politics now resemble the behaviour of the compulsive gambler who finds himself in a casino at Las Vegas or Atlantic City. Who can expect the gambler to refrain from 'irresponsible' behaviour, given the temptations that he faces? But, just as the compulsive gambler can know his own proclivities and stay home, so can those who ultimately make political decisions, the citizens, know the proclivities of our ordinary politicians and keep their fiscal activities within bounds of prudence by the enactment of constitutionally restraining rules.

NOTES

1. This chapter was initially published in the volume, *The Political Economy of Capital Formation: Direct and Indirect Effects of Taxation*, ed. Dwight R. Lee (San Francisco: Pacific Institute, 1985). I am grateful to the Pacific Institute for permission to republish the material without substantial change.
2. For more extended treatment of the divergent classical and Keynesian attitudes towards public debt, *see* James M. Buchanan, *Public Principles of Public Debt* (Homewood: Richard D. Irwin, 1958); for extended treatment of the impact of the Keynesian theory of policy on governmental creation of deficits, *see* James M. Buchnan and Richard E. Wagner, *Democracy in Deficit* (New York: Academic Press, 1977).
3. The present value of the liabilities represented by the debt instruments may not be so high as the maturity values of the debt. There will be a difference here to the extent that government borrows at rates of interest lower than the rate appropriate for discounting future tax liabilities, which would normally be the market rate of return. To the extent of this difference in present values, the government has not issued what we may call 'real debt' but has, instead, imposed a tax on persons living during the period of the public consumption. The extreme case is of course that in which the government 'sells' bonds to the central bank for zero or very low nominal rates.
4. For a generalized discussion of costs that makes the distinctions between pre-choice and post-choice costs, *see* James M. Buchanan, *Cost and Choice* (Chicago: University of Chicago Press, Midway Reprint, 1975).
5. For an analysis of such a sequence, *see* Ch. 19.

19 Debt, Demos, and the Welfare State[1]

I. INTRODUCTION

In this chapter I shall restate an old argument that seems to be too often overlooked in the complexities of this century's normative public finance. In the process I hope to be able to add the relevant public choice twists. The classical economists' abhorrence of public debt had very solid intellectual foundations. Threats to the long-term stability of social order are signalled upon any deliberate decision of a democratic government to finance *ordinary* spending by public debt. To put the argument in its most dramatic form, the welfare state guarantees its own demise upon the issue of its first dollar's worth of debt.

The distinction between democratically organized governments and non-democratic or monolithically organized governments has not been sufficiently emphasized with reference to the political implications of debt financing. Principles of prudent finance must be more restrictive in a democratically organized polity, by the nature of this form of decision-making, than the analogous principles for a private person or, by inference, for an authoritarian government. In other words, debt is more dangerous for democracies for the quite simple reason that *demos* faces a more severe problem of 'personal identity' than does either an individual or a monolithic government.

In what we may loosely call the 'Keynesian vision', public debt was held to be categorically different from private debt. Precepts for financial prudence for the individual with respect to private debt creation were held to be inapplicable for governments with regard to public debt issue. Government could, in this paradigm, violate the precepts much more readily than a private person. In one of my first books, *Public Principles of Public Debt* (1958), I argued that the Keynesian vision was analytically in error.[2] I demonstrated that in principle public debt and private debt are equivalent. Although I did not make the extension as such, my argument in that book might have been taken to suggest that precepts for financial prudence should be similar for individuals and for governments, no matter how the latter reach decisions.

210

In that book, and in related later works, I did not fully incorporate the implications of decision-making structures on predicted adherence to or violations of any set of rules for financial prudence. Equivalent financial institutions may predictably generate quite different results within different decision-making structures. My aim in this chapter is to develop this argument with specific reference to the institution of public debt in a democracy and in an economic setting that does not dictate resort to extraordinary finance (e.g. wars, major depressions, natural disasters). In the context of the last third of this century, the focus of analysis is on the debt financing of welfare state spending.

In its essentials, the argument is very elementary. In order to avoid the deluge of qualifications and complications that would emerge in any attempt to make the argument directly relevant to current policy, in section II I shall present a highly simplified and abstracted model. Section III analyzes public debt issue in the setting of the simplified model described in section II. The effects of democratic decision structure on escape from the debt dilemma are examined in section IV. Prospects for default are discussed in section V, and qualifications on the whole analysis are introduced in section VI. Section VII concludes the paper with an application of the argument to financing issues that face Western democratic nations in the last decades of this century.

II. A SIMPLIFIED SETTING

Throughout the analysis I shall assume that the economy is closed and stationary. Population is stable, and there is no net capital formation and no new technology. There are no unanticipated external threats to order that require extraordinary resource usage, and there are no internal natural disasters that dictate governmental intervention on a massive scale.

The government is organized as a representative majoritarian democracy. Collective decisions are made by majority voting rules in a legislative body. These decisions are implemented by an executive-administrative bureaucracy that may or may not have powers to manipulate the legislative agenda. Representative members of the legislature are elected by majority voting rules in periodic elections in well-defined constituencies.

Historically, I assume that government has levied taxes for the financing of both minimal or protective state services (external and internal defence, law and order) and other state services (public goods and transfers). More critical are the assumptions relating to money creation. In orthodox treatments we refer to three separate instruments through which government may finance the provision of services: taxation, money creation, and public debt. In order to isolate the analysis of public debt it is useful to combine taxation and money issue. I do this by assuming that *all* persons in the economy recognize money creation explicitly as a form of tax. Hence, they react to money issue precisely as if it were a tax. There is no money illusion. Recognizing this, governmental decision-makers will treat money issue no differently from any other tax.

Political equilibrium in this setting is reached when the median voter in the legislature, given the agenda on spending patterns with which he is confronted, values the 'good' represented by a dollar's increase in outlay equally with the 'bad' of a dollar's increase in taxes. At the initial 'tax-financed equilibrium', the representative politician is unwilling to levy higher rates of tax in order to finance additional outlays by government. In the analysis to follow, I assume that the tastes or preferences of the electorate do not change in the sequence of periods under examination.

III. PUBLIC DEBT INTRODUCED

To this point I have assumed that government does not issue debt to finance ordinary and recurring outlays. (It may or may not have issued debt in past periods to finance extraordinary outlays; whether or not it may have done so is irrelevant to my argument.) The pressures to expand the level of ordinary and recurring outlays, and particularly those summarized under the 'welfare state' rubric, are ever-present. Politicians, of almost any persuasion, would be pleased to be able to respond positively to these constituency demands, and they would do so were it not for the necessary accompanying 'bad' involved in the higher tax rates that would be entailed.

Onto this setting I want to allow debt issue to be introduced as a new financing option. Some academic-intellectual-economist, let us say, comes up with a new justification for debt creation in financing recurrent outlays. Clearly, political actors, confronting continuing pressures for expansions in spending, will tend to look favourably on any such argument. They will want to treat debt issue as a shift outwards in their 'possibility frontier'. The newly suggested financing instrument may seem to offer them a means of securing 'goods' without 'bads'.[3]

I am concerned here with the displacement of the tax-financed budgetary equilibrium that is politically determined. In this context it seems reasonable to model political response to public debt in terms of some relationship to the relative size of issue.[4] It is assumed here that within some defined deficit share of national product (GNP), say, 5 per cent, individuals in the relevant political choice-setting will react to public debt issue *less* negatively than they do to the levy of taxes or to money creation at current margins of imposition. Beyond this defined limit (5 per cent of GNP), the relevant citizens will react *more* negatively to debt creation than to taxation.[5]

Under these assumptions about political response, a new political equilibrium, in Period 1, after the availability of debt-financing has been introduced, will be characterized by (1) an increase in the rate of spending on recurrent services, (2) the creation of a determinate amount or quantity of public debt (up to the defined limit), and (3) a reduction in rates of tax and in tax-financed revenues. Some share of the funds that the government raises by debt in Period 1 will be used to finance the expanded rate of spending and some share will be used to finance the reduction in revenues from taxes.

Assume that the amount of debt issued in Period 1 is D. These funds are drawn from the private sector of the economy, funds that would otherwise have been channelled either into financing current consumption or current capital investment. In other words, the government borrowing is genuine. Persons who purchase the debt instruments do so in a wholly *voluntary* transaction. They give up current (Period 1) command over resources in explicit exchange for the interest return on the security that is purchased. The government makes a contract with each purchaser of a debt instrument; it promises to return the full principal plus the stipulated interest. (Under our assumption about the absence of money illusion, any inflation will be fully anticipated and its effects fully incorporated into nominal rates of interest on securities; or, for simplicity, we could assume that all government debt instruments are fully indexed.)

So far, so good, or so it seems. The government has exploited the newly available financing instrument and constituency demands both for extensions in service flows and for tax-rate reductions that have been met. The government has shifted to a new position of budgetary equilibrium. All of this happens in Period 1.

Consider, however, the situation that will emerge in Period 2. Taxes (including inflation as a result of money creation) will finance only that level of services tax-financed in Period 1. Revenues from taxes must be supplemented by the amount of D in order to maintain the flow of total services reached in Period 1. Government may finance D by resort, once again, to borrowing. But the debt that was incurred in Period 1 will remain in existence, and this initial debt must, at the least, be serviced in Period 2. Holders of debt instruments must be paid the promised interest returns. How will this necessary debt-service spending be financed? If government has borrowed up to the indicated political breakpoint in Period 1 (5 per cent of GNP in our example), it cannot extend its borrowing rate beyond D in Period 2 without disturbing the established political equilibrium. In order to meet its combined spending obligations in Period 2 (G + D + rD), government might either increase tax rates or cut the rate of outlay, but either of these changes would also disturb the equilibrium reached in Period 1.

As the equilibrium is necessarily displaced, adjustments will tend to occur along the available margins. A new Period 2 equilibrium will be characterized by (1) a lower rate of outlay on the provision of recurrent services than that rate attained in Period 1, (2) higher rates of tax than the rates reached in Period 1, and (3) the same amount of new debt issue in Period 2 as in Period 1. If the government does not, for any reason, issue debt up to the breakpoint limit in Period 1, it can be predicted to expand debt issue in Period 2, a process that will continue period by period until the breakpoint is finally reached.

Essentially the same relationship between the equilibria attained in Period 2 and that attained in Period 1 will describe the relationship between any two periods in the initial sequence. Because the required interest charges on public debt will increase period by period, the equilibrium rate of outlays will continue to fall period by period, and the equilibrium rate of tax will continue to rise. Table 1 illustrates the temporal pattern of adjustment.

At some point, the outlays on the provision of services must fall below that which prevailed in the period before debt issue was suggested, and at the same time tax rates must be higher than they were in the pre-debt sequence of periods. The equilibrium flow of public services to the citizenry will be permanently lower and taxes will be permanently higher than they would be if there had been no 'invention' of debt financing for ordinary services.

Table 1: Temporal pattern of adjustment in government finance

	Taxes R	Outlays on services (inc. transfers) G	Debt D	Interest iD	Total Outlay
Period 0	R_0	G_0	0	0	G_0
Period 1	$R_1 < R_0$	$G_1 > D_0$	D_1	0	$G_1 = G_0 + D_1$
Period 2	$R_2 > R_1$	$G_2 < G_1$	$D_2 = D_1$	iD_1	$G_2 + D_2 + iD_1$
Period 3	$R_3 > R_2$	$G_3 < G_2$	$D_3 = D_2$	$iD_1 + iD_2$	$G_3 + D_3 + iD_1 + iD_2$
....					
Period M	$R_0 < R_m > R_{m-1}$	$G_0 > G_m < G_{m-1}$	$D_m = D_{m-1}$	$i \sum_{1}^{m-1} D$	$G_m + D_m + i \sum_{1}^{m-1} D$

Further, there will be no end to the sequence short of government's default on its debt obligations or the total demise of the government's provision of services to the citizenry. Debt will never be 'paid off' so long as political equilibrium is attained, period by period. Total debt will necessarily increase, by the breakpoint amount in each period, which means that interest charges on outstanding debt must increase correspondingly. This sequence will continue even after all governmental provision of services has ceased; taxes will continually increase to finance debt service charges, and these charges will themselves continually mount as new debt is issued each period to finance some part of the charges on previously issued debt. In the limit, *all* of the national product would be devoted to debt service.

The model is of course extreme in the assumption that neither citizens-voters nor prospective lenders to government modify their behaviour over the sequence. We should expect that, as the sequence progresses, citizens would react more and more negatively to debt creation, in part because fears of default on the part of prospective lenders to government would make public borrowing increasingly costly. At some point in the sequence there would be no politically equilibrating issue of debt possible. At this point, the increase in debt service charges would, of course, also cease. But, if default is to be avoided, the community must *forever* live with *higher* taxes and *lower* flows of public service supply than would have been the case had the community adhered to the 'classical wisdom' that shunned all resort to debt financing of ordinary outlays.

In all of this I am doing nothing more than restating one of the most fundamental principles in capital theory. In the familiar version the principle states that putting aside a dollar's worth of current consumption for capital formation will permanently increase the flow of potentially available income. In terms of the debt application here, the principle states tht incurring a dollar's worth of debt with which to finance current consumption will permanently decrease the flow of potentially available income. To discharge the debt obligation, it will be necessary to create funds that might otherwise have been made available for productive capital formation or to withdraw capital already invested in productive earning uses. In effect, the debt financing of consumption is equivalent to the destruction or the 'eating up' of capital. The true 'wealth of the nation' is necessarily reduced by the use of any debt financing of current flows of governmental services.

IV. DEMOS AND DEBT

In its general form discussed in section III, the simple principle of non-productive debt applies independently of any structure of decision-making. The principle stands as a warning to the person who might contemplate financing current consumption by borrowing as well as a warning for any government that might be tempted to use debt finance for ordinary spending. The resort to debt financing of this type is particularly insidious for democratically organized governments, however, for reason that do not exist for private persons or for governments that are essentially organized as private domains of individuals or small groups. The differences here do not arise from the logic of the debt relationship as such but from the temporal horizons that inform decision-making in the separate cases.

Consider first the individual who succumbs to the temptation to borrow to enhance a current consumption flow. He will succeed in increasing the flow of such services over an initial sequence of periods, but he will, himself, face the subsequent-period liabilities for interest and amortization charges. As a person with a continuing identity through time, the individual will readily sense the permanent obligation that debt involves. Once he has done so, the individual may also understand the logic of the means through which he may escape from the debt dilemma. He will be able to recognize that, just as he was the initial-period beneficiary of additional services at the expense of his subsequent-period potential, he will also be able to enjoy future-period income increments to the extent that debt obligations are paid off or retired.

Note that there need be no debt retirement indicated by a rationally based utility-maximizing calculus, even if the individual recognizes the subsequent costs he must bear as a result of past financing of consumption by borrowing. If there is no shift in preferences, the individual may well choose to bear the burden of debt permanently rather than undergo the sacrifice of current services that would be necessary to pay off or to discharge outstanding debt. As stressed above, the initial creation of debt is equivalent to eating up capital; analogously, the paying off of debt is equivalent to the creation of capital. The individual who carries an existing debt obligation may or may not choose to discharge this obligation.

If, however, the basic preferences of the individual should change, the situation is such that he can trade off current consumption costs against future-period benefits. The relevant trade-off is within the temporal perspective of the individual who thinks of himself as a continuing consciousness through time. It is this particular feature of the setting that introduces the distinctive difference between the calculus of the private person who bears existing debt and the calculus of decision-makers in democratic governmental structures. In the latter, the trade-off is not within the temporal perspective of the decision-makers, as such. Hence, any decision to discharge or to retire outstanding public debt must involve the imposition of sacrifice on current-period taxpayers and/or public service beneficiaries in 'exchange' for promised benefits to be enjoyed by future-period taxpayers–beneficiaries. But these persons need not be the same as those who must bear the debt-repayment costs. Faced with this reality, debt retirement would seem bizarre as a means of equilibration on the part of political leaders.

Consider a well-defined example of the situation we are analyzing here. In past periods government has issued debt and has used the funds to finance flows of ordinary public services (including transfers). There is an outstanding debt obligation of the present government, represented in the value of debt instruments held by creditors. It is now proposed that a systematic policy of debt retirement be put in place, that a sinking fund or some such means be set up to ensure that over some appropriately scheduled period of time all outstanding government debt would be fully amortized. A government that is directly responsible to the median preferences of the legislature could not possibly implement such a proposal. Members of the legislature are elected for specifically defined terms, and there is no way of ensuring that the member or members who hold median positions in, say, Period M, will occupy similar positions in the new legislature of Period M + 1. By the very nature of democratic process in which elections are periodically scheduled, decisions made in each period of time must be reflective of the preferences of the members of the legislature in being at each such period, and, indirectly, of the coalition of voters who support the existing legislative majority.

To understand fully the situation that the legislative decision-maker faces, suppose that a debt-retirement schedule is contemplated. If he supports such proposal, current-period taxpayers and beneficiaries must be subjected to onerous fiscal burden. They must be coerced into reducing flows of current consumption and private investment. But, regardless of this current-period cost, suppose that such a debt-retirement scheme is put in place. Time passes and a new legislature is elected; the median preferences in the legislature shift, and the new legislature supports a policy of renewed debt expansion made possible by the prudential debt repayment of the previous body. There is no return or reciprocal side of the projected 'exchange' that the prudential majority in the first period thought to be possible when the debt amortization proposal was adopted. Almost necessarily, and quite apart from the familiar individual life-cycle problems that lead to future discounting, any legislative body's decisions will be characterized by a short-term horizon. Fiscal prudence simply cannot be made to pay off in democracy.

The elementary logic of debt and the elementary analysis of democratic decision-making suggest that unless moral and/or constitutional constraints intervene, public debt will be incurred and, once incurred, that such debt will never be retired. The income of the community will be lower than it would be if resort to public debt financing should have been altogether prohibited.

V. DEBT, DEMOS, AND DEFAULT

The above conclusions are based, however, on the presumption that has been made throughout the analysis to this point, the presumption that the government will not default on its debt obligations, once these are incurred. The selfsame operations of democratic process, however, will tend to ensure that default will be likely to take place, and especially in the absence of strong moral constraints. Consider the sequence of events that the analysis has projected. The government issues debt to finance increases in current levels of outlays on services and tax reductions. As debt service charges mount, rates of outlays on services gradually fall and taxes gradually increase. New issues of debt continue to be floated until the threshold of political response is reached, after which time the budget is put in balance with a lowered level of services and a higher level of taxes than before the sequence was commenced. Debt will not be retired due to the necessarily shortened time horizon of political decision-makers.

But what about default? By defaulting on its debt, the government can eliminate the burden of its interest charges. The capital values of its creditors (internal and/or external) are confiscated, but the capital values (negative) reflected in the future tax liabilities are increased. The flow of services can be expanded once again, and tax rates can be decreased, each margin being adjusted as a result of the elimination of the interest burden of the debt. The governmental budget is balanced at a new equilibrium, and a lengthy regime of fiscal prudence is necessarily commenced due to the fact that government could not, even if it desired to do so, borrow again, once having defaulted on its debt. Over time, however, and particularly in democracies where governmental regimes shift, potential creditors will lose their memories of the default. Government will, once again, find itself able to borrow funds to finance expansions in current outlays and tax reductions. The sequence will commence all over again.

VI. SOME QUALIFICATIONS

The cyclical sequence traced out in this analysis depends, strictly speaking, on the properties of the abstract model being approximated in a real-world setting. Several qualifications to the analysis are required as the various assumptions of the model are dropped. To the extent that real economic growth takes place, both the magnitude of debt and the period over which fiscal profilgacy can continue are of course extended. Government can continue to expand its issue of debt, explicit or implicit, to much higher limits without reaching the breakpoint or threshold where political resistance to further debt generates a necessary retrenchment in the rate of outlay on services and a necessary increase in real tax rates. Once debt has reached this limit, further real growth in the economy can gradually reduce the real burden of servicing the existing debt through time.

I have also assumed that money creation is treated as a tax by all persons in the economy. In a plausible real-world setting, deficits are financed only in part by genuine borrowing from the public. Deficits are also financed in part by monetization, and this process is not considered as being equivalent to ordinary taxation by the public. This process also has the effect of allowing the government to default on its debt obligations held by creditors who had purchased debt instruments in previous periods. Debt creation and default proceed simultaneously in the world that we observe. Nonetheless, the model is useful in that it allows us to separate the two processes.

I have also assumed that government is democratic in the sense that fiscal decisions are made period by period in response to constituency pressures. There are no constitutional constraints against debt issue, and there are no strong moral constraints against 'irresponsible' finance. To the extent that such constraints exist and inhibit resort to debt for the financing of non-productive services, the whole sequence traced out in the analysis may be prevented. Indeed, one of my purposes here is to indicate the need for such constraints on democratic process.

VII. WESTERN DEMOCRACIES IN THE 1980s

Despite these necessary qualifications on the simple and highly abstract analysis, however, I should argue that there are important lessons here for citizens in almost all of the Western democracies as we observe fiscal policies in the 1980s. In the United States we see deficits that are roughly the same size as the annual interest charges on the debt. Projected into the future, these deficits guarantee that the interest charges will surely increase as a share of total budgets. The rate of provision of services has already been curtailed, at least in terms of rate of expansion, and this curtailment will surely be continued. Tax rates have been lowered only in nominal terms, and seem almost certain to increase in real terms. Government defaulted on a substantial share of its debt in the great inflation of the 1970s, and creditors are coming to be increasingly aware of this prospect. There has been no movement towards a repayment of debt, and none can be anticipated. The welfare state has clearly reached its apogee, and it is in its demise. The flow of services to citizens from government will be lower over the ensuing decades than might have been the case had there not been the onset of fiscal irresponsibility in the 1960s and 1970s.

The situation is not much different in other Western countries. Government borrowing requirements in Great Britain, West Germany, France, and Japan are comparable to those in the United States. It is of course difficult to project any precise or exact time or date of a 'crisis', when default becomes general and the sequence is recommenced. Fiscal or budgetary policy in this respect cannot be divorced from monetary policy, and the ultimate crisis of confidence in fiscal policy is intimately tied to confidence in monetary policy regimes. Monetary reform in some basic structural sense may possibly hasten rather than retard the onset of genuine fiscal crisis.

My purpose here is not, however, to be a purveyor of gloom and doom. There is hope for constructive constitutional reform if citizens and leaders in democratic countries can recognize the temptations of fiscal and monetary profligacy and act to impose constraints on their own government's freedom of action in both respects. The sequence of irresponsibility has already proceeded so far, however, that no 'quick fix' is possible, even with the best of intentions and even if, tomorrow, all citizens should adopt a genuinely constitutional attitude. At best, the impositions of constitutional constraints can represent first stages in a long and painful sequence during which the mistakes of decades can be partially rectified.

The argument that deficits do not matter becomes dangerous nonsense in the context of democratic decision-making. If politicians are fully convinced that deficits do not matter, they will simply spend without taxing.[6] In the long term, debt-financed deficits are much more serious for supply-side considerations than either tax increases or spending cuts. In the latter cases, we take our medicine in the here and now; with debt, we have cake now and pay for it later, one way or the other.

NOTES

1.　　The material in this chapter was initially published in German translation under the title, 'Verschuldung, Demos, und Wohlfahrtsstaat' in *Chancen und Grenzen des Sozialstaats*, eds. Peter Koslowski, Philipp Kreuzer, and Reinhard Löw (Tübingen: J. C. B. Mohr [Paul Siebeck], 1983), pp. 117–32. I acknowledge permission to publish the English original here.

　　　　I am indebted to Geoffrey Brennan, Australian National University, Canberra, for comments on the initial drafts.

2.　　James M. Buchanan, *Public Principles of Private Debt* (Homewood: Richard D. Irwin, 1958).

3.　　Note that I am not primarily concerned with the strength of public debt illusion. My argument holds if any such illusion exists in a sense relevant to its potential effects on the political decision process. The model does not therefore rule out the presence of persons who behave in accordance with the Ricardian theorem on the equivalence of debt and taxes. To the extent that such persons are present in the community, their political influence will make politicians less prone to exploit the debt financing option. However, so long as the behaviour of others in the political community is described by debt illusion, political leaders will tend to treat the availability of the new financing option as an expansion of their possibilities to meet constituency demands.

　　　　The implicit model of political equilibrium has affinities with that developed more fully by Gary Becker; *see* G. Becker, 'A Theory of Competition Among Pressure Groups for Political Influence', *Quarterly Journal of Economics*, XCVIII (Aug. 1983), 371–400.

4.　　If this relative-size-of-debt model of response is not introduced, we should find it necessary to analyze the total shift from tax finance to debt finance once we drop the assumption of full capitalization.

5. This two-step-reaction path is analytically more tractable in this general discussion than one that allows for continuous change in reaction over the relevant range.

6. For exhaustive elaboration of this simple but central point, *see* James M. Buchanan and Richard E. Wagner, *Democracy in Deficit* (New York: Academic Press, 1977).

20 Economists on the Deficit[1]

Measured by the topicality of the issue, the conference reported in *The Economic Consequences of the Deficit* was ideally timed. Unfortunately, the substantive contribution falls short of its temporal standard. Despite the title for the conference and the volume, the economic consequences of public debt and deficits that are relevant for individual choice behaviour seem to be largely neglected. The political economy of deficit financing is handled much more satisfactorily by the political scientists represented in the book (Aranson, Shepsle, Rabushka) than by the economists. These three authors make relevant contributions to ongoing political and policy discussion, whereas the efforts of the economists seem strangely out of focus with either explanatory analysis or normative argument.

My remarks are intended to apply to economists generally; the particular contributors to the conference volume are neither better nor worse than most of their disciplinary peers, and their separate papers exhibit a high standard of professional competence. Because none of them addresses the 'economic consequences' in straightforward terms, however, their efforts remain peripheral. In the initial paper, Preston Miller argues that deficits matter because they modify expectations. In the second paper, Alan Blinder looks at monetization, and his paper contains an interesting game-theoretic model of monetary-authority – fiscal-authority interaction that might have been more fully developed. Vance Roley examines the crowding out issue with a set of simulation models. Alan Auerbach and Laurence Kotlikoff analyze the comparative effects of investment and saving incentives in relation to deficit financing. Jerome Stein, Scott Hein, Frederick Mishkin, and Franco Modigliani offer comments that are consistent with the level of analysis in the main papers. Murray Weidenbaum provides a summary anatomy of the deficit that we observe in the 1980s.

For my purposes, Roger Noll's comment on the Aranson and Rabushka papers is both the best and the worst of the volume. It is best because Noll offers me the most inviting direct target for criticism, and worst because the comment reflects most specifically what is wrong with modern economists' treatment of debt and deficits. Noll even provides me with a text:

A secondary argument is that deficits represent an intergenerational transfer from the future to the present. I will ignore the latter; it confuses the means of finance with the political selection of a division between consumption (private and public) and investment (private and public). The less said about this argument the politer. (p. 205)

Those of us who have advanced such arguments may appreciate Noll's politeness in not exposing our errors, but, unfortunately, until and unless such attempts are made, we must continue to think that it is Noll and his mainstream peers who have persistently refused to get their elementary analysis straight.

For more than a quarter century I have been puzzled by the refusal of so many of my fellow economists to accept the elementary principles of public borrowing.[2] The consequences of public debt and government deficits are much better understood by the public than by professional economists, an anomaly that is sensed by Preston Miller in his first paper.

What does the public understand that the economists do not? It is embarrassingly necessary to go back to square one. Borrowing, as an institution, allows temporal patterns of spending to differ from temporal patterns of income flows. Through borrowing, spending may be made larger than income flow in one period, with offsetting reduction below income flow in some later period or periods. This simple definitional principle holds regardless of the purpose to which the enhanced spending flow is directed during the period of the borrowing operation. If the enhanced spending is used to purchase income-yielding assets, the asset-related income may be sufficient to offset the non-asset-related income flow required for amortization of the debt. On the other hand, if the enhanced spending is used for consumption in the initial period, there is no offsetting income yield later, and the net effect must be to reduce spending below non-related income flow.

There is no difference between private and public borrowing in this setting. This fact is recognized and fully appreciated by the public that expresses its continuing concern with debt-financed deficits. The political decision-makers during the 1960s, 1970s, and 1980s have destroyed capital value through the debt financing of public consumption. There are three separate but closely related sources of confusion that make recognition of this elementary logic difficult for sophisticated economists. First, many economists have not yet escaped from the aggregation fallacies of Keynesian macroeconomics. Second, most economists remain with the benevolent despot image for policy analysis; relatively few have incorporated public choice principles in their discussion. Third, and most importantly, economists have failed to apply opportunity cost theory correctly in this particular application.

Modern macroeconomists have made diligent efforts to derive micro foundations for predicted effects of shifts in economy-wide constraints. It remains surprising that they have largely overlooked the choice-theoretic foundations of the collective decision process. Only individuals maximize utilities subject to constraints, and only individuals respond to shifts in the set of constraints. It seems but a small step from this presupposition to the recognition that only individuals can act so as to impose such shifts, if, indeed, such shifts are anything other than genuinely exogeneous parameters of the environment. Political decisions are made by individuals placed in political roles, and benefits and costs relevant to such decisions must be those faced by such individuals. To analyze changes in 'social aggregates' as if these aggregates exert direct influences on those individuals who can and do make choices is to engage in ambiguity at best and confusion at worst.

The simplistic fact that the resources used by 'government' during a single period of time must be non-used by 'private persons' during that same period is totally irrelevant for any determination of the temporal incidence of the costs of the goods and services that the governmental resource use embodies. Taxation involves a current-period imputation of the post-choice costs; debt issue allows these costs to be postponed. Debt-financed public outlay takes place with no current-period reduction in private outlay, either voluntarily or coercively, 'in exchange' for the benefits of such outlay. Current-period reductions in private outlay made by purchasers of debt instruments are made 'in exchange' for the promises of future yields, and have no relation at all to the promised benefit of the debt-financed outlay by government. The reciprocating payment 'in exchange' for the current-period services made possible by debt-financed government outlay is made only by future-period taxpayers.

This difference in the temporal location of the costs of public spending is the primary economic consequence of debt financing. The sources and the uses of the revenues that enter the debt-financing flow of funds may also be worthy of attention, but these remain secondary to the primary effect. If, in purchasing government securities, lenders draw down rates of investment relatively more than taxpayers would reduce investment under equal-revenue tax-financing, private capital accumulation will be reduced. This crowding-out difference may be important for some purposes, but the primary effect does not depend on this result. Even if the purchasers of government securities should purchase these from the same consumption-investment mix that would provide the source for the alternative equal-revenue tax financing, the temporal pattern of costs remains quite different in the two cases.

Comparable results apply for the uses to which the borrowed funds may be put. Obviously, if borrowed funds are used for public consumption, there is no offsetting income yield in future periods that might be used to provide a basis for financing the debt service and amortization. If, on the other hand, borrowed funds are put into income-yielding assets, such offsetting income flows may be present. In the latter case, if the yield is sufficiently large, aggregate income flows need not be reduced and may even be increased by the combined public-spending-debt-financing operation on the part of government. By comparison with the tax financing of the same income-yielding public asset, however, debt financing places a claim or obligation against income flows in future periods.

The elementary analytics of the comparison between tax and debt financing of public outlay is unaffected by the presence or absence of fiscal illusion. If persons fully anticipate the future-period tax liability that debt financing embodies, and if these are fully capitalized into current asset values, the motivation for political support of deficit finance is weakened. That is to say, if such capitalization takes place (i.e. if the Ricardian theorem advanced by Barro and others in its modern formulation is correct), the political economy of deficits would be different from the political economy under fiscal illusion. Also, the aggregate rate of capital formation might be different in the presence and in the absence of such illusion. But the primary effect of debt financing remains unchanged; indeed, the whole discussion of the Ricardo-Barro theorem is based on an acceptance of the temporal dislocation of costs that debt financing facilitates.

My reason for summarizing the analysis is to indicate that it does not seem to inform much of the discussion of the economists in the volume under review. Acceptance of the elementary principles suggests a whole set of economic consequences that remain untouched. Faced with ever-mounting debt charges, which amount to precommitted claims against income, how will future-period decision-makers act? Will the debt obligations be honoured, or will explicit or implicit default take place? Surely analysis that treats payment of debt as mere 'transfers' lends indirect support for the default alternative. By contrast, default carries quite a different implication if payments to holders of debt instruments are treated as costs that must be paid by individuals as members of the polity in some final reckoning of the fiscal accounnt.

In fairness, my basic criticism should be limited to the economists. The contributions of the political scientists either explicitly or implicitly incorporate the elementary analytics of debt in their discussions. Shepsle's comment, in particular, warrants brief attention. Deficit financing of government outlay is treated as being analogous to grazing on the commons, and Shepsle looks at possible property-rights solutions, again analogously to those often applied to common resource use problems. He suggests that the 1960s changes in the rules of the House of Representatives in the United States Congress effectively modified the property-rights structure of the whole appropriations process. He then suggests that a return to concentrations of congressional power might be more effective than the proposed constitutional amendment for budget balance, supported here by Rabushka. As Gordon Tullock inquires, however, when shown a draft of this review, how does Shepsle's solution extend to other Western democracies?

The central problem in the political economy of deficit control is that of securing requisite agreement on reform by those groups that must give up the current-period command over resources that deficit financing makes possible. We must face the reality that deficit financing of a large share of governmental outlay is the status quo, even if the observed regime cannot be characteristic of either economic or political equilibrium. The problem of getting agreement is by no means an easy one for the idea-room designers of budgetary reform, quite apart from practical politics. The contribution of mainstream economists to the necessary discussion will be negligible if not negative unless their attention is returned to fundamental principles.

NOTES

1. This chapter was initially written as a review article of Laurence H. Meyer (ed.), *The Economic Consequences of Government Deficits* (Boston: Kluwer-Nijhoff Publishing Co., 1983), pp. xiii, 242. It was prepared on invitation of the book-review editor of *The Journal of Monetary Economics*. Despite the invitation that I write the review article, the submitted version was twice rejected for publication. This editorial behaviour indicates that my views on debt and deficits remain outside the prevailing orthodoxy; indeed, so much so that they are not to be exposed.

2. For my earlier efforts, see James M. Buchanan, *Public Principles of Public Debt* (Homewood: Irwin, 1958) and James M. Buchanan and Richard Wagner, *Democracy in Deficit* (New York: Academic Press, 1977). See also, James Ferguson (ed.), *Public Debt and Future Generations* (Chapel Hill: University of North Carolina Press, 1964); this book collects many of the papers that were generated by my 1958 book, in both opposition to and support of my argument.

Part Five
The Individual and the State

21 Individual Choice in Private, Agency, and Collective Decisions[1]

I. INTRODUCTION

In this chapter I shall examine and analyze, by way of both comparison and contrast, the choice behaviour of an individual in three separate roles or positions: (1) as a private, autonomous unit within a well-defined legal structure that protects and enforces the assignment of rights; in its idealized conceptualization this model is that of the individual buyer or seller in a regime of effectively competitive markets; (2) as a designated agent, who acts for a well-defined community that includes others than himself (and may not, in the limit, include himself at all); (3) as a single chooser in a group of several persons with decisions for the group emerging from some rule through which the individual choices are combined or amalgamated. The idealized conceptualization of this third model is the choice of behaviour of the individual voter in a large-number political constituency that generates collective decisions via a majority or plurality voting rule.

My emphasis is on the influence of role or position on the choice behaviour of the individual. For purposes of analytical clarity, it is useful to think of the same person as he or she may be placed in each of the three institutional structures, or in any combination of these. My emphasis is on the differences that the alternative institutional structures exert on the choice-influencing opportunity costs that the individual confronts. I shall not address directly the whole set of normative issues involved in any comparison of institutional structures.

Much of my analysis will of course cover familiar ground, both from my own previous works and in the works of many other scholars.[2] A 'varied reiteration' may be helpful, however, and in the process I hope that remaining ambiguities can be clarified.

II. INDIVIDUAL CHOICE IN A PRIVATE ROLE

The model of individual private choice is widely familiar, and it is of course the stock-in-trade of the economic theorist. Although the individual whose behaviour is analyzed may be involved in a social interaction that contains many other persons, there is no 'personal' dealing in the limiting case. As my professor, Frank Knight, was fond of remarking, 'in competition there is no competition'. The individual's choice behaviour can be analyzed to be analogous to that of Robinson Crusoe on his island before Friday appears on the scene. In the idealized competitive market, the individual is one among many as a buyer in each and every market that he enters as a potential purchaser; he is also one among many as a seller in each and every market that he enters as a potential seller. By definition in the limit, the individual has no control over the terms of trade at which he buys and/or sells any good or service. From this it follows that he is not conscious that his own behaviour exerts an influence on other persons. He senses no power over any other person, and he does not sense that any other indentifiable person has power over his own well-being. Any action taken by a person will have connected with it a pattern of pecuniary benefits and harms, but these are precisely offsetting; there is no net external benefit or harm consequent on an individual's behaviour in idealized market choice.

From this description we may directly draw the inference that the recognized costs and benefits of any choice are private in the sense that these can affect directly only the utility or satisfaction of the individual who chooses among the options that are available. The opportunity cost to the chooser, in this setting, is the utility losses that are suffered in the prospect of foregoing the non-chosen option or alternative.[3]

In this idealized model of the market place, there is a direct correspondence between the assigned *responsibility* for choice and the observed *incidence* of the direct effects of the action consequent on choice. Unless the individual chooses and acts, there are no consequences, either for his (her) own well-being or for that of anyone else. There is no explicitly chosen course of action that will be followed unless action is taken.[4] The line of responsibility is clear. The direct incidence is located squarely on the person who chooses and acts. There are, in the very definition of the model, no direct effects on anyone else, despite the complex web of interdependence that the network of interrelated exchanges may describe. The model becomes the extreme opposite of the 'house of cards'; in the fully competitive market, a change in the position of any single 'card' (person) cannot affect the location (position) of any other.

III. INDIVIDUAL CHOICE IN A PURE AGENCY ROLE

As a second idealized setting within which individual choice behaviour may be analyzed, consider the pure agency role. In this, a selected person is assigned full *responsibility* for making the relevant choices that will initiate action, but all members of the relevant community understand that the agent in the limit will bear none of the direct *incidence* of the effects. Any benefits and harms that occur as a result of the choice are borne, exclusively by others than the agent who is authorized to make the decisions. In this limiting model, all directly observable utility flows (positive or negative) are externalities, to use familiar terminology from economic theory, whereas in the first model, by contrast, all such flows are 'internalities'.

The agent who chooses–acts for others, and whose choices must affect the well-being of others, cannot directly experience the post-choice costs of his choices in the same sense as the privately choosing actor in the first model. In either case, the choice-influencing or pre-choice opportunity cost must be understood to be the loss in the chooser's utility involved in the prospect of sacrificing or foregoing the non-chosen option or alternative. In the private-choice model previously discussed, however, this choice-influencing cost is related to the individual's own discounted value of the post-choice flow of services that he or she might expect to enjoy from the sacrificed alternative. In the agency model, by contrast, the agent will anticipate no change in the flows of services for his or her own usage, regardless of his or her choice. The post-choice, post-action changes in the flows of services in periods subsequent to choice are exclusively concentrated on those persons for whom the agent is authorized to act, or possibly on others outside the community.

The agent will, nonetheless, make a choice by balancing off the estimated costs and benefits of the alternatives. But what are the opportunity costs that he or she confronts? Consider an example. A group of friends asks you to recommend (to be their agent, to choose) a seafood or a steak restaurant. They do so in the knowledge that you are not, yourself, going with the group to dinner. You become a pure agent in this choice. The opportunity cost of the steak restaurant will be the utility value that you the chooser place, at the moment of choice, on the impossibility of (suggesting) choosing the fish restaurant.

The pure agent's choice need not be related to the anticipated incidence of benefit flows to those for whom he or she is acting. Consider several possible responses in our example, whether these are stated explicitly or implicitly. The agent may say (1) 'If I were going I should go to the steak restaurant'. Or he may say (2) 'I think that you would like the steak restaurant better'. Or he may say (3) 'I think the steak is better for you'. Or he may say to himself (4) 'I like the waitress at the steak restaurant'. Note that only the second of these 'reasons' for choosing the steak restaurant would be analogous to the private choice behaviour that might be made by those upon whom the incidence of choice falls. Note also that only with the second reason would there be a feedback leading to the correction of error. If the group returns and tells the agent, 'we did not like that restaurant you suggested', the choice would be corrected on another occasion only if the second reason should have been dominant in the initial choice. If the agent made the selection for any of the other reasons listed, or any one of many others not listed, the post-choice knowledge that those affected were not happy with the choice would not reflect an error on the part of the agent. There would be no feedback effect leading to 'correction' if similar options should be confronted in subsequent periods.

The divorce between the responsibility for making choice and the incidence of the effects of choice under the agency institution provides the basis for the search for rules that will constrain the agent's choices. The agent may be directed by a rule which states that choice *should* be made in 'the interest of the group of persons who bear the incidence'. In this setting, the cost to the choosing agent in not selecting that option that is estimated to be most beneficial to the group of persons affected becomes the utility loss estimated in the prospect of the punishment or sanction for violation of the rule. To the extent that vagueness and ambiguity in the rule itself make the detection and subsequent punishment of violation difficult, the existence of a rule for choice behaviour of agents may obscure the essential arbitrariness of agents' power over those for whom they make choices.

More effective means of controlling agents are located in some departure from the pure agency role on the one hand and from the limitation of appointment on the other. If an agent who is authorized to choose for the group is required to be a member of the group, and if there is some general sharing of benefits and costs, the agent will be at least within the group that bears the direct effects of choices. This inclusion will serve to restrict, and possibly severely, the range over which choices may fall. A further step involves relating the incidence of effects more closely to the agent's responsibility through the institution of residual claimancy status, as in the case of profit-seeking firms. A person may be authorized to act on behalf of a community of persons, with the incidence of choices being differentially adjusted so as to ensure that the agent will share more than a *pro rata* share of gains and losses, measured above and below some contractually determined benchmark. These arrangements effectively replace agency choice with private choice.

A more familiar institutional control over agency power lies in the rules that allow persons affected to remove the agent and to install a replacement appointee. An agent who operates under such a rule must always reckon on the prospect that he or she will be removed by those for whom he or she has been authorized to act. In making any decision, one aspect of opportunity cost will be an estimate of the prospect that such a decision will precipitate removal from office. This prospect of being kicked out places limits on the arbitrary powers of the agent to choose in accordance with personal whims, but the precise form of such limits will depend on the specific features of the rules.

My concern here is not with the particular institutions or agency. My emphasis is instead limited to the demonstration that agents must act in accordance with a utility calculus that is wholly different from that faced by a person who acts in a private choice capacity. At best, the rules for restricting the behaviour of agents can restore some elements of correspondence between an agent's behaviour and that of a person who is both responsible for and affected by the choices that are made. To the extent that any divorce between responsibility and incidence remains present, however, the utility calculus must remain different in the two cases.

IV. INDIVIDUAL CHOICE BEHAVIOUR IN A COLLECTIVE DECISION ROLE

The choice behaviour of the individual in a collective-decision setting is different from that discussed under either the private choice or the agency choice role. In terms of the responsibility for choice, and subsequent action, and in terms of the incidence of effects, the individual who acts in a collective-decision role, at least in the idealized model, bears *neither* the responsibility for decision (and action) *nor* the basic incidence of the effects of action. It is the basic *irresponsibility* of individual choice in this setting that warrants special consideration here.

In both private choice and agency choice, the individual who chooses does so in the knowledge that the course of action selected from among a set of alternatives will be the course of action that will in fact be carried out. Other persons in the relevant social community also recognize the location of responsibility for decision and adjust their behaviour appropriately. The person who purchases an apple with 25 cents does so in the knowledge that he will get an apple in exchange for a transfer of 25 cents to the seller. Similarly, the person who is authorized to act as an investment agent knows that he may choose to shift $10,000 from stocks to bonds in a portfolio and that, upon his orders, such a shift will actually be made. There is a direct linkage between choice and its consequences.

This linkage is broken in the collective-decision setting. Consider a single voter in a many-voter constituency, and one in which collective results are determined by a majority or a plurality voting rule. The collectivity, as a unit, faces alternatives A and B. The one of the two that secures the higher number of votes is to be installed as the collectivity's 'choice'.

The individual as a voter, however, will not be able to influence the outcome save in exceptional cases. He or she may 'choose' A over B in the polling booth, but, independently of this polling-booth behaviour, the selection between these alternatives will be determined by the operation of the decision rule. If A should win by more than a single vote, not a single person in the constituency can treat his or her own behaviour as having been decisive, regardless of how it might have been directed. There is an analogue of sorts here with the anonymity of the individual buyer or seller in the pure market setting discussed earlier, in that no person directly influences the well-being of any other person. In the idealized competitive setting of private choice, however, each person does, through his or her own choice behaviour, influence directly *his or her own* well-being. In the collective decision setting, by contrast, the individual's choice, as such, directly influences neither others or himself (herself). Yet it remains the case that the individual's well-being, along with that of others, is affected, and possibly dramatically, by the action of the collectively as a unit.

Consider an example. Suppose that a voter anticipates that alternative A will yield a net benefit stream that he or she presently values at $1,000, while alternative B is anticipated to yield a net benefit stream of only $800 in present value. In ordinary language, and employing rationality postulates, we may conclude that the individual 'prefers' A to B. But as he or she *votes for* A over B, if indeed he or she bothers to vote at all, $800 will not be treated as the opportunity cost of expressing the choice for A over B. This result follows for the simple reason that the voter is not placed in a position of choosing A or B in the sense of being responsible for the outcome. As a single voter among many voters, the individual cannot influence the outcome finally selected. The voter is not here acting as the agent for others in the collectivity, despite the 'publicness' of the results once chosen. The individual is not even acting on his or her own behalf in expressing preferences. There is *no* direct consequence on individual choice.[5]

It is questionable whether the very word 'choice' is appropriate with reference to that which the individual does in the pure collective decision setting. A 'preference' is expressed over the alternatives, but there is no direct evaluation. Voting choice becomes at least partially analogous to a person who is asked, 'Would you prefer a rainy or a bright day?' Suppose the response is 'A bright day'. In a sense, this response does provide information about the person even though it is acknowledged by all concerned that this expressed preference can have no effect whatsoever on the weather. But it seems clear that, in making the response to such a question, the person is likely to be less serious and less calculating than would be the case in a market-like response to an offer or bid.

The failure of voting processes to take adequate account of varying intensities of preference among different persons has been thoroughly analyzed in public choice theory. Persons in a majority coalition may prefer A over B only slightly, whereas persons in the defeated minority may prefer B over A intensely. But unless side payments and/or vote trading take pace, ordinary voting rules cannot incorporate such differential intensities into patterns of outcomes.

My emphasis here is quite different from that of the preference-intensity discussion. The latter has implicitly assumed that expressions of preferences in a voting booth do reflect a relative evaluation of the options on the part of a voter, at least in an ordinal sense. If a person votes for A over B, the presumption is that A is anticipated to yield more utility than B. This amounts to saying that if the person in question should be given dictatorial powers, as appointed agent for the collectivity, he or she would *choose* A over B. It is, however, inappropriate to draw such an inference. The 'choice' settings confronted by the individual in the voting booth and by the individual in the role of the agent for the community are very different. In the first, the acknowledged absence of linkage between preference-expression and results removes any incentive to become informed about the properties of the alternatives (the familiar rational ignorance) and tends to encourage essentially frivolous (non-evaluative) behaviour, which may include moralistic posturing. In the latter setting, by dramatic contrast, the direct linkage between choice and result forces the individual-as-agent to behave 'economically', by which I mean only that account is taken of the elementary reality of scarcity, that the opportunity costs are at least subjectively reckoned, within the presumably integrated mind of the decision-maker.

In the collective decision setting, even if we totally ignore the absence of linkage between 'choice' and result for the individual voter, with its implications for the rationality of behaviour, it may be impossible for the voter to make an estimate of the opportunity costs of the alternatives that are confronted by the group. The selection of A will preclude the selection of B, and the anticipated benefits of B are the opportunity costs of A. This logic seems straightforward enough if we think of A and B as being mutually exclusive alternatives (e.g. candidates for a single office or parties in an election) and if we implicitly assume that collective decisions are restricted to the AB selection. Consider, however, a setting where A is defined as 'approval of an outlay of X dollars on defence', and B is defined as 'disapproval of the proposed outlay'. It is evident here that the opportunity cost of A, measured in anticipated foregone benefits of B, cannot be known or even estimated until and unless the disposition of revenues that might otherwise go to the outlay on defence is specified. These funds may go towards tax reduction, to welfare outlay, or to outlay on any of many other public services. The anticipated benefits of these various alternatives may be very different for the individual voter, and hence, the opportunity cost of A must remain highly uncertain. This feature of the individual decision calculus is not present in either market choice or in agency choice because of the embodiment of all margins of choice within the single responsible choosing entity, a single mind. The approval of a private outlay of 'Z dollars on beer' is made in the presumed knowledge of the chooser as to just what outlays are to be reduced to allow the expanded outlay on beer. With collective choice, by contrast, the individual may know what *his own* preferred sacrificed alternative is, but he cannot know how others will array alternatives and, hence, how they might vote. There is no 'group mind' which has any conscious sense of identity sufficient to allow an internalization of the relevant choice margins.

When the absence of linkage between individual behaviour and result is combined with the necessary difficulty in estimating opportunity costs, the essentially irresponsible nature of collective decisions becomes apparent, and quite apart from the more widely discussed (but largely irrelevant) prospect of collective 'irrationality' in the sense of the voting cycle. The pattern of decisions taken under majority or plurality voting rules may bear little or no relationship to any underlying 'true evaluation' of the citizens, if there exists no voting cycle at all.

V. THE SPONTANEOUS EMERGENCE OF MARKET AND POLITICAL OUTCOMES

There are important parallels as well as important differences between the two non-agency models that have been analyzed. As noted earlier, in idealized private choice (the market), a person acts on his or her own behalf, and, in the limit, this action exerts no direct influence on anyone else in the interacting group. Despite the privateness of individual choice, however, the action of all persons does generate what may be called a 'social outcome', a 'resource allocation', an 'income distribution'. This aggregative result is not *chosen* or *selected* by anyone. The outcome emerges spontaneously from separate, privately taken choices, made without conscious attention to the overall result.

Recognition of this relationship between individual choice and aggregative result is of course a part of elementary economic theory. Its parallel in the collective decision setting is not so widely recognized. As the analysis in Part IV has shown, the individual, as voter, exercises no direct influence on his or her own or others' well-being by behaviour in the voting booth. Despite the essential insignificance of each individual's behaviour, however, the behaviour of all persons does, as in the market-choice model, generate a result or outcome (alternative A or B is selected). But this result emerges from the voting rule; it is not explicitly chosen by anyone. Collective or political outcomes that are generated by individual behaviour under majority or plurality voting rules in large-number consitituencies are therefore *spontaneous* in one sense that is analogous to those 'economic' outcomes generated by individual behaviour in a market economy with enforceable property rights.

The basic difference lies in the incidence of effects in these contrasting decision structures. In the idealized market structure, the individual's own well-being is not directly affected by the recognizable behaviour of others. He or she has no instrumental reason to be interested in the spontaneously generated 'allocation of resources', which become simply an aspect of the environment within which he or she finds himself situated. The individual may maximize utility or surplus by behaving rationally within the constraints that are confronted. By dramatic contrast, in the collective-decision setting, the individual knows that his or her own well-being depends directly or critically on how others, in aggregate, behave in the voting·booth, even when it is recognized that , individually, no single person acts if he or she has an affect on the outcome at all.

VI. DEPENDENCE

The three separate models of decision-making can usefully be compared in terms of their dependence relations for the individual. In an idealized market order, the individual is connected indirectly with many other persons in a very complex network of interrelated markets. The individual is not, however, directly dependent on the behaviour of any other person and, hence, is not affected by the moral stance of any buyer or seller with whom he makes exchanges. The buyer or seller whom the individual faces need not include his across-trade partner in what I have called the 'moral community' (see Ch. 11). The market embodies a 'moral order' that requires only mutuality of respect for the law that enforces rights and contracts. Within these minimal limits, the individual participant in the idealized market is therefore *morally independent* while at the same time remaining beneficiary of the advantages of social interaction.

By contrast, in either the agency or the collective-decision structure, the individual becomes directly dependent on the behaviour of other persons, singly in the agency model, aggregatively in the collective decision model. In the agency model, the possible advantages of having responsibility lodged in an identifiable chooser, one who may be held accountable within certain limits, is counterbalanced by the disadvantage that the agent's personal discretion may directly affect the person for whom decisions are to be made. The latter becomes *morally dependent* on the agent, necessarily so.

In the collective-decision structure, the individual is affected by the results that emerge from the operations of a voting rule, but he or she is not necessarily brought within the moral community of any identifiable voter or participant in the process. There is no direct moral dependence analogous to that which is present in the agency model. But neither is there the substantial moral independence that characterizes the individual's position in the market. There is here a direct dependence on the aggregative behaviour of others which renders the individual more vulnerable than in either of the other two settings. He or she has no resort to alternatives, as in the market, and he or she has no directly identifiable perpetrator of benefit or harm, as in the agency setting. In this respect, the politics of democracy, even as idealized, is indeed somewhat like the weather.

VII. INSTITUTIONAL REALITIES

I have analyzed individual behaviour in three idealized models of decision. In institutional reality, the individual will rarely, if ever, be confronted with a 'pure' choice in any of the three idealizations. In ordinary economic interactions, persons may be able to affect others in the nexus directly and in turn be directly affected by them. Economic rents exist, and may loom large, especially in a short time period. Relevant technological externalities may not be fully internalized. In putative agency roles, persons may, and normally will, bear some of the incidence of their own behaviour directly. In collective-decision settings, persons may be strategically located so that individual actions do have consequences. Even without such positions, persons may often act as if their own behaviour matters individually.

I have utilized the idealized rather than the fuzzy models because the analysis is more tractable and because it is helpful in allowing the trade-offs to be defined for some ultimate purpose of deriving normative implications for direction of institutional reform. I have made and shall make no such normative inferences in this chapter. This step would require both analysis and data beyond the abstract formulations of the individual choice models. The divergence between the empirically observed settings for individual decision-making and the abstract and idealized models that I have analyzed would have to be estimated. Further, and importantly, the normative implications to be drawn would depend on the imputed motivations for individual behaviour, either generally or specifically in the models of decision examined.

If individuals are assumed to behave solely in *homo economicus* terms, in all of their decision-taking roles, there would seem, on first argument, a strong normative case for the widest possible usage of market and market-like institutions. Such enthusiasm may be immediately dampened, however, by Adam Smith's emphasis on the necessary mutuality of respect for law, without which markets cannot function. Such law-abiding behaviour cannot in itself be readily derived from a pure *homo economicus* model. On the other hand, the possibility that individuals may behave as strict economic men, regardless of the institutional setting, gives necessary pause to those who would enthusiastically endorse agency or collectivized institutions as substitutes for markets. Persons do not become saints as they shift roles, or at least not so readily as some of our academic colleagues might wistfully hope.

There is much work to be done; persons do behave differently under differing institutions that place them in differing roles because the roles do modify the constraints and also may affect motivations. But the saints among us may not be those selected as our agents (indeed, the opposite seems more likely), and too few of us may behave as 'responsible citizens' when the incentives to do so are absent. Finally, when both the analytical and the empirical work is done, the preferred direction for institutional reform will require the difficult balancing of the values of independence, self-reliance, and liberty on the one hand, against those of community, fraternity, and dependence on the other. Individuals simultaneously want to be free and to belong to a community; they do not want to be anonymous slaves. The challenge to social philosophers and social reformers has been, is, and will be that of satisfying the former demands without promoting institutional change that guarantees the latter condition.

NOTES

1. Material in this chapter was initially presented at a conference on 'Individual and Collective Rationality', organized by Club Turati in Turin, Italy, in January 1983. It was also presented at the Chicago meeting of the American Political Science Association in September 1983.

    I am indebted to Robert Sugden and Viktor Vanberg for helpful comments on earlier drafts.

2. In particular, *see* James M. Buchanan, 'Individual Choice in Voting and the Market', *Journal of Political Economy*, LXII (Aug. 1954), 334–43; reprinted in Buchanan, *Fiscal Theory and Political Economy* (Chapel Hill: University of North Carolina Press, 1960), pp. 90–104. *See also* Geoffrey Brennan and James M. Buchanan, 'Voter Choice: Evaluating Political Alternatives', *American Behavioural Scientist*, 28 (Dec. 1984), 185–201.

3. *See* James M. Buchanan, *Cost and Choice* (Chicago: University of Chicago Press, Midway Reprint, 1975) for a general discussion of opportunity cost and its relation to choice behaviour.

4. For my purposes at this point, there is no necessary distinction between routine and innovative choice and action. By simply repeating the choice patterns and the subsequent action patterns that have been chosen in prior periods, the individual is effectively choosing among alternatives. For other purposes, of course, the distinction between passive and active choice behaviour becomes important.

5. For extended discussion, *see* Geoffrey Brennan and James M. Buchanan, 'Voter Choice: Evaluating Political Alternatives', *op. cit.*

22 Contractarianism and Democracy[1]

I. INTRODUCTION

If politics is to be interpreted in any justificatory or legitimizing sense without the introduction of supra-individual value norms, it must be modelled as a process within which individuals, with separate and potentially differing interests and values, interact for the purpose of securing individually valued benefits of cooperative effort. If this presupposition about the nature of politics is accepted, the ultimate model of politics is *contractarian*. There is simply no feasible alternative.

This presupposition does not, however, directly yield implications about the structure of political arrangements and hence about 'democracy' in the everyday usage of this term. We must acknowledge that in terms of ordinary language usage, 'non-democratic' political institutions may be analytically derived from fully consistent contractarian premises.

Hobbes offers, of course, the classic example. Finding themselves in the war of each against all, persons contract with the sovereign; they give up natural liberty for the order and security that the sovereign promises. Decisions taken by the sovereign subsequent to this initial contract are not 'democratic', in any meaningful sense of the term. While useful in setting the stage for discussion here, however, the Hobbesian contractual metaphor need not be extended to Hobbes' own gloomy predictions concerning the prospects for limiting the power of the sovereign. The Hobbesian metaphor suggests, nonetheless, that so long as the sovereign remains within the agreed and assigned limits of the initial contract, so long as the role remains the maintenance and enforcement of internal order, 'democratic' attributes of the sovereign's decision-making would be out of place and, indeed, would be counter-productive.

The principle here may be placed in a more general setting, and it warrants some discussion because failure to understand the principle has been, and continues to be, the source of widespread confusion. In the most inclusive definitional sense, 'politics' embodies all activities within institutions that are co-extensive with membership in the collectivity, the organized polity. Politics includes, therefore, the whole structure of legal institutions, the law, as well as political institutions defined in the ordinary sense. It is essential, however, that three quite different stages or levels of collective action be distinguished one from another.

First, there are those activities that involve the enforcement of the law that exists. This classification includes the legitimate activities of the Hobbesian sovereign, those that are included in what I have called the 'protective state', which Nozick has called the 'minimal state', and which some nineteenth-century philosophers called the 'night-watchman state'. In the familiar game analogy, the role here is that of the umpire or referee, who is appointed to enforce the rules, to police the playing of the game.

Second, there are those activities that involve collective action within the limits of the law that exists. I have referred to this set of activities as belonging to the 'productive state'. Hayek refers to 'legislation' as distinct from 'law'. In terms familiar to economists, this set of activities involves the financing, supply, and provision of 'public goods and services', those goods and services that may not be supplied efficiently by the activities of individuals and private groups acting within the existing legal rules.

Third, there are those activities that involve changes in the law itself, changes in the set of legal rules that exist. In American usage, this set can perhaps best be described as 'constitutional law', although Hayek uses the general term 'law' in this context. In the game analogy, the activities here are those that involve changes in the rules of the game that has been and is being played.

In the chaotic intellectual and political setting of the mid-1980s we can observe that the three sets of activities are confusedly intermingled. Those agents whose proper role should be confined to the first set feel no compunction whatever (and are encouraged to feel none by their scholastic mentors) in acting within the third set. Modern legal-judicial practice places us all in an ongoing game where the umpires themselves continually change the rules and, indeed, openly proclaim this to be their annointed social role. Those representative agents, legislators, whose role properly falls within the second set of activities, do not themselves consciously acknowledge the existence of limits. Modern politicians are encouraged to legitimize any and all extensions of legislative activity so long as 'democratic' procedures prevail. Hence, both judicial and legislative agents invade the territory that the third category describes, and both groups do so under cloaks of claimed legitimacy. It is difficult to imagine a deeper and more widespread confusion than that which now exists, not only among the citizenry but, tragically, among those who might and do exert disproportionate influence on opinion.

We must recognize the intellectual confusion for what it is, and we must studiously avoid the temptation to apply contractarian derivations prematurely to observed institutions that have been warped out of all fit with their proper roles. The derivations must first be applied to meaningful categories. Therefore, within the three-part classification of politics outlined, I shall proceed to examine possible contractarian bases for democratic decision rules, if indeed such bases exist.

II. THE ENFORCEMENT OF LAW

I have already suggested, in earlier reference to Hobbes, that there is no obvious role for 'democratic' decision-making procedures in the state's role as law enforcer. In its activities as umpire, the state, through its agents, determines when the existing rules are violated and punishes those who are the violators, again within the rules. In such activity, truth-judgements are involved. Was the law violated or was it not violated? Varying institutional arrangements may be evaluated in terms of comparative efficacy. The appointed expert judge and the multi-person jury may be alternative means of generating desired patterns of results.

To introduce 'democratic' decision procedures, with *all* members of the polity equally weighted (*ex ante*) in collective choices, in the determination of law violations, would be quasi-contradictory to the very meaning of law. To allow a designated plurality, or majority, of all citizens to decide whether a single citizen or a group has or has not broken the law would almost directly imply that 'law' does not exist independently. Such an institutional arrangement would indeed allow for tyrannization by the designated plurality or majority.

It seems evident that these arrangements could never emerge from any contractual agreement that persons enter voluntarily. The first normative principle that emerges from the contractarian perspective is that any agreed delegation of authority to the state or its agents be *limited by law*. I shall not in this chapter go through the derivation of this precept. I note only that the principle emerges directly without the necessity of assuming risk averseness in the standard sense.

III. COLLECTIVE ACTION WITHIN THE LAW

The law, inclusively defined, may include a range for collective or state action, a range that is not in itself independent of the rules for reaching decisions within the range that is allowed. There may be goods and services that can only be or can most effectively be provided under the auspices of the collectivity as a unit. There may be 'public goods' in the modern economists' meaning of this term, and decisions as to how such goods are to be provided may be assigned to the state. The question at issue here involves the possible role for democratic procedures in the making of such decisions. Will individual contractors necessarily adopt majority rule for those political choices that may be confronted within allowable ranges of state action?

The direct answer to this question is clearly negative. Majority rule may well emerge from contractual agreement entered into by all citizens. But it does so only as one among a set of plausibly acceptable decision rules, any one or all of which might be chosen with equal validity. The removal of the sacrosanct status accorded to majority rule was one of the main purposes of Buchanan and Tullock's *The Calculus of Consent* (1962). As the analysis there demonstrated, the rule that emerges from contractual agreement reflects the results of cost-benefit calculations on the part of the contractors. Because differing sorts of potential collective actions embody differing predicted cost and benefit patterns, there may be scope for the co-existence of several collective decision rules. For many decisions, simple majority voting, both in the selection of political representatives and in the operation of legislative assemblies, may well offer the most effective instruments. For other choices, however, which may be predicted to embody potentially more important consequences in costs and benefits, qualified majorities may be required for positive collective action. For still other ranges of state activities, authority may well be delegated to single agents or agencies.

Majority rule, as a uniquely legitimate principle for the making of political decisions, cannot be derived from the contractarian perspective as such. The perspective is not so empty as it seems, however. It would be difficult, indeed, to derive a delegation of wide-ranging decision-making authority to an hereditary monarchy or to a family-defined aristocracy from any contractual process in which all members of the polity participate. Much the same could be said concerning delegation to a self-perpetuating, essentially cooptive, ruling elite. Delegation to a selected oligarchy that is regularly rotated through some guaranteed electoral process might possibly emerge in a contract, although the limits within which such an oligarchy might operate would tend to be more tightly drawn than those under more inclusive decision structures.

A critical element in any contractarian perspective, regardless of where the criteria are applied, is *political equality*, and especially in the *ex ante* sense. In an idealized contractual setting, the individual is modelled as making a choice among alternative decision rules without knowing how the operation of particular rules will impact on his own personal interests or values. In the Rawlsian limit, the person does not know who he will be in the settings where the chosen rule is to be operative. In the somewhat less rarified Buchanan-Tullock idealization, the person may himself be identified, but there is such uncertainty about the effects of rules on separate individual positions that particular interests cannot be related to particular rules. In either case, the contractual process will tend to exclude from consideration decision rules that explicitly deny some persons or groups *ex ante* access to political process. In the Rawlsian logic, the contractor, not knowing whether he will find himself red, white, green, or black, is unlikely to agree on any rule that does not assign equal weights, *ex ante*, to persons from all groups. In the Buchanan-Tullock logic, the red, white, green, or black person will not agree to assign choices over policies in set X to a rule that fails to incorporate *ex ante* equal weighting, since he cannot know how choices within the set will impact on his own well-being.

Majority rule satisfies the criterion of *ex ante* political equality provided that the voting franchise is co-extensive with membership in the polity. As previously noted, however, other alternatives also meet this criterion. With all decision rules other than unanimity, however, *ex post* political equality is violated. The interests and values of those whose choices dominate the outcome are ultimately accorded more weight than those whose choices are ignored. If A is selected by a majority vote of 60 per cent, those in the coalition who supported A secure more than those in the 40 per cent minority who supported B.

If, however, *ex ante* equality is ensured through the open franchise, and if political decisions are effectively decentralized over both issues and time, *ex post* differential weights on particular outcomes may be no cause for concern. Over a whole pattern or sequence of political choices (plays in the ongoing game), the ensured *ex ante* equality may map into some proximate *ex post* equality of weights.

IV. CHANGES IN LAW

Discussion in the preceding section summarizes the argument developed in *The Calculus of Consent* (1962), from almost a quarter-century's hindsight and with an attempted focus on the question addressed in this chapter. Now, as then, democracy defined as *ex ante* political equality can be contractually derived, whereas democracy, defined as majority rule, passes muster only under a restricted set of circumstances and is in no sense uniquely related to contractual agreement. As we move to the constitutional stage, where the relevant set of choices are those relating to changes in the law, in the rules that constrain both private and public activity, there is *no* place for majority rule or, indeed, for any rule short of unanimity.

It is at this stage, and only at this stage, that the ultimate contract takes place, either in conceptualization or in actuality. It is here that the basic exchange or cooperative paradigm for politics takes on dramatically different implications from those generated by the truth-judgement or the zero-sum paradigm. If politics in the large, defined to encompass the whole structure of governance, is modelled as the cooperative effort of *individuals* to further or advance *their own* interests and values, which only they, as individuals, know, it is evident that *all* persons must be brought into agreement.

The simple analogy with market exchange illustrates the point. It would seem obvious that both parties to an exchange of apples and oranges must agree on the terms of trade if the reallocation of endowments generated by trade is to qualify as value enhancing for both parties. An enforced 'exchange', whether by a third party or by only one of the two traders, cannot satisfy the individualistic value-enhancing criterion.

The complex exchange that describes a change in the constitution (in the rules) is not different in this fundamental respect from a simple exchange between two traders. A change in the rules (the law) that is applicable to all members of the polity can be judged as value enhancing only on the expressed agreement among all participants. There is no contractually derivable justification or legitimization for basic structural rules of governance that cannot meet the restricted consensus test. Any justification or legitimization of rules changes that fails the unanimity test must call upon non-contractarian criteria of evaluation, which must be *non-individualistic* in origin, or at least, non-individualistic in any universalizable sense.

V. FROM THE ABSTRACT TO THE REAL

As noted, the analysis to this point is developed with reference to the highly abstract three-stage classification of politics. In this setting the relationships between contractarianism and democracy can be presented in relatively straightforward fashion. The observed world of politics, however, embodies a confused and confusing mixture of the three stages, with law enforcement, legislation, and law-making undertaken by almost all political agents. Despite the confusion, attempts are made to assign meaningful descriptive attributes such as 'democratic' or 'non-democratic' to political arrangements as they are rather than to the idealized models which do not, have not, and possibly could not exist. In this intensely practical realm of discourse, the relationships cannot be nearly so sharply traced.

Nonetheless, we can isolate and identify critical attributes of observed political process that must be present if any contractarian legitimization is to be advanced. The most important requirement is that law exist, in a meaningful sense of the term. That is to say, both the private and the public activities of individuals must be limited by *constitutional constraints*. State or collective power to operate without limits, *regardless of the particular decision rule*, could never find contractarian justification. I have referred elsewhere to the 'electoral fallacy', which has been the source of major misunderstanding, the notion that, so long as 'democratic' decision rules are guaranteed, anything goes. Even here, however, there would have to be constitutional prohibitions against changing such rules.

Within the constitutionally or legally authorized exercise of governmental or state power, political arrangments must be characterized by political equality of all those who are included in the polity's membership, at least in some ultimate *ex ante* sense. This requirement need not, as noted earlier, guarantee that all persons carry equal weight in a defined collective choice. Nor does the requirement guarantee against overt coercion of some persons or group by the collectivity. What is required here is that all persons possess equal access to political influence over a whole pattern or sequence of collective choices. In practical terms, this means that the franchise be open to all, that political agents be rotated on some regular basis, and that gross bundling of separate collective choices be avoided.

Finally, there must exist an observed and honoured distinction between collective actions carried out within the allowed constitutional constraints, within the law, and collective or group actions that involve changes in the law itself. A polity in which neither practising politicians nor political-legal scholars distinguish between legislation and law cannot be justified on contractarian grounds. If the distinction here is made, and widely acknowledged, the effective decision rule for changing the basic law must be observed to be more inclusive than the rule for making collective decisions within the law. The abstract contractarian logic need not be pushed to its extreme here, which would require that constitutional changes be reached only through unanimous agreement.

To summarize, a political-legal order can broadly be classified as 'contractarian' if the following attributes are observed to be present:

(1) Both private and public agents are constrained in their activity by the law, by operative constitutional limits.

(2) Within the law, all members of the polity have equal access to decision-making structures, and all have equal weights in the determination of collective decisions in the appropriately defined *ex ante* sense.

(3) There is a recognized distinction between collective action within the law and action taken to change the law, with the decision rule for the latter being necessarily more inclusive than the former.

VI. LIMITED AND UNLIMITED CONTRACTARIAN APPLICATION

Note that the criteria for classification listed above do *not* include reference to the history of how existing rules might have emerged. To say that a political-legal order that satisfies the listed criteria qualifies as 'contractarian' is to say something about the *operation* of that order. And there is moral-ethical content in such a statement. But confusion has emerged through a failure to recognize the severely limited scope of such contractarian justification. To say that, given the rules that exist (which must include the distribution of endowments among persons who operate, privately and collectively, within the rules), an observed political-legal order, in its operation, may be conceptually 'explained-interpreted-justified-legitimized' by a contractarian-exchange model of interaction, is to say nothing whatsoever about the moral-ethical aspects of the distribution of the nominally claimed endowments of persons in some conceptualized 'pre-operative' stage of politics.

A simple analogy with market exchange may again be helpful here. Suppose that there are two potential traders, each one of whom has an endowment of apples and oranges. Mr A has, before trade, ninety-three apples and forty-three oranges. Mr B has, before trade, two apples and four oranges. After trade, Mr A has ninety apples and forty-four oranges; Mr B has five apples and three oranges. The limits of the ethical-moral jutification of free and non-fraudulent exchange is contained in the argument that *both* parties *gain* in the trading operation. There is no implication that the distribution of endowments, either before or after trade, is justified or made legitimate by the prospects for trade or by its reality.

To extend the contractarian criteria beyond the limited application to the operation of existing political-legal rules, to derive the implied contractarian features of the structure itself, is the task that John Rawls set for himself. There is no call for my own judgement here concerning an evaluation of his success or failure. In my own efforts I have, perhaps not always consistently, been content with the more limited application. But my sympathy with and affinity for Rawls' effort has been, I hope, evident. At base, we share, along with fellow contractarians of all stripes, an unwillingness normatively to evaluate politics with non-individualistic standards or positively to interpret politics exclusively as the clash of conflicting interests.

NOTE

1. Material in this chapter was initially presented at a Liberty Fund Conference on 'Individual Liberty and Democratic Order' in Crystal City, Virginia, in June 1984.

23 Constitutional Democracy, Individual Liberty, and Political Equality[1]

I. INTRODUCTION

In this country 'democracy' is a positively charged emotive term. It is employed in putative description of political regimes that vary widely in structure, purpose, and operation. Few regimes are to be found that openly claim status as 'non-democratic', and even those regimes that avoid total distortion of language often promise movement towards 'democratic' procedures. From observed usage alone, therefore, the term seems to be largely empty of discriminatory content. Any meaningful discussion of alternative political structures must commence with an examination and evaluation of fundamental normative precepts of political philosophy. It is necessary to get behind the emotive connotation of 'democracy' and to look at the philosophical origins of the whole conception.

I shall suggest that 'democracy' emerges as a uniquely desired political ordering of interaction only in a particular set of circumstances. This set requires acceptance of specific philosophical presuppositions along with an understanding of the workings of the institutions of politics, broadly defined. So understood, the term 'constitutional' *must* be prefixed to the term 'democracy' if the latter is to be sustainable in an internally consistent normative argument. Stated in somewhat more concrete detail, my argument is that 'democracy' assumes evaluative significance only under the presupposition that individual liberty is, itself, of value, and, further, that effective political equality, which is the operative principle of democracy, can be meaningfully secured only if the range and scope for collective political action are constrained or limited by constitutional boundaries. As indicated, there are two separate elements in my argument: the first may be classified to be broadly philosophical in nature; the second is intensely practical, and draws on much of the modern research in public choice and related areas of inquiry.

In section II, I discuss the philosophical or epistemological presuppositions without which 'democracy' or 'democratic procedures' would find no normative foundations. In sections III and IV, and accepting the initial presupposition, I discuss the relationship between the normative principle of political equality and the structure of political organization. In sections V and VI, I discuss problems and implications of constitutional design, especially as this topic is informed by modern public choice theory. In section VII, I treat the issue of limits to the range of political decisions or actions, and I evaluate the state of modern discussion. Finally, in section VIII, I offer summary conclusions.[2]

II. INDIVIDUAL PERSONS AS SOURCES OF VALUE

The first and most critical presupposition that provides a foundation for any genuine democratic theory is that which locates sources of value exclusively in individuals. If there exist, or if there are presumed to exist, non-individualistic sources of value, democratic political procedures become at best one set of possible instruments for discovering such independent values, a set that may not be any more efficient than several other alternatives. Much of the so-called 'political theory', through the centuries, has been developed in such a non-individualistic tradition. In this tradition, politics, broadly and inclusively defined, involves a search for 'truth', and the activity of politics, in its modern conceptualization, becomes analogous to that of science, an activity that is acknowledged to be a discovery process.[3]

It should be evident that democratic procedures, which involve at least some counting of heads, some use of individually expressed preferences over alternatives, are not directly related to the search for some independently existing and abstract objective of 'politics', an objective that is presumed omnipresent in the whole of the non-individualistic tradition in political theorizing. In some settings, a counting of heads, along with a discussion among ordinary persons, may be judged to be instrumentally superior to the delegation of authority to a single expert or to a group of experts. In other settings, however, the reverse pattern of decision authority may well be deemed more desirable in the sense of its ability to generate efficient patterns of results. The use of the judge and the jury in criminal law cases illustrates this point well. The guilt or innocence of an accused must be determined by some institutional process. In some legal structures, the use of a multi-person jury, operating within well-defined voting rules, may be more efficacious in yielding 'correct' results over a sequence. In other legal structures, the power of decision is lodged in a single agent, a judge, who is considered to be more capable of rendering 'correct' verdicts. There is no *a priori* basis for a claim that either one of these two institutional means of determining guilt or innocence is instrumentally superior to the other.

By extension of this argument, it should be clear that if the existence of some independent political objective, whether this be called 'truth' or 'the common good', is implicitly postulated, and if politics is intellectually modelled as the search for this objective, then ordinary electoral process that are widely interpreted to describe 'democracy' need not be judged to be either necessary or desirable. Effective political decision-making authority may be lodged in a committee of experts, a set of philosopher-kings, a single party's ruling clique, a military junta, or in a single monarch, any one of which structures may be held better able to attain 'that which is good for all members of the community' than ordinary electoral processes with inclusive voting franchise. In this way the institutional form or structure of governance is divorced from process, and 'democracy' can be reintroduced, not as process at all but as an emotively charged term designed putatively to distinguish between alternative end-objects for politics. Hence, a ruling committee can lay claim to 'democracy' if it acts 'for the good sought by the people', as opposed to acting 'for the interests of the ruling class', with the proviso, of course, that the definition of what is 'good for the people' is made by the ruling committee.

The authoritarian-totalitarian regimes that cloak their activities in the rhetoric of 'democracy' are a natural outgrowth of the non-individualistic tradition of a political theory that has been advanced at least since the ancient Greeks. My argument stems from the conviction that there is no generalizable *instrumental* defence of democratic political procedures. A normative case in support of electoral process, where individual preferences are counted, must be non-instrumental. That which is sought for in politics is not and cannot be that which exists independently of the values of the individuals who make up the political community. The object or aim of politics is the furtherance or achievement of the separate and several objects of the individuals who participate variously in the collective enterprise. There is and can be no other object if we are to develop a general normative defence of democratic governance, understood in the process sense of the term.

If the suggested presupposition is accepted—that is, if individuals are presumed to be the only ultimate source of evaluation—the argument for electoral processes as means through which values (preferences, interests) may be expressed becomes straightforwrd. Here the question is not one of how to find or to discover 'truth' through politics; it is not one of determining what is the 'best' one from among several political options; it is not the quest for 'the common good'. Here the question is, instead, one of using the institution of politics, or governance, as means through which separate persons, as members of an organized political community, may jointly achieve their individually desired purposes. In this individualistic and contractarian model for politics, that which emerges from the interaction process is, quite simply, that which emerges. It is inappropriate to classify any one outcome or end-state as 'better than' another. There is no supra-individual scalar that can be introduced as a criterion for any such ranking.

In this model of politics, any method of decision making that does *not* incorporate the expressed preferences of all persons in the polity, at least in some ultimate sense, must involve overt discrimination. Those who participate in the collective or group decision process have the opportunity to express *their own evaluations* of the alternatives that are confronted. Those who are not allowed to participate have no such opportunity; their preferences and interests must go unrepresented. Note that the operation of non-electoral processes of decision is categorically different in this model and in the truth-discovery model previously discussed. The activity of a ruling committee or junta, conceived as a search for an independently existing objective, may find instrumental defence. The same activity, conceived as the expression and subsequent imposition of the values of the self-chosen elite, finds no comparable normative support.

The individualist-contractarian model of politics, for the reasons noted, cannot incorporate discriminatory limits on participation, regardless of the relative size of the decision-making group. The normative argument advanced above may seem acceptable in application to a small committee or junta, but it may, initially, seem to be attenuated in application to large number constituencies. Suppose, for example, that democratic electoral procedures are observed to operate but that only one-half (say, males) of the adult members of the polity are franchised. In the truth- or goodness-discovery model of politics, this system may be expected to yield results that are approximately identical to those that would be generated under inclusive franchise. Hence, there would be little to choose between inclusive and discriminatory franchise. By contrast, in the individualistic-contractarian model the values of those persons who remain disenfranchised cannot be reflected in the results from the very fact of non-participation.

The normative argument for democratic electoral processes, as a means of allowing individuals to express their own values, the only values that exist, becomes at the same time an argument for an inclusive franchise, or, more generally, for individual political equality.

III. POLITICAL EQUALITY AND THE POTENTIAL FOR CONFLICT AMONG INDIVIDUAL VALUES

With the presupposition that individuals are the only sources of value, the normative argument for universal adult franchise and for electoral process in which all persons participate seems to emerge. The extension and application of this argument to the institutions of politics and governance remain to be examined. Serious errors have been made in too-hasty extensions of the argument, as I shall demonstrate in the following discussion.

If there are no non-individualistic sources of value, 'out there', waiting to be discovered in the truth or goodness discovery enterprise of politics, we should expect that individuals, as separate conscious beings, will have differing values, interests, and preferences, at least within wide limits. Politics, inclusively defined, involves the whole set of activities in which separate persons participate as a collective body or organization. That is to say, politics and governance involve the determination of rules, institutional structure, and particular outcomes that are to be applied to all persons in the collective. There is, by definition, a single political choice among relevant alternatives that are confronted. In the terminology of modern economics, politics, by definition, involves 'publicness', whether 'public good' or 'public bad'.

The singularity and commonality of political decision is extremely important and makes it necessary to distinguish effective political equality from nominal political equality. Because of the possible conflict among separate individual interests and values, any political decision must override at least some of those who participate in the process. Nominal political equality only ensures that all persons may participate equally in the ultimate choices to be made. This point is perhaps best illustrated in a setting where all persons vote in a referendum on a single issue, with the collective outcome to be settled by simple majority rule. All persons equally express their preferences as between two outcomes presented; but those who are out-voted find that their own desired outcome is not selected. They must acquiesce in a result that runs counter to their own interests or values. Clearly, with respect to the particular choice examined, those whose interests are submerged gain little or nothing from their participation in the electoral procedure.

Here it is necessary to introduce a second and complementary philosophical presupposition, and one that is a direct implication of the first. If individuals are the only sources of value, it follows by implication, if not directly, that the satisfaction of individual values carries positive normative weight. That is to say, a situation in which individual preferences are met becomes normatively superior to a situation in which preferences are overruled, other things equal. From this straightforward statement, implications for political organization may be drawn.

Consider the simple referendum example, one in which the preferences of a majority for alternative A are satisfied, while the preferences of a minority for alternative B are overruled. Clearly such a result is normatively inferior to one in which alternative A could be chosen for members of the majority and alternative B could be chosen for members of the minority, if, indeed, such a result should be structurally-institutionally possible. The normative principle that individual values should be allowed to find expression in results necessarily has implications for the design of political institutions.

Conflicts among separate individual values should be reduced or eliminated to the maximum extent that is possible. And, since conflicts of interests depend in part on the structure within which interaction takes place, there are direct implications for structural design.

Return to the referendum example and suppose that the objects for choice are: A, which is a holiday in June, and B, which is a holiday in August. As the example suggests, if this pairwise comparison is treated as a mutually exclusive choice between two 'public goods', conflict necessarily arises. But as the illustration also suggests, conflict need not be present unless there is some non-reducible 'publicness' involved. That is to say, A and B, as defined, need not be mutually exclusive alternatives for the whole membership of the polity. Unless there are compelling reasons for the requirement that all persons take the same holiday, conflicts among individual values may be eliminated by the elementary expedient of allowing those who wish to take the holiday in June and those others who so desire to take the holiday in August. This solution guarantees effective equality in the satisfaction of individual preferences. It clearly goes well beyond the minimal equality that participation in the voting process ensures. To the extent that the potential for conflict among individual values and preferences can be reduced by structural design, there will be less need to be concerned about the requirement that individuals, whose interests are overruled in collective decisions, must voluntarily acquiesce so long as they possess rights of participation.

IV. DEMOCRACY WITHIN LIMITS: THE LOGIC OF CONSTITUTIONAL CONSTRAINTS

The elevation of individual values to a central normative significance in any comprehensive political theory has, therefore, direct implications for the institutional structure of human interaction. If conflict among separate interests is a variable, alternative structures of interaction may be ordered in a meaningful fashion. 'Democracy', defined as a process that allows equal expression of separate individual values in choices that are *necessarily* mutually exclusive and that necessarily generate results applicable to all members of the polity, may be severely limited in scope and range. Such limitation is a mark of the political 'success' of the social interaction process, inclusively considered, rather than the opposite. Indeed, the perversity of much modern discussion is well illustrated by the claim that the extension of 'democracy' to previously non-politicized areas of interaction is somehow praiseworthy, when, of course, such extension is a signal that the potential for interpersonal and inter-group conflict is enhanced rather than reduced.

The normative argument for democratic decision procedures of decision-making would be substantially weakened, if not totally eliminated, if *all* forms of social interaction should be either actually or potentially considered to fall within the range of political choice. If all activities should be politicized, individuals would of course find some normative value in guaranteed rights of equal participation in the choice process—that is, in electoral institutions—but there would also be the certainty that individual interests would be thwarted in many separate areas of activity. An evaluative comparison between a procedural democracy that is literally unlimited in this sense, and other governmental forms that explicitly limit the range of politicization, even if the choices made within that range are non-democratic, may well cut in favour of the second alternative. The normative case for democratic procedures emerges strongly only if it is understood that the range over which political-collective decisions are to be made is appropriately constrained. The attachment of the word 'constitutional' as a prefix to 'democracy', with the implied meaning that this carries if properly interpreted, immeasurably strengthens the normative case. This conclusion follows even if we are willing to make the assumption that genuinely unlimited politicization could indeed remain procedurally democratic, rather than shift inexorably towards totalitarian reality cloaked in democratic rhetoric.

It is of course no accident that constitutional democracy, as an observed governmental form, emerged in the post-Enlightenment period, and that it finds intellectual support in the eighteenth-century discovery of the spontaneous coordination properties of the market economy. Simply stated, the principle of spontaneous coordination suggests that the economy operates so as to allow separate individual interests to be reconciled peacefully without any need for political determination of the allocation of resources, the choices of products, and the distribution of goods. The range of necessary political decisions on economic matters is dramatically reduced in a polity that gives a predominant place to a market or enterprise economy.

The economy will not of course organize itself in total independence of the political-legal order. There is a necessary political role involved in enforcing individuals rights and contracts and in producing those goods and services that are inherently public or collective in nature, including the legal system itself. The role of politics in this severely limited sense was well recognized by the classical economists who discovered and promulgated the ordering principle of the market economy.

There exist, however, no 'natural' barriers that will emerge to ensure that politics, as it actually operates, will stay within the limits defined by any 'public goods' requirements. Indeed, quite the opposite seems to characterize political reality. There seems to arise a 'natural' proclivity for individuals, groups, and the political entrepreneurs representing them, to extend the range and scope of collective-political action beyond any conceivable publicness boundaries, if publicness is defined in any economically meaningful sense. (Any politicization of an activity converts what might have been private into a public activity. Hence, politics always involves publicness, artifically defined.) The arms, agencies, and authority of the state will be utilized to secure, or in attempts to secure, differential gains for members of particular coalitions, with little or no regard for normatively appropriate boundaries on governmental action.

Such overextension can be prevented only if the range and scope for politics, for collective, governmental, or state activity is subjected to enforcible constitutional constraints. As I have already suggested, there seems to be relatively little normative support for democratic electoral procedures as such, until and unless some limits are placed on the range of activities over which politics may operate.

V. DEFINING THE LIMITS: THE PROBLEM OF CONSTITUTIONAL DESIGN

The general principle that politics should be limited by constitutional rules may be readily accepted, and for the reasons discussed in section IV above. The translation of this principle into political practice is quite a different matter. There are no technologically sharp dividing lines between those activities that involve public goods and those possible activities that can, with proper institutional design, be left to non-political interaction processes, such as the market. As I have indicated earlier, the fundamental role for politics, inclusively defined, is that of providing the legal framework within which individuals can go about their ordinary business of seeking to further the values they choose to seek, without overt conflict. The enforcement of rights and contracts is a necessary task for government in any liberal regime. The argument extends quite normally to the guarantee of internal and external order.

Beyond such minimal-state or protective-state limits, however, there exists a broad area for potential political activity that may or may not be admissible with appropriately defined constitutional constraints. Should or should not there be an explicit role for collective action in setting the value of the monetary unit? In enforcing and ensuring that the economy is effectively competitive? In regulating natural monopolies? In preserving environmental amenities? In protecting health and safety? In promoting equality of opportunity, especially through the support of education? In alleviating poverty?

It is precisely in such areas as these that the problem of constitutional design is squarely met. There may be consensus on the legitimacy of governmental action in the maintenance of order (the protective state) and on the illegitimacy of government action in the regulation and control of purely private behaviour, such as the individual's choice of his location, occupation, and consumption bundle. At the same time, there may arise intense dispute about the range for the potential governmental role over the whole set of in-between activities, such as those listed.

Persons who may broadly be classified as 'social democrats' will want governments to remain free of any constitutional constraints on the activities falling within this set. By comparison, persons who may be broadly classified as 'liberal', in the European sense, or as 'libertarian', in the modern American usage, will want governments to be constitutionally restricted over at least some subset of the activities noted.

I shall neither criticize nor defend a particular dividing line between those activities that may be appropriately politicized and those that should be left free from politics. I do want to suggest, however, that quite apart from fundamental ideological persuasion, the degree to which any person will, ideally, seek to limit the activity of government by constitutional constraints depend on the *predictive model of politics* that informs his analysis.

VI. THE IMPLICATION OF MODERN PUBLIC CHOICE THEORY FOR CONSTITUTIONAL DESIGN

The theory of public choice becomes directly relevant for my discussion at this point. This theory provides at least the elements of a predictive model, or models, of how democratic electoral politics works in reality. Public choice examines the behaviour of persons as they take on varying roles as 'public choosers', as actual or potential voters, as organizers or members of pressure groups, as party leaders, as aspiring or elected politicians, as bureaucrats. The theory allows us to make some predictions about patterns of outcomes that may be generated under varying sets of institutional rules through which final collective-political decisions are reached.

There are direct normative implications of public choice theory for the issues of constitutional design previously discussed. Those who have previously accepted, if often unconsciusly, a naïvely romantic model of political activity, and who may, on that account, have remained largely unconcerned about effective constitutional constraints on governments, can scarcely do so once the full impact of modern public choice theory is acknowledged. In a very real sense, public choice theory offers a 'theory of governmental-political failure' that is on all fours with the 'theory of market failure' that emerged from the theoretical welfare economics of the 1950s. By comparison with the conventional wisdom of the 1960s, there can no longer be a *prima facie* case for political-governmental intrusion into the whole range of in-between activities that fail to be handled ideally by the operation of the nonpoliticized market. The whole question of limits here must be addressed pragmatically, in part on a case-by-case basis and in part through a long-term and reflective consideration of the costs and benefits that are predicted under alternative regimes of democratic procedures.

VII. CONSTITUTIONAL GUARANTEES OF DEMOCRATIC PROCEDURES AND OF THE POLITICAL LIMITS

Those persons who object to the explicit introduction of or an extension of constitutional limits over the range and scope of political activity often at the same time strongly support constitutional guarantees of democratic decision-making procedures as such. In the literal sense, therefore, these persons are also 'constitutionalists', and they would acknowledge the necessity of affixing the word 'constitutional' to 'democracy'. Without effective guarantees of electoral processes, a majority coalition, once in office, could, of course, simply abolish all elections and establish itself in permanent authority. In this context, those persons who most strongly oppose constitutional constraints on the activities of governments accept the necessity of constitutional constraints on the procedures of politics. There are few who claim to adhere to democratic values, however these values may be described, who are not at the same time constitutionalists of one sort or another. There is then no inherent or internal inconsistency in the position that urges the imposition of constraints on the range of activities open to political authority. Just as a majority coalition may, unless it is restricted, abolish electoral feedbacks that ensure the potential for rotation in office, so may an effectively operating political coalition seek to extend its authority beyond any plausibly acceptable boundaries described by the publicness notion.

Even when the basic analysis here is accepted, however, and even when the operating flaws in both non-political and political interactions are understood, there will remain the prospect for disagreement over constitutional design. Only those who might yet retain a romantically naïve faith in the progress of 'social science' could expect convergence of opinion on the proper range of governmental action. The argument that has persisted for centuries is not likely to be resolved in any emergence of 'scientific consensus'. At its best, scientific analysis can reduce the level of intellectual conflict.

Nonetheless, spokesmen for modern public choice theory can, I think, legitimately claim that the 'state of the debate' has been considerably advanced over the course of the post-middle decades of this century. To the extent that the issues are discussed as issues of constitutional design rather than issues of policy choice with little or no regard to the rules and institutions within which choices are made, the dialogue has taken a major leap forwards, by almost any criteria. To discuss policy alternatives or options independently of processes in which policy choices take place almost necessarily involves reversion to or maintenance of the notion that non-individualistic sources of value and valuation exist, whether these be expressed as the efficiency criteria of the economists or as the common-good vector of the philosophers. Quite apart from the introduction of an external value scale, however, any discussion of policy choices independently of rules must embody the romantic conception that individual decision-makers, in their roles as 'public choosers', will totally disregard the incentives offered by the rules structure and that they will somehow be guided only by whatever scalar ordering that exists to inform their behaviour.

By comparison and by contrast, consider the level and content of the normative argument among constitutionalists who continue to disagree about the appropriate limits on state or political action. The argument here is based on the presupposition that there exist no non-individualistic values, and also that individuals will respond to the incentives that they confront. The argument further incorporates the modern analysis of how differing rules and institutions of public choice affect the incentives for persons who participate.

The normative argument then reduces to one that involves an ultimate choice among alternative structures of rules (to constitutional choice) rules that will in turn serve to limit collective action. As I noted earlier, we need not expect consensus, even among those who work within the given presuppositions and who are informed by essentially the same analysis. Productive dialogue can proceed, however, unencumbered by the excesses of romantic folly that have wrought such havoc in the intellectualized discussions of 'democracy' over the ages.

Such a constructive dialogue must embody some attempts to derive plausibly acceptable criteria for constitutional choices. If alternative sets of rules are the ultimate objects of choice, how are these rules to be ordered? What is the scalar here? Or, even at one stage further back in the discourse, what principles are to guide the construction of an ordering of alternative sets of rules? It is, I think, an indication of intellectual progress when we can point to modern efforts to examine precisely these issues.[4]

VIII. DEMOCRACY IN CONSTITUTIONAL PERSPECTIVE

In summation of my argument in this paper, let me suggest that 'democracy' assumes normative meaning only in a constitutional perspective. I suggest further that those who limit meaningful usage of the term to those political regimes that embody electoral processes in which individuals participate as ultimate public choosers, must implicitly if not explicitly adopt such a perspective. Surely it would be difficult to locate a 'non-constitutional democrat', a person who does indeed value the rights of persons to participate in collective action but who, at the same time, does not seek to limit the range of political behaviour, even to the extent of incorporating guarantees that rights to participate are maintained.

The philosophical presuppositions that are implicit in any normative argument for constitutional democracy are by no means universally shared, even by persons in effectively democratic regimes, and even by those scholars whose task it is to clarify and to explain the intellectual underpinnings of social reality. There is widespread intellectual confusion, even at the level of academic 'political theory' (or perhaps especially at this level). However, until and unless we can unpack and sort out the intellectual foundations, there is relatively little to be gained in engaging in debates at the stage of choice among policy alternatives.

As I have noted, progress has been and is being made in the academic-intellectual-philosophical discussion. 'Constitutional democracy' is now a meaningful term with positive normative weight for more people than was the case in the middle years of this century. With time, and with luck, those of us who profess to be the academic-intellectual defenders of constitutional democracy, as the uniquely preferred regime of political-social-economic order, may find that our ivory tower conceptions can measure up, in broad terms, to the inchoate sentiments of ordinary persons everywhere, sentiments that place liberty from political oppression very high on any value scale.

NOTES

1. This material was initially published in *Jahrbuch für Neue Politische Ökonomie*, Band 4, pp. 35–47 (Tubingen: J. C. B. Mohr, Paul Siebeck, 1985), ed. E. Boettcher. I acknowledge permission to reprint the material here.

2. I have discussed the central subject matter of this chapter in several prior published works, although not, of course, in precisely the manner developed here. For a more general understanding of my position, I suggest the following works be consulted: James M. Buchanan and Gordon Tullock, *The Calculus of Consent* (Ann Arbor: University of Michigan Press, 1962); James M. Buchanan, *The Limits of Liberty* (Chicago: University of Chicago Press, 1975); German translation *Grenzen der Freiheit*, J. C. B. Mohr, 1984); James M. Buchanan, *Freedom in Constitutional Contract* (College Station: Texas A & M University Press, 1978); Geoffrey Brennan and James Buchanan, *The*

Reason of Rules (Cambridge University Press, forthcoming).

Also, see *Constitutional Economics: Containing the Economic Powers of Government*, ed. Richard McKenzie (Lexington: Lexington Books, 1984). This volume of conference papers is directly relevant to the subject matter of this chapter.

3. *See* Ch. 5 above.
4. For the first question, *see* Buchanan and Tullock, *The Calculus of Consent, op. cit.*, and subsequent discussion. Also, for a modern treatment, *see* Brennan and Buchanan, *The Reason of Rules, op. cit.*

For the second question, *see* John Rawls, *A Theory of Justice* (Cambridge, Mass. Harvard University Press, 1971), along with the vast literature that this seminal book has spawned.

24 Political Economy and Social Philosophy[1]

I. INTRODUCTION

Scientific economics was born as a by-product of social philosophy. Adam Smith found it necessary to explain how markets work in order to carry his argument for the dismantling of the mercantilist regulatory apparatus. Some of Smith's followers in classical political economy overextended his teaching and treated their subject as an inflexible 'natural' science. Whereas the mercantilists had failed to understand how free markets generate order, the extremists among the classical economists failed to understand that the institutions of markets were not themselves immutable. However, the socialist impetus of the late nineteenth and twentieth centuries was in part provided by a false rather than a true comparison of market institutions and practicable political alternatives. Only in the last part of this century did 'political economy' emerge into its current status as a continuing and necessary element in the philosophical evaluation and comparison of *attainable* institutional structures. Modern public choice theory provided insights into the working of politics much as Adam Smith offered initial insights into the working of markets. We now know that neither market nor political institutions match up to the performance of their conceptually idealized models, a simple truth of course, but one that social scientists and philosophers have so often failed to recognize.

The ultimate question in social philosophy remains that of how we should organize ourselves, one with another, so as to secure peace, freedom, and prosperity? To so much as put this question presupposes that we can in fact modify the structure within which our mutual interdependence takes form. The question itself denies by implication the validity of the propostion that we are locked into an inevitable process of historical necessity, as well as the one that suggests that we and our institutions are products of a biological and cultural evolution that we disturb only at our peril. The social philosopher has a moral obligation to believe that social reform is possible and that discussion can be helpful both in tempering the romantic yearnings for perfectibility and in suggesting avenues for practical constructive change.

261

In this paper I shall attempt to place modern political economy in what I consider to be its appropriate role in such an ongoing discussion. I shall first identify ideas that must be discarded if such a role is ever to be attained. In this respect I distinguish three related strands: the heritage of classical utilitarianism, the ubiquitous and pervasive engineering urge, and the elitist mentality. Scourged of these demons, the potential contributions of modern political economy to the ongoing normative discussion of the ultimate question can be sketched.

II. THE UTILITARIAN CALCULUS

It is unfortunate that Benthamite utilitarianism emerged to obfuscate the central ideas of classical political economy before these ideas had permeated into the general public consciousness. The calculus of pleasure and pain came to be attached to the evaluation of the market process, with the predicted result that the fundamental philosophical argument for markets was almost lost from mind and for over a century. Markets are basically *political* institutions, and they serve to allow persons to interact voluntarily one with another without the detailed supervision of the state. Markets should never have been evaluated primarily and instrumentally for their ability, as institutions, to maximize pleasure over pain, or indeed to maximize anything else that is interpersonally comparable.

Modern neoclassical economics did, of course, finally escape from the philosophical straightjacket imposed by the Benthamite utilitarian calculus. Unfortunately, however, it retained the maximization paradigm as a central element in models of individual behaviour, a retention that seemed to created a methodological void between individual 'economizing' and social or political 'economizing'. There seemed nothing that the economists could legitimately say about the organization of social interdependence. Without a utilitarian value scale, the notion of efficiency in resource use seemed empty of normative content.

Pareto was rediscovered to have offered what seemed to be a way out of the dilemma, and theoretical welfare economics emerged, an economics that seemed to incorporate normative content within an absolutely minimal set of ethical presuppositions. Application of the Pareto criterion for the classification of both social states and shifts in these states did not require interpersonal comparisons of utilities or the conversion of individuals utilities into some unique social dimension. Individuals might be modelled as maximizing their own utilities (or anything else), but so long as the Pareto criterion remains satisfied, a state could be judged Pareto-optimal or Pareto-efficient. So long as the criterion applied to a move or shift was met, such a move could be classified as Pareto-superior.

Economists remained unsatisfied with the Pareto construction, however, and for at least two distinct reasons, both of which, in some sense, relate to the utilitarian heritage of the whole discipline of economics. With no social value standard, there is no social maximand. Alternative structural arrangements cannot be arrayed on some better-to-worse scalar. Furthermore, an arrangement meeting the Pareto criterion does so because of the particular configuration of the individually claimed endowments that describe such an arrangement. It follows that there exists a subinfinity of positions or sets of arrangements that meet the simple Pareto test. Relative to the robust utilitarian norm, the Pareto criterion allowed the economist to say very little. Importantly, the Pareto construction closed off any potentiality of evaluating distributions of individual endowments or claims. Given any distribution, or, more generally, any definition of individuals, the Pareto norm introduces some normative content into the economist's examination of institutions, even if this content remains severely limited. But, as among differing distributions, the norm remains silent. As I shall summarize in section III below, economists moved quickly, and sometimes confusedly, to remedy this presumed deficiency in the Paretian normative apparatus.

A second and distinctly different problem with the Pareto norm also finds its origins in the utilitarian heritage. Utilitarianism fosters a delusion of quantitative measurability that did not disappear with the demise of interpersonal comparability. Even if it is acknowledged that Mr A's 'utility' is not comparable with Mr B's 'utility', analysis proceeded as if Mr A's 'utility' is itself an objectively measurable and quantifiable magnitude. After all, 'utility' is defined as 'that which a maximizer maximizes', and the maximization paradigm implies a quantifiable maximand. The difficulties of any crude or simplistic measurement of individual utilities were of course recognized, but the basic dimensionality issue remained obscured. Economists who were reluctant to measure individual utilities directly were, nonetheless, willing to introduce cardinally measurable arguments into individual utility functions. Once this step is taken, the application of the Pareto norm can be made without relation to observed individual evaluation, which, methodologically, becomes equivalent to a reintroduction of the apparently discarded utilitarian calculus.

The point here is perhaps sufficiently subtle to warrant simple illustration. Consider a community with two persons, A and B, along with an external observer economist. there are two producible commodities, X and Y, and two inputs, those from A and those from B, designated as *a* and *b*. The quantities of commodities may be changed by variations in inputs supplied. The utility functions of A and B contain, at most, four arguments, X, Y, *a* and *b*. If the economist signs the arguments, with X and Y signed positive, *a* signed negatively for A, and *b* signed negatively for B, arrangements may be arrayed in accordance with the Pareto norm. There may be an arrangement that enables *both* A and B to secure more X *and* more Y while supplying less *a* and less *b* than that arrangement observed to be in existence. The economist seems to be able to say that a shift from the existing arrangement to the alternative one is a Pareto improvement.

The quasi-utilitarian step is that which allows the economist first to identify and then to sign the arguments in individual utility functions. If this step can be taken, the economist must presume to know something about individual utilities, and it seems but a small step from this to the presumption that he knows all. The indirect quantification of individual value scales through the specification of arguments in utility functions was encouraged, and its methodological status obscured, by the mathematization of economics, which was itself fostered by the maximization paradigm.

It seemed possible at the apogee of theoretical welfare economics at mid-century to lay down objectively meaningful conditions that must be met if an allocation is to satisfy the Pareto norm of optimality or efficiency. From this perspective it seemed to be possible for the economist observer to make diagnoses of market failures and to suggest specific changes that might be Pareto superior. As the illustration above suggests, however, all is not so simple. What if the identification and the signing of the arguments in individual utility functions are all wrong? What if Mr A does not positively value X, and, indeed, what if X is a 'bad' rather than a 'good' in his utility function? Suppose that Mr B enjoys working; hence *b* is a 'good' rather than a 'bad', as postulated in the exercise. Once such questions as these are raised, even the limited scope of Paretian welfare analysis seems to be largely emptied of normative substance.

It is at this point that Wicksell comes to the rescue but not in a manner that satisfied the modern welfare theorist. If the Paretian construction is translated into the Wicksellian framework, the economist escapes from the apparent necessity to know anything about individual functions. I shall return to this interpretation of normative political economy later in section VI.

III. THE ENGINEERING URGE

I listed the engineering urge as one of three related strands of intellectual motivation that must be eliminated if political economy and the work of its disciplinary practitioners can assume an appropriate role in social philosophy. I use 'engineering' here rather than the more inclusive words 'science' or 'scientific' because it conveys more accurately the behavioural implications. In an ultimate sense, all science is aimed at control, at assistance in the solving of problems; but at least at the level of academic endeavour, scientists may seek knowledge for its own sake. By contrast, the engineers find their *raison d'etre* in solving problems or, at one stage removed, in suggesting solutions to decision-makers faced with problems. It is in this sense that modern economists have sought pervasively to assume roles as putative problem solvers, as policy advocates, as advisers to governments, directly or indirectly.

I noted above that modern economists were unhappy with the Paretian construction because they consider the construction to be insufficiently robust. They did not accept the implied inability to say anything about distributional arrangements, and they did not like the subinfinity of optimal positions forced upon them by the feedback dependence of classifications on distributions. Relatively early in theoretical welfare economics, attempts were made to get beyond the Paretian limits by introducing the 'social welfare function', a construction that was aimed precisely at allowing the economist to make normative evaluations of distributional arrangements. The Paretian construction was incorporated into the new edifice, but the social welfare function was designed to enable its user to rank or array among themselves all states or positions that meet the lower-level Pareto norm.

It should have been clear from the outset, from the very meaning of the Pareto criterion, and especially if interpreted in Wicksellian terms, that no unique social welfare function could be derived that allowed for an expression of individuals values and which remained internally consistent in its orderings. Nonetheless, Arrow's formal proof was required to establish this proposition, and, despite the widespread acceptance of such proof, economists continued (and continue) to utilize the social welfare function as a device that seemed to offer a basis for normative statements. Why did this practice persist so long, and why does it still persist? Why did economists reintroduce essentially the same evaluation procedures that were used by the utilitarians and which seemed thoroughly discredited? Presumably they did so, at least in part, because of their urge to be able to offer what seemed to be 'scientific' solutions to what seemed to be social problems. They wanted to be able to proceed in a manner analogously to that of their academic colleagues in engineering. Even when, at one level of discourse, these economists would acknowledge that there are as many social welfare functions as there are members of the community, they continued to use the ordering constructions. Empty as these might be, the exercise appeared to give satisfaction to those economists who were, and are, intellectually at sea without some engineering paradigm within which to ply their trade.

A second and totally different reflection of the basic engineering urge among modern economists also warrants brief attention here. At a practical level, this expression may swamp in significance the one previously discussed. Fully acknowledging that no evaluative norms can be applied to distributional arrangements, and also that the arrangements that exist determine the meaning of the efficiency scale, some economists have proceeded to use the scale as a policy norm. That is to say, the slogan has been 'a dollar's worth is a dollar's worth, full speed ahead, and ignore the distributional consequences!'

All of the serious cost-benefit analysis that has been central to much applied economics in the decades since the Second World War can be interpreted to fall within this classification. Many man-hours of economists have been turned to the evaluation of public investment projects on the basis of this methodology. Note that this applied welfare economics, like its counterpart labelled theoretical welfare economics, presumes the legitimacy of the quasi-utilitarian step made when arguments in individual utility functions are defined and signed. In the work under the rubric here discussed, this step is straightforward. Individuals are postulated to be net wealth maximizers, and, for the collectivity, that which is presumed to be the maximand is the aggregate net wealth, as measured in monetary values. With such a measuring rod in hand, the economist indeed becomes the 'social engineer'.

IV. THE ELITIST MENTALITY

The economists who have worked or who work within either of the two research programmes sketched above have been and remain highly sophisticated analysts. Why have they remained so reluctant to acknowledge the fragility of the epistemological foundations for their exercises? In part, they remain utilitarians; in part, they seek roles as engineers. But equally important is what I have called an elitist mentality, that described not only the economists but also the inclusive membership of the modern academy, along with that of the intelligentsia broadly defined. There has been a general unwillingness to accept the implications of the rejection of classical utilitarianism. Economists, along with their peers, have been unable to evacuate the putative claim to normative knowledge that seemed to be offered by the utilitarian delusion. They continue to think themselves superior in normative wisdom to ordinary persons who possess none of the requisite analytical skills.

I am not directly concerned here with the cruder forms of elitism, represented by paternalistic and patronizing attitudes of members of the academic-intellectual establishment towards the great unwashed. Economists as such have not been nearly so flagrant in espousing these attitudes as their peers in other disciplines. The elitist mentality that I want to identify and to discuss is much more subtle, and those scholars whose attitudes it describes need have no conscious sense of being themselves elitist in any of the standard uses of the term. Indeed, my terminology may be deemed misleading, since I am discussing a general characterization of politics, broadly defined, as a truth-discovery process.

To the extent that the purpose of collective action, of 'politics', is interpreted, even if unconsciously, to be a seeking after 'truth', it follows that those who engage themselves more actively in the process, and especially in the intellectual inquiries accompanying the process, are somehow 'closer' to 'that which is to be discovered' than those who remain passive in their behaviour and their reflections. It is as if all who engage in 'politics' are 'scientists', while those who do not directly participate are 'non-scientists'. Just as the layman defers to the scientists in all matters appropriate to science, so the non-participant in politics 'should' defer to those who participate in the discourses on matters of the political realm.

The economist who models his behaviour in an analogue to the scientist must be confident that his investment in human capital yields a positive return. If, indeed, there is a 'most efficient' set of structural arrangements 'out there' waiting to be discovered by economic research the economist is surely more capable of suggesting possible changes that will move the community towards that desideratum than is the person who claims no prior knowledge.

To rid modern political economy of this 'scientific' mind-set, which is subtly different from the more simple engineering urge already discussed, requires much more than the rejection of utilitarianism. What is required is a fundamental reshaping of the research programme of the whole disicpline of 'politics', of which economics and political economy are but component parts.

V. THE PRINCIPLE OF SPONTANEOUS ORDER

I suggested that political economy assumes its proper place in social philosophy only if the three related strands or elements identified in the neoclassical orthodoxy can be removed from the mind-set of those who remain within the disciplinary boundaries. I also suggested that developments in the research programme of political economy late in this century have been such as to allow this place to be assumed. In defending this statement I am obliged to outline what political economy is and how it can make its contribution to the more inclusive and ongoing dialogue.

As indicated earlier, the central principle of classical political economy remains untouchable. The principle demonstrates that the separate actions of individuals may be coordinated through a structure of interrelated markets contained within a legal-governmental system that enforces property rights and contracts. The implications of this principle for social philosophy are straightforward. To the extent that individual actions can be coordinated by decentralized organization of emergent markets, the necessity for political coordination and/or reconciliation is reduced. To the extent that markets work, there is no need for the state. Markets allow persons to interact, one with another, in a regime that combines freedom and order, provided only that the state supply the protective legal umbrella.

Note that the exposition of this central principle of political economy does not require any identification of arguments in individual utility or preference functions or any summation of individual values in some unique social dimension. Individuals coordinate their efforts so as to achieve mutual gains, as they individually define the content of such gains. Importantly, there is no need for individuals to agree explicitly or implicitly on an allocation or a distribution. These emerge as results of a process of trading, and individual preferences are exerted, not on the characteristics of such end-states, but instead on the subjectively defined objects of each person's own value scale, a scale that may itself emerge only as trade takes place. The market allows each particpant to seek to further 'that which he wants', given the constraints that he confronts, and 'that which A wants' need not be brought into agreement with 'that which B wants' at all. Indeed, the efficacy of market process is located in its facilitation of the satisfaction of divergent preferences.

The principle of the spontaneous order of the market process depends critically, however, on some explicit presuppositions that cannot be neglected in any systematic philosophical treatment. The organization of markets coordinates separate individual activities within the protective umbrella of a legal order without a specification of arguments in utility functions, but it does require that individuals themselves are defined in terms of some set of initial endowments, claims, rights, or characteristics.

Who is an individual? Who is a person? Who is a potential market participant? Response to these questions may seem at first glance to be as difficult as response to that which the classical utilitarian purports to answer: What does an individual want?

There is, nonetheless, a quantum difference between the epistemological requirements in the two cases. The utilitarian who would define the arguments in individual preference functions presumes a degree of psychological knowledge that is internal, whereas the non-utilitarian requires nothing beyond an empirical identification of the acting subject. The *individual* or 'that entity which engages in potential exchange' can be conceptually defined by the legal structure that sets out allowable limits on behaviour. The individual, in this context, is that choosing-acting unit that may voluntarily exchange or trade his legal endowments, rights, or claims, including those to the produce of his own application of personal talents (work) with others for some reciprocal offering (money, other claims, other inputs in a joint venture).

The argument here does suggest, however, that a legal-governmental order, one that contains within its allowable limits of enforcibility some specification of the distribution of rights and claims among individuals, is logically prior to any meaningful discussion of the process of market interaction among persons. Note that this priority of the legally protected assignment of rights does not carry the implication that the state itself is empowered arbitrarily to modify this assignment.

The central principle of political economy remains valid under *any* observed or imagined assignment of rights and claims. To the extent that individuals are *separately* assigned any legally protected rights or claims and voluntary contractual exchanges in these separately assigned rights and claims are enforced, emergent exchange arrangements will generate results that will maximize the values of the persons within the constraints described by their initial assignments. The principle applies equally to the production, sale, and final distribution of goods from the small garden plots of persons in the Soviet Union to the production, sale, and final distribution of the far wider range of goods and services that are allowed in Western economies.

The normative thrust of the principle depends critically on two presuppositions, one empirical, the other ethical. The empirical presupposition states that units of the human species are separable in a meaningful and observable sense. That is to say, just as we can talk about separate dogs, cats, or trees, we can talk about separate persons as independently existent biological units. The presupposition simply calls attention to the elemental fact of what we might call 'natural partitionability' within the species. The ethical presupposition states that these 'natural individuals' are the ultimate sources of valuation, clearly much more controversial than its empirical counterpart. If, however, individuals are not acknowledged to be the sources of value, the central principle of political economy has no normative meaning. If some external or supra-individual value standard is postulated, the coordination processes of the exchange network need not produce results that have any meaningful relationship to such standard. Or, if some individuals' values are somehow deemed to be 'superior' to those of others, there is no valuation process implicit in market equilibrium.

Even upon acceptance of these presuppositions, however, there may exist a subinfinity of possible assignments of rights and claims among persons. The particular assignment that describes a status quo is, in some fundamental sense, arbitrary. Given any such assignment, the decentralized market or exchange order operates so as to further the values of the individual participants, so defined, whatever these values might be. But the question remains of whether the political economist can offer any normative guidance in the assignment of rights and claims among persons?

VI. THE WICKSELLIAN CRITERION FOR INSTITUTIONAL CHANGE

Having shed the utilitarian value standard, and having accepted the presuppositions that individuals who can be identified are the sources of value, the political economist cannot array differing institutional structures, including assignments of individuals' rights and claims, in accordance with any non-individualistic value scale. He cannot call on some criterion of 'efficiency' unless he takes the quasi-utilitarian step noted earlier.

The contractarian framework advanced by Knut Wicksell can be helpful at precisely this point.[2] The political economist may call on his specialized talents to isolate and to identify changes in the institutional structure that might meet the Pareto test for superiority, interpreted in Wicksellian terms. Given any assignment of rights to persons, the political economist may advance an hypothesis to the effect that *all* persons in the community can be made better off, by their own reckoning, by a proffered shift in institutional arrangements. This hypothesis can then be put to the test; if arrangements can be worked out so that all members of the community agree to make the change, the test is passed; the hypothesis is corroborated. If the test fails, the political economist returns to his drawing board and searches for alternative rearrangements, or finally, if none are found, he concludes that that which he observes is optimal in the Pareto-Wicksell sense.[3]

Care must be taken, however, not to claim too much for the contractarian escape route offered in the Wicksellian construction. The political structure of modern societies is such that suggested reforms in institutions can rarely, if ever, be put to the Wicksellian unanimity test. Indeed, we might argue, at the more fundamental level of rules for constitutional decision-making, that the Wicksellian test, in itself, would not probably be Wicksell-efficient.[4] Where then does this leave the political economist who remains unwilling to take the quasi-utilitarian step? If he cannot actually carry out the Wicksellian test and observe the results, he is left with the notion of conceptual agreement. Critics have suggested that attempts to define changes upon which 'persons might have agreed', if test were possible, are on all fours with attempts to define and sign arguments in individual utility functions.

The Wicksellian contractarian framework seems, nonetheless, superior for normative purposes to the quasi-utilitarian framework of orthodox welfare economics because it allows for a sharper conceptual separation of value-enhancing and distributional changes to be made. In a sense, of course, the Wicksellian approach to normative economics is a straightforward extension of the exchange nexus. In working out the requisite compromises, side payments, deals, many-issue adjustments that may be necessary to secure general consent to a proposed institutional shift, individual participants are essentially exchanging elements of a vector that describes the total package. To the extent that such compromises are possible, we are assured that the change finally made is value-enhancing. But the Wicksellian procedure dictates that pure redistribution, defined in utility dimensions, simply cannot occur with general consent of all parties. No such implication can be drawn from the application of utilitarian procedures, which has been the source of much of the confusion in normative discourse.

VII. JUSTICE AND THE STATUS QUO

Because political economy as such cannot contribute directly to the normative discussion about alternative assignments of rights and claims among persons—that is, about pure distributional issues—we may be tempted to conclude that its role in social philosophy is severely limited. To the extent that social philosophy concentrates on considerations of distributive or social justice, where can political economy be of assistance? The implied relegation to secondary place in relevant discussion would be premature, however, once we recognize that very little of the observed discussion of 'social justice' by philosophers other than political economists has more than remote relevance to any ultimate choice. Far too frequently, social philosophers have implicitly presumed that their normative discussion of idealized principles of justice are applicable to social worlds that we inhabit. There are two related flaws in such a presumption. First, no person, agency, or collectivity chooses among differing assignments of rights and claims. Second, we live and interact one with another in historical time and place. We cannot jump out of our history and commence again.

I have often argued that any discussion of institutional change must embody the recognition that *we start from here*, and that *here* defines both place and time. There is a distribution of rights, endowments, and claims among persons, along with historically determined rules that dictate limits on exchanges in such rights. The distribution is an existential reality. It is that which exists; there is, and could be, no other.

Considerations of justice in distribution must therefore be couched in terms of possible *changes* from the statue quo. In this context, the two presuppositions advanced earlier will simply not permit normative judgements on any *redistributional* change to be made. The basis for this somewhat shocking (and disturbing to many) result is that any reduction in the expressed or revealed well-being of one person or group for the purpose of enhancing the well-being of another person or group, unless it is wholly voluntary (in which case it could not be called redistribution) can only be 'legitimized' by resort to some standard of valuation external to and independent of the valuations of the individuals involved in the social interaction.

I should emphasize that the acknowledgment of an inability to evaluate genuinely redistributional changes in the status quo on other than purely individual scales should not be interpreted as providing some ethical-moral defence of that assignment of rights and claims that exist. By any individual's private value scale, the existing assignment may be worse than a whole set of alternatives. The absence of the potential for voluntary or agreed-on consent to change indicates only that the existing assignment is the unique point in the directionally divergent individual scalars.

VIII. RULES, END-STATES, AND CONTRACTARIAN REFORM

The role for political economy, now interpreted in the Wicksellian-contractarian paradigm, need not be so limited as the above discussion may suggest to those who think of distributional issues exclusively or primarily in end-state terms. As noted earlier, 'distributions' are not 'chosen' by any person or group. Distributions emerge from the operation of framework rules or institutions within which separate persons interact. The potential objects for collective choice, and hence for reform or change, are these rules or institutions. Differing rules will of course generate differing predicted patterns of distribution, often in some stochastically defined sense.

Precisely because rules are the objects for collective choice, the scope for potential agreed-on contractual change is considerably more inclusive than that which might be applicable for end-state comparisons. That is to say, it is easier for persons to agree on rules which will, in their turn, allow differing patterns of end-state distributions to emerge, than it is for persons to agree on end-states themselves; or, to put the point differently, the focus of attention on rules serves to relegate overt redistributional conflict to secondary stages of consideration.

The basic reason why agreement can emerge more readily upon a choice of rules or processes than upon end-state assignments lies in the relatively greater uncertainty about individuals' identifiable positions under the operations of alternative rules. Almost by definition, an individual's own position in an end-state is well identified. By comparison, the operation of a quasi-permanent rule that generates stochastic patterns of end-states, each with distributional characteristics, necessarily makes it difficult for the individual to identify and predict accurately just what his own position might be. Because of this inherent uncertainty, the individual will be led to evaluate alternative sets of rules in accordance with a somewhat more inclusive sense of his own interest than that which might inform his simple choice among well identified end-states.[5]

In a contractarian and rule-orientated perspective, therefore, it is possible that consensus on a set of institutional arrangements will emerge that will, in operation, embody interpersonal transfers that may be loosely described as redistributional. But it is critically important that this 'constitutional redistribution' be categorically distinguished from post-constitutional 'political redistribution', which can never be normatively sanctioned. Note, however, that the normative argument in support of arrangements that embody constitutional redistribution stems from the agreement on these arrangements in the constitutional or rule-making dialogue. Such argument does not and cannot stem from any external and supra-individualistic value scale.

IX. POLITICAL ECONOMY IN SOCIAL PHILOSOPHY

Political economy is a necessary ingredient in any informed discussion of the ultimate question of social philosophy. It need not of course be sufficient. As conceptualized in the contractarian-constitutionalist paradigm, political economy offers a coherent structure within which the interactions of persons may be analyzed. It allows the generalization and extension of the exchange model of market interaction to the more encompassing institutions of politics and governance. As with the simpler exchange models of markets, specific results can neither be positively predicted nor normatively evaluated. That which emerges emerges, and evaluative criteria can only be applied to processes of the interaction and not to the characteristics of the end-states that are generated.

The structure is not normatively empty, however, and institutional arrangements that incorporate or allow for the coercive overriding of individual values do not find ready legitimation in the contractarian or generalized exchange framework. Legitimacy can only be derived, at one level or another, from the voluntary consent of individuals. But the fundamental question of who is an individual remains exogenous to the whole contractarian exercise. In this context, political economy, along with contract theory, depends critically on the two presuppositions noted earlier in the paper. If there are 'natural persons' in some biological sense, what are the margins for extension? Are there 'natural boundaries' that separate persons one from another? Are there 'natural rights?' These questions remain relevant even for the social philosopher who staunchly holds to a methodologically individualist position. But, are individuals the only sources of value? Do extra-individual sources exist? Are there moral absolutes?

Political economists can contribute only indirectly to the discussion on such grand questions. Such discussion becomes meaningful, however, only if it is informed by an understanding of the principles of political economy.

NOTES

1.   Material in this chapter was first presented at CIVITAS Conference on 'Economics and Philosophy', in Munich, West Germany, 22–24 July 1984. It was initially published in the conference volume. I acknowledge permission to reprint the material here.

       I am indebted to Viktor Vanberg for comments on an earlier draft.

2.   Cf. Knut Wicksell, *Finanztheorietische Untersuchungen* (Jena: Gustav Fischer, 1896).

3.   The role for the political economist sketched here was first advanced in an early paper, 'Positive Economics, Welfare Economics, and Political Economy', *Journal of Law and Economics*, II (1959), 124–38; reprinted in my *Fiscal Theory and Political Economy* (Chapel Hill: University of North Carolina Press, 1960), pp. 105–24.

4.   *See* James M. Buchanan and Gordon Tullock, *The Calculus of Consent* (Ann Arbor: University of Michigan Press, 1962).

5.   Elements of the analysis of Buchanan-Tullock, Rawls, and Nozick are combined in the position outlined here. In *The Calculus of Consent* (1962), Tullock and I examined the choice among political decision rules, and we discussed the prospect for agreement on rules that is enhanced by the uncertainty of individuals' positions under the operations of alternative arrangements. John Rawls in *A Theory of Justice* (Cambridge, Mass.: Harvard University Press, 1971), introduced the veil of ignorance, rather than uncertainty, to analyze prospects for ultimate contractual agreement on basic principles of justice. Robert Nozick in *Anarchy, State, and Utopia* (New York: Basic Books, 1974) developed the basic distinction between choices among processes and choices among end-states.

Index